Praise for *Effective Modern C++*

So, still interested in C++? You should be! Modern C++ (i.e., C++11/C++14) is far more than just a facelift. Considering the new features, it seems that it's more a reinvention. Looking for guidelines and assistance? Then this book is surely what you are looking for. Concerning C++, Scott Meyers was and still is a synonym for accuracy, quality, and delight.

—Gerhard Kreuzer
Research and Development Engineer, Siemens AG

Finding utmost expertise is hard enough. Finding teaching perfectionism— an author's obsession with strategizing and streamlining explanations—is also difficult. You know you're in for a treat when you get to find both embodied in the same person. *Effective Modern C++* is a towering achievement from a consummate technical writer. It layers lucid, meaningful, and well-sequenced clarifications on top of complex and interconnected topics, all in crisp literary style. You're equally unlikely to find a technical mistake, a dull moment, or a lazy sentence in *Effective Modern C++*.

—Andrei Alexandrescu
Ph.D., Research Scientist, Facebook, and author of *Modern C++ Design*

As someone with over two decades of C++ experience, to get the most out of modern C++ (both best practices and pitfalls to avoid), I highly recommend getting this book, reading it thoroughly, and referring to it often! I've certainly learned new things going through it!

—Nevin Liber
Senior Software Engineer, DRW Trading Group

Bjarne Stroustrup—the creator of C++—said, "C++11 feels like a new language." *Effective Modern C++* makes us share this same feeling by clearly explaining how everyday programmers can benefit from new features and idioms of C++11 and C++14. Another great Scott Meyers book.

—Cassio Neri
FX Quantitative Analyst, Lloyds Banking Group

Scott has the knack of boiling technical complexity down to an understandable kernel. His *Effective C++* books helped to raise the coding style of a previous generation of C++ programmers; the new book seems positioned to do the same for those using modern C++.

—*Roger Orr*
OR/2 Limited, a member of the ISO C++ standards committee

Effective Modern C++ is a great tool to improve your modern C++ skills. Not only does it teach you how, when and where to use modern C++ and be effective, it also explains *why*. Without doubt, Scott's clear and insightful writing, spread over 42 well-thought items, gives programmers a much better understanding of the language.

—*Bart Vandewoestyne*
Research and Development Engineer and C++ enthusiast

I love C++, it has been my work vehicle for many decades now. And with the latest raft of features it is even more powerful and expressive than I would have previously imagined. But with all this choice comes the question "when and how do I apply these features?" As has always been the case, Scott's *Effective C++* books are the definitive answer to this question.

—*Damien Watkins*
Computation Software Engineering Team Lead, CSIRO

Great read for transitioning to modern C++—new C++11/14 language features are described alongside C++98, subject items are easy to reference, and advice summarized at the end of each section. Entertaining and useful for both casual and advanced C++ developers.

—*Rachel Cheng*
F5 Networks

If you're migrating from C++98/03 to C++11/14, you need the eminently practical and clear information Scott provides in Effective Modern C++. If you're already writing C++11 code, you'll probably discover issues with the new features through Scott's thorough discussion of the important new features of the language. Either way, this book is worth your time.

—*Rob Stewart*
Boost Steering Committee member (*boost.org*)

Effective Modern C++

Scott Meyers

Beijing · Boston · Farnham · Sebastopol · Tokyo

Effective Modern C++

by Scott Meyers

Published by O'Reilly Media, Inc., 1005 Gravenstein Highway North, Sebastopol, CA 95472.

O'Reilly books may be purchased for educational, business, or sales promotional use. Online editions are also available for most titles (*http://oreilly.com/safari*). For more information, contact our corporate/institutional sales department: 800-998-9938 or corporate@oreilly.com.

Editor: Rachel Roumeliotis	**Indexer:** Scott Meyers
Production Editor: Melanie Yarbrough	**Interior Designer:** David Futato
Copyeditor: Jasmine Kwityn	**Cover Designer:** Ellie Volkhausen
Proofreader: Charles Roumeliotis	**Illustrator:** Rebecca Demarest

November 2014:   First Edition

Revision History for the First Edition
2014-11-07:   First Release
2014-12-12:   Second Release
2015-01-20:   Third Release
2015-04-03:   Fourth Release
2015-05-08:   Fifth Release
2015-06-30:   Sixth Release (ebook-only)
2015-07-10:   Seventh Release (ebook-only)
2015-10-23:   Eighth Release
2016-01-29:   Ninth Release
2017-01-13:   Tenth Release
2017-03-03:   Eleventh Release (PDF-only)
2018-05-11:   Twelfth Release

See *http://oreilly.com/catalog/errata.csp?isbn=9781491903995* for release details.

978-1-491-90399-5

[LSI]

For Darla,

black Labrador Retriever extraordinaire

Table of Contents

From the Publisher

Using Code Examples

This book is here to help you get your job done. In general, if example code is offered with this book, you may use it in your programs and documentation. You do not need to contact us for permission unless you're reproducing a significant portion of the code. For example, writing a program that uses several chunks of code from this book does not require permission. Selling or distributing a CD-ROM of examples from O'Reilly books does require permission. Answering a question by citing this book and quoting example code does not require permission. Incorporating a significant amount of example code from this book into your product's documentation does require permission.

We appreciate, but do not require, attribution. An attribution usually includes the title, author, publisher, and ISBN. For example: "*Effective Modern C++* by Scott Meyers (O'Reilly). Copyright 2015 Scott Meyers, 978-1-491-90399-5."

If you feel your use of code examples falls outside fair use or the permission given above, feel free to contact us at *permissions@oreilly.com*.

O'Reilly Safari

 *Safari* (formerly Safari Books Online) is a membership-based training and reference platform for enterprise, government, educators, and individuals.

Members have access to thousands of books, training videos, Learning Paths, interactive tutorials, and curated playlists from over 250 publishers, including O'Reilly Media, Harvard Business Review, Prentice Hall Professional, Addison-Wesley Professional, Microsoft Press, Sams, Que, Peachpit Press, Adobe, Focal Press, Cisco Press, John Wiley & Sons, Syngress, Morgan Kaufmann, IBM Redbooks, Packt,

Adobe Press, FT Press, Apress, Manning, New Riders, McGraw-Hill, Jones & Bartlett, and Course Technology, among others.

For more information, please visit *http://oreilly.com/safari*.

How to Contact Us

Comments and questions concerning this book may be addressed to the publisher:

> O'Reilly Media, Inc.
> 1005 Gravenstein Highway North
> Sebastopol, CA 95472
> 800-998-9938 (in the United States or Canada)
> 707-829-0515 (international or local)
> 707-829-0104 (fax)

To comment or ask technical questions about this book, send email to *bookquestions@oreilly.com*.

For more information about our books, courses, conferences, and news, see our website at *http://www.oreilly.com*.

Find us on Facebook: *http://facebook.com/oreilly*

Follow us on Twitter: *http://twitter.com/oreillymedia*

Watch us on YouTube: *http://www.youtube.com/oreillymedia*

Acknowledgments

I started investigating what was then known as C++0x (the nascent C++11) in 2009. I posted numerous questions to the Usenet newsgroup `comp.std.c++`, and I'm grateful to the members of that community (especially Daniel Krügler) for their very helpful postings. In more recent years, I've turned to Stack Overflow when I had questions about C++11 and C++14, and I'm equally indebted to that community for its help in understanding the finer points of modern C++.

In 2010, I prepared materials for a training course on C++0x (ultimately published as *Overview of the New C++*, Artima Publishing, 2010). Both those materials and my knowledge greatly benefited from the technical vetting performed by Stephan T. Lavavej, Bernhard Merkle, Stanley Friesen, Leor Zolman, Hendrik Schober, and Anthony Williams. Without their help, I would probably never have been in a position to undertake *Effective Modern C++*. That title, incidentally, was suggested or endorsed by several readers responding to my 18 February 2014 blog post, "Help me name my book," and Andrei Alexandrescu (author of *Modern C++ Design*, Addison-Wesley, 2001) was kind enough to bless the title as not poaching on his terminological turf.

I'm unable to identify the origins of all the information in this book, but some sources had a relatively direct impact. Item 4's use of an undefined template to coax type information out of compilers was suggested by Stephan T. Lavavej, and Matt P. Dziubinski brought Boost.TypeIndex to my attention. In Item 5, the `unsigned-std::vector<int>::size_type` example is from Andrey Karpov's 28 February 2010 article, "In what way can C++0x standard help you eliminate 64-bit errors." The `std::pair<std::string, int>`/`std::pair<const std::string, int>` example in the same Item is from Stephan T. Lavavej's talk at *Going Native 2012*, "STL11: Magic && Secrets." Item 6 was inspired by Herb Sutter's 12 August 2013 article, "GotW #94 Solution: AAA Style (Almost Always Auto)." Item 9 was motivated by Martinho Fernandes' blog post of 27 May 2012, "Handling dependent names." The Item 12 example demonstrating overloading on reference qualifiers is based on Casey's answer to the question, "What's a use case for overloading member functions on reference qualifiers?," posted to Stack Overflow on 14 January 2014. My Item 15 treatment of C++14's expanded support for `constexpr` functions incorporates information I received from Rein Halbersma. Item 16 is based on Herb Sutter's C++ *and Beyond 2012* presentation, "You don't know `const` and `mutable`." Item 18's advice to have factory functions return `std::unique_ptrs` is based on Herb Sutter's 30 May 2013 article, "GotW# 90 Solution: Factories." In Item 19, `fastLoadWidget` is derived from Herb Sutter's *Going Native 2013* presentation, "My Favorite C++ 10-Liner." My treatment of `std::unique_ptr` and incomplete types in Item 22 draws on Herb Sutter's 27 November 2011 article, "GotW #100: Compilation Firewalls" as well as Howard Hinnant's 22 May 2011 answer to the Stack Overflow question, "Is std::unique_ptr<T> required to know the full definition of T?" The `Matrix` addition example in Item 25 is based on writings by David Abrahams. JoeArgonne's 8 December 2012 comment on the 30 November 2012 blog post, "Another alternative to lambda move capture," was the source of Item 32's `std::bind`-based approach to emulating init capture in C++11. Item 37's explanation of the problem with an implicit detach in `std::thread`'s destructor is taken from Hans-J. Boehm's 4 December 2008 paper, "N2802: A plea to reconsider detach-on-destruction for thread objects." Item 41 was originally motivated by discussions of David Abrahams' 15 August 2009 blog post, "Want speed? Pass by value." The idea that move-only types deserve special treatment is due to Matthew Fioravante, while the analysis of assignment-based copying stems from comments by Howard Hinnant. In Item 42, Stephan T. Lavavej and Howard Hinnant helped me understand the relative performance profiles of emplacement and insertion functions, and Michael Winterberg brought to my attention how emplacement can lead to resource leaks. (Michael credits Sean Parent's *Going Native 2013* presentation, "C++ Seasoning," as his source.) Michael also pointed out how emplacement functions use direct initialization, while insertion functions use copy initialization.

Reviewing drafts of a technical book is a demanding, time-consuming, and utterly critical task, and I'm fortunate that so many people were willing to do it for me. Full or partial drafts of *Effective Modern C++* were officially reviewed by Cassio Neri, Nate Kohl, Gerhard Kreuzer, Leor Zolman, Bart Vandewoestyne, Stephan T. Lavavej, Nevin ":-)" Liber, Rachel Cheng, Rob Stewart, Bob Steagall, Damien Watkins, Bradley E. Needham, Rainer Grimm, Fredrik Winkler, Jonathan Wakely, Herb Sutter, Andrei Alexandrescu, Eric Niebler, Thomas Becker, Roger Orr, Anthony Williams, Michael Winterberg, Benjamin Huchley, Tom Kirby-Green, Alexey A Nikitin, William Dealtry, Hubert Matthews, and Tomasz Kamiński. I also received feedback from several readers through O'Reilly's Early Release EBooks and Safari Books Online's Rough Cuts, comments on my blog (*The View from Aristeia*), and email. I'm grateful to each of these people. The book is *much* better than it would have been without their help. I'm particularly indebted to Stephan T. Lavavej, Rob Stewart, and Tomasz Kamiński, whose extraordinarily detailed and comprehensive remarks lead me to worry that they spent nearly as much time on this book as I did. Special thanks also go to Leor Zolman, who, in addition to reviewing the manuscript, double-checked all the code examples.

Dedicated reviews of digital versions of the book were performed by Gerhard Kreuzer, Emyr Williams, and Bradley E. Needham.

My decision to limit the line length in code displays to 64 characters (the maximum likely to display properly in print as well as across a variety of digital devices, device orientations, and font configurations) was based on data provided by Michael Maher.

Since initial publication, I've incorporated bug fixes and other improvements suggested by Kostas Vlahavas, Daniel Alonso Alemany, Takatoshi Kondo, Bartek Szurgot, Tyler Brock, Jay Zipnick, Barry Revzin, Robert McCabe, Oliver Bruns, Fabrice Ferino, Dainis Jonitis, Petr Valasek, Bart Vandewoestyne, Kjell Hedstrom, Marcel Wid, Mark A. McLaughlin, Miroslaw Michalski, Vlad Gheorghiu, Mitsuru Kariya, Minkoo Seo, Tomasz Kamiński, Agustín K-ballo Bergé, Grebënkin Sergey, Adam Peterson, Matthias J. Sax, Semen Trygubenko, Lewis Stiller, Leor Zolman, Kisung Han, Rein Halbersma, Ben Craig, Nicolai Josuttis, Marek Scholle, Lucas Panian, Gerhard Kreuzer, Calum Laing, Gennaro Prota, Alex Dumov, Harri Berglund, Tim Buchowski, Robin Kuzmin, József Mihalicza, Mitch T. Besser, Jesper Storm Bache, Stephane Aubry, Declan Moran, and Tomasz Grzegorz Markiewicz. Many thanks to all these people for helping improve the accuracy and clarity of *Effective Modern C++*.

Ashley Morgan Long made dining at the Lake Oswego Pizzicato uniquely entertaining. When it comes to man-sized Caesars, she's the go-to gal.

More than 20 years after first living through my playing author, my wife, Nancy L. Urbano, once again tolerated many months of distracted conversations with a cocktail of resignation, exasperation, and timely splashes of understanding and support. During the same period, our dog, Darla, was largely content to doze away the hours I spent staring at computer screens, but she never let me forget that there's life beyond the keyboard.

Introduction

If you're an experienced C++ programmer and are anything like me, you initially approached C++11 thinking, "Yes, yes, I get it. It's C++, only more so." But as you learned more, you were surprised by the scope of the changes. `auto` declarations, range-based `for` loops, lambda expressions, and rvalue references change the face of C++, to say nothing of the new concurrency features. And then there are the idiomatic changes. `0` and `typedef`s are out, `nullptr` and alias declarations are in. Enums should now be scoped. Smart pointers are now preferable to built-in ones. Moving objects is normally better than copying them.

There's a lot to learn about C++11, not to mention C++14.

More importantly, there's a lot to learn about making *effective* use of the new capabilities. If you need basic information about "modern" C++ features, resources abound, but if you're looking for guidance on how to employ the features to create software that's correct, efficient, maintainable, and portable, the search is more challenging. That's where this book comes in. It's devoted not to describing the features of C++11 and C++14, but instead to their effective application.

The information in the book is broken into guidelines called *Items*. Want to understand the various forms of type deduction? Or know when (and when not) to use `auto` declarations? Are you interested in why `const` member functions should be thread safe, how to implement the Pimpl Idiom using `std::unique_ptr`, why you should avoid default capture modes in lambda expressions, or the differences between `std::atomic` and `volatile`? The answers are all here. Furthermore, they're platform-independent, Standards-conformant answers. This is a book about *portable* C++.

The Items in this book are guidelines, not rules, because guidelines have exceptions. The most important part of each Item is not the advice it offers, but the rationale behind the advice. Once you've read that, you'll be in a position to determine whether the circumstances of your project justify a violation of the Item's guidance. The true goal of this book isn't to tell you what to do or what to avoid doing, but to convey a deeper understanding of how things work in C++11 and C++14.

Terminology and Conventions

To make sure we understand one another, it's important to agree on some terminology, beginning, ironically, with "C++." There have been four official versions of C++, each named after the year in which the corresponding ISO Standard was adopted: *C++98*, *C++03*, *C++11*, and *C++14*. C++98 and C++03 differ only in technical details, so in this book, I refer to both as C++98. When I refer to C++11, I mean both C++11 and C++14, because C++14 is effectively a superset of C++11. When I write C++14, I mean specifically C++14. And if I simply mention C++, I'm making a broad statement that pertains to all language versions.

Term I Use	Language Versions I Mean
C++	All
C++98	C++98 and C++03
C++11	C++11 and C++14
C++14	C++14

As a result, I might say that C++ places a premium on efficiency (true for all versions), that C++98 lacks support for concurrency (true only for C++98 and C++03), that C++11 supports lambda expressions (true for C++11 and C++14), and that C++14 offers generalized function return type deduction (true for C++14 only).

C++11's most pervasive feature is probably move semantics, and the foundation of move semantics is distinguishing expressions that are *rvalues* from those that are *lvalues*. That's because rvalues indicate objects eligible for move operations, while lvalues generally don't. In concept (though not always in practice), rvalues correspond to temporary objects returned from functions, while lvalues correspond to objects you can refer to, either by name or by following a pointer or lvalue reference.

A useful heuristic to determine whether an expression is an lvalue is to ask if you can take its address. If you can, it typically is. If you can't, it's usually an rvalue. A nice feature of this heuristic is that it helps you remember that the type of an expression is independent of whether the expression is an lvalue or an rvalue. That is, given a type T, you can have lvalues of type T as well as rvalues of type T. It's especially important to remember this when dealing with a parameter of rvalue reference type, because the parameter itself is an lvalue:

```
class Widget {
public:
  Widget(Widget&& rhs);     // rhs is an lvalue, though it has
  ...                       // an rvalue reference type
};
```

Here, it'd be perfectly valid to take rhs's address inside Widget's move constructor, so rhs is an lvalue, even though its type is an rvalue reference. (By similar reasoning, all parameters are lvalues.)

That code snippet demonstrates several conventions I normally follow:

- The class name is Widget. I use Widget whenever I want to refer to an arbitrary user-defined type. Unless I need to show specific details of the class, I use Widget without declaring it.

- I use the parameter name *rhs* ("right-hand side"). It's my preferred parameter name for the *move operations* (i.e., move constructor and move assignment operator) and the *copy operations* (i.e., copy constructor and copy assignment operator). I also employ it for the right-hand parameter of binary operators:

  ```
  Matrix operator+(const Matrix& lhs, const Matrix& rhs);
  ```

  It's no surprise, I hope, that *lhs* stands for "left-hand side."

- I apply special formatting to parts of code or parts of comments to draw your attention to them. In the Widget move constructor above, I've highlighted the declaration of rhs and the part of the comment noting that rhs is an lvalue. Highlighted code is neither inherently good nor inherently bad. It's simply code you should pay particular attention to.

- I use "..." to indicate "other code could go here." This narrow ellipsis is different from the wide ellipsis ("...") that's used in the source code for C++11's variadic templates. That sounds confusing, but it's not. For example:

  ```
  template<typename... Ts>          // these are C++
  void processVals(const Ts&... params)  // source code
  {                                 // ellipses

      ...                           // this means "some
                                    // code goes here"
  }
  ```

The declaration of processVals shows that I use typename when declaring type parameters in templates, but that's merely a personal preference; the keyword class would work just as well. On those occasions where I show code excerpts from a C++ Standard, I declare type parameters using `class`, because that's what the Standards do.

When an object is initialized with another object of the same type, the new object is said to be a *copy* of the initializing object, even if the copy was created via the move constructor. Regrettably, there's no terminology in C++ that distinguishes between an object that's a copy-constructed copy and one that's a move-constructed copy:

```
void someFunc(Widget w);          // someFunc's parameter w
                                  // is passed by value

Widget wid;                       // wid is some Widget

someFunc(wid);                    // in this call to someFunc,
                                  // w is a copy of wid that's
                                  // created via copy construction

someFunc(std::move(wid));         // in this call to someFunc,
                                  // w is a copy of wid that's
                                  // created via move construction
```

Copies of rvalues are generally move constructed, while copies of lvalues are usually copy constructed. An implication is that if you know only that an object is a copy of another object, it's not possible to say how expensive it was to construct the copy. In the code above, for example, there's no way to say how expensive it is to create the parameter w without knowing whether rvalues or lvalues are passed to `someFunc`. (You'd also have to know the cost of moving and copying `Widget`s.)

In a function call, the expressions passed at the call site are the function's *arguments*. The arguments are used to initialize the function's *parameters*. In the first call to `someFunc` above, the argument is `wid`. In the second call, the argument is `std::move(wid)`. In both calls, the parameter is `w`. The distinction between arguments and parameters is important, because parameters are lvalues, but the arguments with which they are initialized may be rvalues or lvalues. This is especially relevant during the process of *perfect forwarding*, whereby an argument passed to a function is passed to a second function such that the original argument's rvalueness or lvalueness is preserved. (Perfect forwarding is discussed in detail in Item 30.)

Well-designed functions are *exception safe*, meaning they offer at least the basic exception safety guarantee (i.e., the *basic guarantee*). Such functions assure callers that even if an exception is thrown, program invariants remain intact (i.e., no data structures are corrupted) and no resources are leaked. Functions offering the strong exception safety guarantee (i.e., the *strong guarantee*) assure callers that if an exception arises, the state of the program remains as it was prior to the call.

When I refer to a *function object*, I usually mean an object of a type supporting an `operator()` member function. In other words, an object that acts like a function. Occasionally I use the term in a slightly more general sense to mean anything that can be invoked using the syntax of a non-member function call (i.e., "*function-Name(arguments)*"). This broader definition covers not just objects supporting `operator()`, but also functions and C-like function pointers. (The narrower definition comes from C++98, the broader one from C++11.) Generalizing further by adding member function pointers yields what are known as *callable objects*. You can generally ignore the fine distinctions and simply think of function objects and callable objects as things in C++ that can be invoked using some kind of function-calling syntax.

Function objects created through lambda expressions are known as *closures*. It's seldom necessary to distinguish between lambda expressions and the closures they create, so I often refer to both as *lambdas*. Similarly, I rarely distinguish between *function templates* (i.e., templates that generate functions) and *template functions* (i.e., the functions generated from function templates). Ditto for *class templates* and *template classes*.

Many things in C++ can be both declared and defined. *Declarations* introduce names and types without giving details, such as where storage is located or how things are implemented:

```
extern int x;                 // object declaration

class Widget;                 // class declaration

bool func(const Widget& w);   // function declaration

enum class Color;             // scoped enum declaration
                              // (see Item 10)
```

Definitions provide the storage locations or implementation details:

```
int x;                        // object definition

class Widget {                // class definition
  …
};

bool func(const Widget& w)
{ return w.size() < 10; }      // function definition

enum class Color
{ Yellow, Red, Blue };         // scoped enum definition
```

A definition also qualifies as a declaration, so unless it's really important that something is a definition, I tend to refer to declarations.

I define a function's *signature* to be the part of its declaration that specifies parameter and return types. Function and parameter names are not part of the signature. In the example above, `func`'s signature is `bool(const Widget&)`. Elements of a function's declaration other than its parameter and return types (e.g., `noexcept` or `constexpr`, if present), are excluded. (`noexcept` and `constexpr` are described in Items 14 and 15.) The official definition of "signature" is slightly different from mine, but for this book, my definition is more useful. (The official definition sometimes omits return types.)

New C++ Standards generally preserve the validity of code written under older ones, but occasionally the Standardization Committee *deprecates* features. Such features are on standardization death row and may be removed from future Standards. Compilers may or may not warn about the use of deprecated features, but you should do your best to avoid them. Not only can they lead to future porting headaches, they're generally inferior to the features that replace them. For example, `std::auto_ptr` is deprecated in C++11, because `std::unique_ptr` does the same job, only better.

Sometimes a Standard says that the result of an operation is *undefined behavior*. That means that runtime behavior is unpredictable, and it should go without saying that you want to steer clear of such uncertainty. Examples of actions with undefined behavior include using square brackets ("[]") to index beyond the bounds of a `std::vector`, dereferencing an uninitialized iterator, or engaging in a data race (i.e., having two or more threads, at least one of which is a writer, simultaneously access the same memory location).

I call built-in pointers, such as those returned from `new`, *raw pointers*. The opposite of a raw pointer is a *smart pointer*. Smart pointers normally overload the pointer-dereferencing operators (`operator->` and `operator*`), though Item 20 explains that `std::weak_ptr` is an exception.

In source code comments, I sometimes abbreviate "constructor" as *ctor* and "destructor" as *dtor*.

Reporting Bugs and Suggesting Improvements

I've done my best to fill this book with clear, accurate, useful information, but surely there are ways to make it better. If you find errors of any kind (technical, expository, grammatical, typographical, etc.), or if you have suggestions for how the book could be improved, please email me at *emc++@aristeia.com*. New printings give me the opportunity to revise *Effective Modern C++*, and I can't address issues I don't know about!

To view the list of the issues I do know about, consult the book's errata page, *http://www.aristeia.com/BookErrata/emc++-errata.html.*

CHAPTER 1

Deducing Types

C++98 had a single set of rules for type deduction: the one for function templates. C++11 modifies that ruleset a bit and adds two more, one for `auto` and one for `decltype`. C++14 then extends the usage contexts in which `auto` and `decltype` may be employed. The increasingly widespread application of type deduction frees you from the tyranny of spelling out types that are obvious or redundant. It makes C++ software more adaptable, because changing a type at one point in the source code automatically propagates through type deduction to other locations. However, it can render code more difficult to reason about, because the types deduced by compilers may not be as apparent as you'd like.

Without a solid understanding of how type deduction operates, effective programming in modern C++ is all but impossible. There are just too many contexts where type deduction takes place: in calls to function templates, in most situations where `auto` appears, in `decltype` expressions, and, as of C++14, where the enigmatic `decltype(auto)` construct is employed.

This chapter provides the information about type deduction that every C++ developer requires. It explains how template type deduction works, how `auto` builds on that, and how `decltype` goes its own way. It even explains how you can force compilers to make the results of their type deductions visible, thus enabling you to ensure that compilers are deducing the types you want them to.

Item 1: Understand template type deduction.

When users of a complex system are ignorant of how it works, yet happy with what it does, that says a lot about the design of the system. By this measure, template type deduction in C++ is a tremendous success. Millions of programmers have passed arguments to template functions with completely satisfactory results, even though many of those programmers would be hard-pressed to give more than the haziest description of how the types used by those functions were deduced.

If that group includes you, I have good news and bad news. The good news is that type deduction for templates is the basis for one of modern C++'s most compelling features: auto. If you were happy with how C++98 deduced types for templates, you're set up to be happy with how C++11 deduces types for auto. The bad news is that when the template type deduction rules are applied in the context of auto, they sometimes seem less intuitive than when they're applied to templates. For that reason, it's important to truly understand the aspects of template type deduction that auto builds on. This Item covers what you need to know.

If you're willing to overlook a pinch of pseudocode, we can think of a function template as looking like this:

```
template<typename T>
void f(ParamType param);
```

A call can look like this:

```
f(expr);                        // call f with some expression
```

During compilation, compilers use *expr* to deduce two types: one for T and one for *ParamType*. These types are frequently different, because *ParamType* often contains adornments, e.g., const or reference qualifiers. For example, if the template is declared like this,

```
template<typename T>
void f(const T& param);        // ParamType is const T&
```

and we have this call,

```
int x = 0;

f(x);                           // call f with an int
```

T is deduced to be int, but *ParamType* is deduced to be const int&.

It's natural to expect that the type deduced for T is the same as the type of the argument passed to the function, i.e., that T is the type of *expr*. In the above example, that's the case: x is an int, and T is deduced to be int. But it doesn't always work that way. The type deduced for T is dependent not just on the type of *expr*, but also on the form of *ParamType*. There are three cases:

- *ParamType* is a pointer or reference type, but not a universal reference. (Universal references are described in Item 24. At this point, all you need to know is that they exist and that they're not the same as lvalue references or rvalue references.)

- *ParamType* is a universal reference.

- *ParamType* is neither a pointer nor a reference.

We therefore have three type deduction scenarios to examine. Each will be based on our general form for templates and calls to it:

```
template<typename T>
void f(ParamType param);

f(expr);                    // deduce T and ParamType from expr
```

Case 1: *ParamType* is a Reference or Pointer, but not a Universal Reference

The simplest situation is when *ParamType* is a reference type or a pointer type, but not a universal reference. In that case, type deduction works like this:

1. If *expr*'s type is a reference, ignore the reference part.

2. Then pattern-match *expr*'s type against *ParamType* to determine T.

For example, if this is our template,

```
template<typename T>
void f(T& param);       // param is a reference
```

and we have these variable declarations,

```
int x = 27;             // x is an int
const int cx = x;       // cx is a const int
const int& rx = x;      // rx is a reference to x as a const int
```

the deduced types for param and T in various calls are as follows:

```
f(x);                   // T is int, param's type is int&

f(cx);                  // T is const int,
                        // param's type is const int&

f(rx);                  // T is const int,
                        // param's type is const int&
```

In the second and third calls, notice that because cx and rx designate const values, T is deduced to be const int, thus yielding a parameter type of const int&. That's important to callers. When they pass a const object to a reference parameter, they expect that object to remain unmodifiable, i.e., for the parameter to be a reference-to-const. That's why passing a const object to a template taking a T& parameter is safe: the constness of the object becomes part of the type deduced for T.

In the third example, note that even though rx's type is a reference, T is deduced to be a non-reference. That's because rx's reference-ness is ignored during type deduction.

If we change the type of f's parameter from T& to const T&, things change a little, but not in any really surprising ways. The constness of cx and rx continues to be respected, but because we're now assuming that param is a reference-to-const, there's no longer a need for const to be deduced as part of T:

```
template<typename T>
void f(const T& param);   // param is now a ref-to-const

int x = 27;               // as before
const int cx = x;         // as before
const int& rx = x;        // as before

f(x);                     // T is int, param's type is const int&

f(cx);                    // T is int, param's type is const int&

f(rx);                    // T is int, param's type is const int&
```

As before, rx's reference-ness is ignored during type deduction.

If param were a pointer (or a pointer to const) instead of a reference, things would work essentially the same way:

```
template<typename T>
void f(T* param);         // param is now a pointer

int x = 27;               // as before
const int *px = &x;       // px is a ptr to x as a const int


f(&x);                    // T is int, param's type is int*

f(px);                    // T is const int,
                          // param's type is const int*
```

By now, you may find yourself yawning and nodding off, because C++'s type deduction rules work so naturally for reference and pointer parameters, seeing them in written form is really dull. Everything's just obvious! Which is exactly what you want in a type deduction system.

Case 2: *ParamType* is a Universal Reference

Things are less obvious for templates taking universal reference parameters. Such parameters are declared like rvalue references (i.e., in a function template taking a type parameter T, a universal reference's declared type is T&&), but they behave differently when lvalue arguments are passed in. The complete story is told in Item 24, but here's the headline version:

- If *expr* is an lvalue, both T and *ParamType* are deduced to be lvalue references. That's doubly unusual. First, it's the only situation in template type deduction where T is deduced to be a reference. Second, although *ParamType* is declared using the syntax for an rvalue reference, its deduced type is an lvalue reference.

- If *expr* is an rvalue, the "normal" (i.e., Case 1) rules apply.

For example:

```
template<typename T>
void f(T&& param);         // param is now a universal reference

int x = 27;                // as before
const int cx = x;          // as before
const int& rx = x;         // as before

f(x);                      // x is lvalue, so T is int&,
                           // param's type is also int&

f(cx);                     // cx is lvalue, so T is const int&,
                           // param's type is also const int&

f(rx);                     // rx is lvalue, so T is const int&,
                           // param's type is also const int&

f(27);                     // 27 is rvalue, so T is int,
                           // param's type is therefore int&&
```

Item 24 explains exactly why these examples play out the way they do. The key point here is that the type deduction rules for universal reference parameters are different from those for parameters that are lvalue references or rvalue references. In particular, when universal references are in use, type deduction distinguishes between lvalue arguments and rvalue arguments. That never happens for non-universal references.

Case 3: *ParamType* is Neither a Pointer nor a Reference

When *ParamType* is neither a pointer nor a reference, we're dealing with pass-by-value:

```
template<typename T>
void f(T param);              // param is now passed by value
```

That means that `param` will be a copy of whatever is passed in—a completely new object. The fact that `param` will be a new object motivates the rules that govern how `T` is deduced from *expr*:

1. As before, if *expr*'s type is a reference, ignore the reference part.

2. If, after ignoring *expr*'s reference-ness, *expr* is `const`, ignore that, too. If it's `volatile`, also ignore that. (`volatile` objects are uncommon. They're generally used only for implementing device drivers. For details, see Item 40.)

Hence:

```
int x = 27;               // as before
const int cx = x;         // as before
const int& rx = x;        // as before

f(x);                     // T's and param's types are both int

f(cx);                    // T's and param's types are again both int

f(rx);                    // T's and param's types are still both int
```

Note that even though `cx` and `rx` represent `const` values, `param` isn't `const`. That makes sense. `param` is an object that's completely independent of `cx` and `rx`—a *copy* of `cx` or `rx`. The fact that `cx` and `rx` can't be modified says nothing about whether `param` can be. That's why *expr*'s `constness` (and `volatileness`, if any) is ignored when deducing a type for `param`: just because *expr* can't be modified doesn't mean that a copy of it can't be.

It's important to recognize that `const` (and `volatile`) is ignored only for by-value parameters. As we've seen, for parameters that are references-to- or pointers-to-`const`, the `constness` of *expr* is preserved during type deduction. But consider the case where *expr* is a const pointer to a const object, and *expr* is passed to a by-value param:

```
template<typename T>
void f(T param);            // param is still passed by value

const char* const ptr =  // ptr is const pointer to const object
  "Fun with pointers";

f(ptr);                     // pass arg of type const char * const
```

Here, the const to the right of the asterisk declares ptr to be const: ptr can't be made to point to a different location, nor can it be set to null. (The const to the left of the asterisk says that what ptr points to—the character string—is const, hence can't be modified.) When ptr is passed to f, the bits making up the pointer are copied into param. As such, *the pointer itself (ptr) will be passed by value*. In accord with the type deduction rule for by-value parameters, the constness of ptr will be ignored, and the type deduced for param will be const char*, i.e., a modifiable pointer to a const character string. The constness of what ptr points to is preserved during type deduction, but the constness of ptr itself is ignored when copying it to create the new pointer, param.

Array Arguments

That pretty much covers it for mainstream template type deduction, but there's a niche case that's worth knowing about. It's that array types are different from pointer types, even though they sometimes seem to be interchangeable. A primary contributor to this illusion is that, in many contexts, an array *decays* into a pointer to its first element. This decay is what permits code like this to compile:

```
const char name[] = "J. P. Briggs";  // name's type is
                                      // const char[13]

const char * ptrToName = name;        // array decays to pointer
```

Here, the const char* pointer ptrToName is being initialized with name, which is a const char[13]. These types (const char* and const char[13]) are not the same, but because of the array-to-pointer decay rule, the code compiles.

But what if an array is passed to a template taking a by-value parameter? What happens then?

```
template<typename T>
void f(T param);        // template with by-value parameter
```

```
f(name);                        // what types are deduced for T and param?
```

We begin with the observation that there is no such thing as a function parameter that's an array. Yes, yes, the syntax is legal,

```
void myFunc(int param[]);
```

but the array declaration is treated as a pointer declaration, meaning that myFunc could equivalently be declared like this:

```
void myFunc(int* param);          // same function as above
```

This equivalence of array and pointer parameters is a bit of foliage springing from the C roots at the base of C++, and it fosters the illusion that array and pointer types are the same.

Because array parameter declarations are treated as if they were pointer parameters, the type of an array that's passed to a template function by value is deduced to be a pointer type. That means that in the call to the template f, its type parameter T is deduced to be const char*:

```
f(name);            // name is array, but T deduced as const char*
```

But now comes a curve ball. Although functions can't declare parameters that are truly arrays, they *can* declare parameters that are *references* to arrays! So if we modify the template f to take its argument by reference,

```
template<typename T>
void f(T& param);          // template with by-reference parameter
```

and we pass an array to it,

```
f(name);                   // pass array to f
```

the type deduced for T is the actual type of the array! That type includes the size of the array, so in this example, T is deduced to be const char [13], and the type of f's parameter (a reference to this array) is const char (&)[13]. Yes, the syntax looks toxic, but knowing it will score you mondo points with those few souls who care.

Interestingly, the ability to declare references to arrays enables creation of a template that deduces the number of elements that an array contains:

```
// return size of an array as a compile-time constant. (The
// array parameter has no name, because we care only about
// the number of elements it contains.)
template<typename T, std::size_t N>          // see info
constexpr std::size_t arraySize(T (&)[N]) noexcept  // below on
{                                             // constexpr
```

```
    return N;                                      // and
}                                                  // noexcept
```

As Item 15 explains, declaring this function constexpr makes its result available during compilation. That makes it possible to declare, say, an array with the same number of elements as a second array whose size is computed from a braced initializer:

```
int keyVals[] = { 1, 3, 7, 9, 11, 22, 35 };       // keyVals has
                                                   // 7 elements

int mappedVals[arraySize(keyVals)];                // so does
                                                   // mappedVals
```

Of course, as a modern C++ developer, you'd naturally prefer a std::array to a built-in array:

```
std::array<int, arraySize(keyVals)> mappedVals;    // mappedVals'
                                                   // size is 7
```

As for arraySize being declared noexcept, that's to help compilers generate better code. For details, see Item 14.

Function Arguments

Arrays aren't the only things in C++ that can decay into pointers. Function types can decay into function pointers, and everything we've discussed regarding type deduction for arrays applies to type deduction for functions and their decay into function pointers. As a result:

```
void someFunc(int, double);     // someFunc is a function;
                                // type is void(int, double)

template<typename T>
void f1(T param);               // in f1, param passed by value

template<typename T>
void f2(T& param);              // in f2, param passed by ref

f1(someFunc);                   // param deduced as ptr-to-func;
                                // type is void (*)(int, double)

f2(someFunc);                   // param deduced as ref-to-func;
                                // type is void (&)(int, double)
```

This rarely makes any difference in practice, but if you're going to know about array-to-pointer decay, you might as well know about function-to-pointer decay, too.

So there you have it: the auto-related rules for template type deduction. I remarked at the outset that they're pretty straightforward, and for the most part, they are. The special treatment accorded lvalues when deducing types for universal references muddies the water a bit, however, and the decay-to-pointer rules for arrays and functions stirs up even greater turbidity. Sometimes you simply want to grab your compilers and demand, "Tell me what type you're deducing!" When that happens, turn to Item 4, because it's devoted to coaxing compilers into doing just that.

Things to Remember

- During template type deduction, arguments that are references are treated as non-references, i.e., their reference-ness is ignored.

- When deducing types for universal reference parameters, lvalue arguments get special treatment.

- When deducing types for by-value parameters, const and/or volatile arguments are treated as non-const and non-volatile.

- During template type deduction, arguments that are array or function names decay to pointers, unless they're used to initialize references.

Item 2: Understand auto type deduction.

If you've read Item 1 on template type deduction, you already know almost everything you need to know about auto type deduction, because, with only one curious exception, auto type deduction *is* template type deduction. But how can that be? Template type deduction involves templates and functions and parameters, but auto deals with none of those things.

That's true, but it doesn't matter. There's a direct mapping between template type deduction and auto type deduction. There is literally an algorithmic transformation from one to the other.

In Item 1, template type deduction is explained using this general function template

```
template<typename T>
void f(ParamType param);
```

and this general call:

```
f(expr);                        // call f with some expression
```

In the call to f, compilers use *expr* to deduce types for T and *ParamType*.

When a variable is declared using `auto`, `auto` plays the role of T in the template, and the type specifier for the variable acts as *ParamType*. This is easier to show than to describe, so consider this example:

```
auto x = 27;
```

Here, the type specifier for x is simply `auto` by itself. On the other hand, in this declaration,

```
const auto cx = x;
```

the type specifier is `const auto`. And here,

```
const auto& rx = x;
```

the type specifier is `const auto&`. To deduce types for x, cx, and rx in these examples, compilers act as if there were a template for each declaration as well as a call to that template with the corresponding initializing expression:

```
template<typename T>            // conceptual template for
void func_for_x(T param);       // deducing x's type

func_for_x(27);                 // conceptual call: param's
                                // deduced type is x's type

template<typename T>            // conceptual template for
void func_for_cx(const T param); // deducing cx's type

func_for_cx(x);                 // conceptual call: param's
                                // deduced type is cx's type

template<typename T>            // conceptual template for
void func_for_rx(const T& param); // deducing rx's type

func_for_rx(x);                 // conceptual call: param's
                                // deduced type is rx's type
```

As I said, deducing types for `auto` is, with only one exception (which we'll discuss soon), the same as deducing types for templates.

Item 1 divides template type deduction into three cases, based on the characteristics of *ParamType*, the type specifier for `param` in the general function template. In a variable declaration using `auto`, the type specifier takes the place of *ParamType*, so there are three cases for that, too:

- Case 1: The type specifier is a pointer or reference, but not a universal reference.
- Case 2: The type specifier is a universal reference.

- Case 3: The type specifier is neither a pointer nor a reference.

We've already seen examples of cases 1 and 3:

```
auto x = 27;            // case 3 (x is neither ptr nor reference)

const auto cx = x;      // case 3 (cx isn't either)

const auto& rx = x;     // case 1 (rx is a non-universal ref.)
```

Case 2 works as you'd expect:

```
auto&& uref1 = x;       // x is int and lvalue,
                        // so uref1's type is int&

auto&& uref2 = cx;      // cx is const int and lvalue,
                        // so uref2's type is const int&

auto&& uref3 = 27;      // 27 is int and rvalue,
                        // so uref3's type is int&&
```

Item 1 concludes with a discussion of how array and function names decay into pointers for non-reference type specifiers. That happens in auto type deduction, too:

```
const char name[] =         // name's type is const char[13]
    "R. N. Briggs";

auto arr1 = name;           // arr1's type is const char*

auto& arr2 = name;          // arr2's type is
                            // const char (&)[13]


void someFunc(int, double); // someFunc is a function;
                            // type is void(int, double)

auto func1 = someFunc;      // func1's type is
                            // void (*)(int, double)

auto& func2 = someFunc;     // func2's type is
                            // void (&)(int, double)
```

As you can see, auto type deduction works like template type deduction. They're essentially two sides of the same coin.

Except for the one way they differ. We'll start with the observation that if you want to declare an int with an initial value of 27, C++98 gives you two syntactic choices:

```
int x1 = 27;
int x2(27);
```

C++11, through its support for uniform initialization, adds these:

```
int x3 = { 27 };
int x4{ 27 };
```

All in all, four syntaxes, but only one result: an int with value 27.

But as Item 5 explains, there are advantages to declaring variables using auto instead of fixed types, so it'd be nice to replace int with auto in the above variable declarations. Straightforward textual substitution yields this code:

```
auto x1 = 27;
auto x2(27);
auto x3 = { 27 };
auto x4{ 27 };
```

These declarations all compile, but they don't have the same meaning as the ones they replace. The first two statements do, indeed, declare a variable of type int with value 27. The second two, however, declare a variable of type std::initializer_list<int> containing a single element with value 27!

```
auto x1 = 27;          // type is int, value is 27

auto x2(27);           // ditto

auto x3 = { 27 };      // type is std::initializer_list<int>,
                       // value is { 27 }

auto x4{ 27 };         // ditto
```

This is due to a special type deduction rule for auto. When the initializer for an auto-declared variable is enclosed in braces, the deduced type is a std::initializer_list.[1] If such a type can't be deduced (e.g., because the values in the braced initializer are of different types), the code will be rejected:

---

[1] In November 2014, the C++ Standardization Committee adopted proposal N3922, which eliminates the special type deduction rule for auto and braced initializers using direct initialization syntax, i.e., when there is no "=" preceding the braced initializer. Under N3922 (which isn't part of C++11 or C++14, but which has been implemented by many compilers), the type of x4 in the examples above is int, not std::initializer_list<int>.

```
auto x5 = { 1, 2, 3.0 };  // error! can't deduce T for
                          // std::initializer_list<T>
```

As the comment indicates, type deduction will fail in this case, but it's important to recognize that there are actually two kinds of type deduction taking place. One kind stems from the use of `auto`: x5's type has to be deduced. Because x5's initializer is in braces, x5 must be deduced to be a `std::initializer_list`. But `std::initializer_list` is a template. Instantiations are `std::initializer_list<T>` for some type T, and that means that T's type must also be deduced. Such deduction falls under the purview of the second kind of type deduction occurring here: template type deduction. In this example, that deduction fails, because the values in the braced initializer don't have a single type.

The treatment of braced initializers is the only way in which `auto` type deduction and template type deduction differ. When an `auto`–declared variable is initialized with a braced initializer, the deduced type is an instantiation of `std::initializer_list`. But if the corresponding template is passed the same initializer, type deduction fails, and the code is rejected:

```
auto x = { 11, 23, 9 };   // x's type is
                          // std::initializer_list<int>

template<typename T>      // template with parameter
void f(T param);          // declaration equivalent to
                          // x's declaration

f({ 11, 23, 9 });         // error! can't deduce type for T
```

However, if you specify in the template that `param` is a `std::initializer_list<T>` for some unknown T, template type deduction will deduce what T is:

```
template<typename T>
void f(std::initializer_list<T> initList);

f({ 11, 23, 9 });         // T deduced as int, and initList's
                          // type is std::initializer_list<int>
```

So the only real difference between `auto` and template type deduction is that `auto` *assumes* that a braced initializer represents a `std::initializer_list`, but template type deduction doesn't.

You might wonder why `auto` type deduction has a special rule for braced initializers, but template type deduction does not. I wonder this myself. Alas, I have not been able to find a convincing explanation. But the rule is the rule, and this means you must remember that if you declare a variable using `auto` and you initialize it with a braced initializer, the deduced type will always be `std::initializer_list`. It's especially important to bear this in mind if you embrace the philosophy of uniform initialization—of enclosing initializing values in braces as a matter of course. A classic mistake in C++11 programming is accidentally declaring a `std::initializer_list` variable when you mean to declare something else. This pitfall is one of the reasons some developers put braces around their initializers only when they have to. (When you have to is discussed in Item 7.)

For C++11, this is the full story, but for C++14, the tale continues. C++14 permits `auto` to indicate that a function's return type should be deduced (see Item 3), and C++14 lambdas may use `auto` in parameter declarations. However, these uses of `auto` employ *template type deduction*, not `auto` type deduction. So a function with an `auto` return type that returns a braced initializer won't compile:

```
auto createInitList()
{
  return { 1, 2, 3 };      // error: can't deduce type
}                           // for { 1, 2, 3 }
```

The same is true when `auto` is used in a parameter type specification in a C++14 lambda:

```
std::vector<int> v;
…

auto resetV =
  [&v](const auto& newValue) { v = newValue; };      // C++14

…

resetV({ 1, 2, 3 });       // error! can't deduce type
                           // for { 1, 2, 3 }
```

Things to Remember

- `auto` type deduction is usually the same as template type deduction, but `auto` type deduction assumes that a braced initializer represents a `std::initializer_list`, and template type deduction doesn't.
- `auto` in a function return type or a lambda parameter implies template type deduction, not `auto` type deduction.

Item 3: Understand `decltype`.

`decltype` is an odd creature. Given a name or an expression, `decltype` tells you the name's or the expression's type. Typically, what it tells you is exactly what you'd predict. Occasionally, however, it provides results that leave you scratching your head and turning to reference works or online Q&A sites for revelation.

We'll begin with the typical cases—the ones harboring no surprises. In contrast to what happens during type deduction for templates and `auto` (see Items 1 and 2), `decltype` typically parrots back the exact type of the name or expression you give it:

```cpp
const int i = 0;           // decltype(i) is const int

bool f(const Widget& w);   // decltype(w) is const Widget&
                           // decltype(f) is bool(const Widget&)

struct Point {
  int x, y;                // decltype(Point::x) is int
};                         // decltype(Point::y) is int

Widget w;                  // decltype(w) is Widget

if (f(w)) …                // decltype(f(w)) is bool

template<typename T>       // simplified version of std::vector
class vector {
public:
  …
  T& operator[](std::size_t index);
  …
};

vector<int> v;             // decltype(v) is vector<int>
…
if (v[0] == 0) …           // decltype(v[0]) is int&
```

See? No surprises.

In C++11, perhaps the primary use for `decltype` is declaring function templates where the function's return type depends on its parameter types. For example, suppose we'd like to write a function that takes a container that supports indexing via square brackets (i.e., the use of "[]") plus a numeric index, then authenticates the user before returning the result of the indexing operation. The return type of the function should be the same as the type returned by the indexing operation.

`operator[]` on a container of objects of type T typically returns a T&. This is the case for `std::deque`, for example, and it's almost always the case for `std::vector`. For `std::vector<bool>`, however, `operator[]` does not return a bool&. Instead, it returns a brand new object. The whys and hows of this situation are explored in

Item 6, but what's important here is that the type returned by a container's opera-tor[] depends on the container.

decltype makes it easy to express that. Here's a first cut at the template we'd like to write, showing the use of decltype to compute the return type. The template needs a bit of refinement, but we'll defer that for now:

```
template<typename Container, typename Index>   // works, but
auto authAndAccess(Container& c, Index i)        // requires
  -> decltype(c[i])                              // refinement
{
  authenticateUser();
  return c[i];
}
```

The use of auto before the function name has nothing to do with type deduction. Rather, it indicates that C++11's *trailing return type* syntax is being used, i.e., that the function's return type will be declared following the parameter list (after the "->"). A trailing return type has the advantage that the function's parameters can be used in the specification of the return type. In authAndAccess, for example, we specify the return type using c and i. If we were to have the return type precede the function name in the conventional fashion, c and i would be unavailable, because they would not have been declared yet.

With this declaration, authAndAccess returns whatever type operator[] returns when applied to the passed-in container, exactly as we desire.

C++11 permits return types for single-statement lambdas to be deduced, and C++14 extends this to both all lambdas and all functions, including those with multiple statements (even multiple returns, provided all yield the same deduced type). In the case of authAndAccess, that means that in C++14 we can omit the trailing return type, leaving just the leading auto. With that form of declaration, auto *does* mean that type deduction will take place. In particular, it means that compilers will deduce the function's return type from the function's implementation:

```
template<typename Container, typename Index>   // C++14;
auto authAndAccess(Container& c, Index i)        // not quite
{                                                // correct
  authenticateUser();
  return c[i];                  // return type deduced from c[i]
}
```

Item 2 explains that for functions with an auto return type specification, compilers employ template type deduction. In this case, that's problematic. As we've discussed, operator[] for most containers-of-T returns a T&, but Item 1 explains that during template type deduction, the reference-ness of an initializing expression is ignored. Consider what that means for this client code:

```
std::deque<int> d;
...
authAndAccess(d, 5) = 10;   // authenticate user, return d[5],
                            // then assign 10 to it;
                            // this won't compile!
```

Here, d[5] returns an int&, but auto return type deduction for authAndAccess will strip off the reference, thus yielding a return type of int. That int, being the return value of a function, is an rvalue, and the code above thus attempts to assign 10 to an rvalue int. That's forbidden in C++, so the code won't compile.

To get authAndAccess to work as we'd like, we need to use decltype type deduction for its return type, i.e., to specify that authAndAccess should return exactly the same type that the expression c[i] returns. The guardians of C++, anticipating the need to use decltype type deduction rules in some cases where types are inferred, make this possible in C++14 through the decltype(auto) specifier. What may initially seem contradictory (decltype *and* auto?) actually makes perfect sense: auto specifies that the type is to be deduced, and decltype says that decltype rules should be used during the deduction. We can thus write authAndAccess like this:

```
template<typename Container, typename Index>    // C++14; works,
decltype(auto)                                  // but still
authAndAccess(Container& c, Index i)            // requires
{                                               // refinement
  authenticateUser();
  return c[i];
}
```

Now authAndAccess will truly return whatever c[i] returns. In particular, for the common case where c[i] returns a T&, authAndAccess will also return a T&, and in the uncommon case where c[i] returns an object, authAndAccess will return an object, too.

The use of decltype(auto) is not limited to function return types. It can also be convenient for declaring variables when you want to apply the decltype type deduction rules to the initializing expression:

```
Widget w;

const Widget& cw = w;

auto myWidget1 = cw;                     // auto type deduction:
                                         // myWidget1's type is Widget
```

```
decltype(auto) myWidget2 = cw;    // decltype type deduction:
                                  // myWidget2's type is
                                  //    const Widget&
```

But two things are bothering you, I know. One is the refinement to `authAndAccess` I mentioned, but have not yet described. Let's address that now.

Look again at the declaration for the C++14 version of `authAndAccess`:

```
template<typename Container, typename Index>
decltype(auto) authAndAccess(Container& c, Index i);
```

The container is passed by lvalue-reference-to-non-`const`, because returning a reference to an element of the container permits clients to modify that container. But this means it's not possible to pass rvalue containers to this function. Rvalues can't bind to lvalue references (unless they're lvalue-references-to-`const`, which is not the case here).

Admittedly, passing an rvalue container to `authAndAccess` is an edge case. An rvalue container, being a temporary object, would typically be destroyed at the end of the statement containing the call to `authAndAccess`, and that means that a reference to an element in that container (which is typically what `authAndAccess` would return) would dangle at the end of the statement that created it. Still, it could make sense to pass a temporary object to `authAndAccess`. A client might simply want to make a copy of an element in the temporary container, for example:

```
std::deque<std::string> makeStringDeque();    // factory function

// make copy of 5th element of deque returned
// from makeStringDeque
auto s = authAndAccess(makeStringDeque(), 5);
```

Supporting such use means we need to revise the declaration for `authAndAccess` to accept both lvalues and rvalues. Overloading would work (one overload would declare an lvalue reference parameter, the other an rvalue reference parameter), but then we'd have two functions to maintain. A way to avoid that is to have `authAndAccess` employ a reference parameter that can bind to lvalues *and* rvalues, and Item 24 explains that that's exactly what universal references do. `authAndAccess` can therefore be declared like this:

```
template<typename Container, typename Index>    // c is now a
decltype(auto) authAndAccess(Container&& c,     // universal
                             Index i);          // reference
```

In this template, we don't know what type of container we're operating on, and that means we're equally ignorant of the type of index objects it uses. Employing pass-by-value for objects of an unknown type generally risks the performance hit of unnecessary copying, the behavioral problems of object slicing (see Item 41), and the sting of our coworkers' derision, but in the case of numeric indices, following the example of the Standard Library for index values (e.g., in operator[] for std::string, std::vector, and std::deque) seems reasonable, so we'll stick with pass-by-value for them.

However, we need to update the template's implementation to bring it into accord with Item 25's admonition to apply std::forward to universal references:

```
template<typename Container, typename Index>    // final
decltype(auto)                                  // C++14
authAndAccess(Container&& c, Index i)           // version
{
  authenticateUser();
  return std::forward<Container>(c)[i];
}
```

This should do everything we want, but it requires a C++14 compiler. If you don't have one, you'll need to use the C++11 version of the template. It's the same as its C++14 counterpart, except that you have to specify the return type yourself:

```
template<typename Container, typename Index>    // final
auto                                            // C++11
authAndAccess(Container&& c, Index i)           // version
  -> decltype(std::forward<Container>(c)[i])
{
  authenticateUser();
  return std::forward<Container>(c)[i];
}
```

The other issue that's likely to be nagging at you is my remark at the beginning of this Item that decltype *almost* always produces the type you expect, that it *rarely* surprises. Truth be told, you're unlikely to encounter these exceptions to the rule unless you're a heavy-duty library implementer.

To *fully* understand decltype's behavior, you'll have to familiarize yourself with a few special cases. Most of these are too obscure to warrant discussion in a book like this, but looking at one lends insight into decltype as well as its use.

Applying decltype to a name yields the declared type for that name. Names are typically lvalue expressions, but that doesn't affect decltype's behavior. For lvalue expressions more complicated than names, however, decltype generally ensures that the type reported is an lvalue reference. That is, if an lvalue expression other than a name has type T, `decltype` reports that type as T&. This seldom has any impact, because the type of most lvalue expressions inherently includes an lvalue reference qualifier. Functions returning lvalues, for example, always return lvalue references.

There is an implication of this behavior that is worth being aware of, however. In

```
int x = 0;
```

x is the name of a variable, so `decltype(x)` is `int`. But wrapping the name x in parentheses—"(x)"—yields an expression more complicated than a name. Being a name, x is an lvalue, and C++ defines the expression (x) to be an lvalue, too. `decltype((x))` is therefore `int&`. Putting parentheses around a name can change the type that `decltype` reports for it!

In C++11, this is little more than a curiosity, but in conjunction with C++14's support for `decltype(auto)`, it means that a seemingly trivial change in the way you write a `return` statement can affect the deduced type for a function:

```
decltype(auto) f1()
{
  int x = 0;
  ...
  return x;          // decltype(x) is int, so f1 returns int
}

decltype(auto) f2()
{
  int x = 0;
  ...
  return (x);        // decltype((x)) is int&, so f2 returns int&
}
```

Note that not only does f2 have a different return type from f1, it's also returning a reference to a local variable! That's the kind of code that puts you on the express train to undefined behavior—a train you certainly don't want to be on.

The primary lesson is to pay very close attention when using `decltype(auto)`. Seemingly insignificant details in the expression whose type is being deduced can affect the type that `decltype(auto)` reports. To ensure that the type being deduced is the type you expect, use the techniques described in Item 4.

At the same time, don't lose sight of the bigger picture. Sure, `decltype` (both alone and in conjunction with `auto`) may occasionally yield type-deduction surprises, but that's not the normal situation. Normally, `decltype` produces the type you expect.

This is especially true when `decltype` is applied to names, because in that case, `decltype` does just what it sounds like: it reports that name's declared type.

Things to Remember

- `decltype` almost always yields the type of a variable or expression without any modifications.

- For lvalue expressions of type `T` other than names, `decltype` always reports a type of `T&`.

- C++14 supports `decltype(auto)`, which, like `auto`, deduces a type from its initializer, but it performs the type deduction using the `decltype` rules.

Item 4: Know how to view deduced types.

The choice of tools for viewing the results of type deduction is dependent on the phase of the software development process where you want the information. We'll explore three possibilities: getting type deduction information as you edit your code, getting it during compilation, and getting it at runtime.

IDE Editors

Code editors in IDEs often show the types of program entities (e.g., variables, parameters, functions, etc.) when you do something like hover your cursor over the entity. For example, given this code,

```
const int theAnswer = 42;

auto x = theAnswer;
auto y = &theAnswer;
```

an IDE editor would likely show that x's deduced type was `int` and y's was `const int*`.

For this to work, your code must be in a more or less compilable state, because what makes it possible for the IDE to offer this kind of information is a C++ compiler (or at least the front end of one) running inside the IDE. If that compiler can't make enough sense of your code to parse it and perform type deduction, it can't show you what types it deduced.

For simple types like `int`, information from IDEs is generally fine. As we'll see soon, however, when more complicated types are involved, the information displayed by IDEs may not be particularly helpful.

Compiler Diagnostics

A generally effective way to get a compiler to show a type it has deduced is to use that type in a way that leads to compilation problems. The error message reporting the problem nearly always mentions the type that's causing it.

Suppose, for example, we'd like to see the types that were deduced for x and y in the previous example. We first declare a class template that we *don't define*. Something like this does nicely:

```
template<typename T>      // declaration only for TD;
class TD;                 // TD == "Type Displayer"
```

Attempts to instantiate this template will elicit an error message, because there's no template definition to instantiate. To see the types for x and y, just try to instantiate TD with their types:

```
TD<decltype(x)> xType;    // elicit errors containing
TD<decltype(y)> yType;    // x's and y's types
```

I use variable names of the form *variableName*Type, because they tend to yield error messages that help me find the information I'm looking for. For the code above, one of my compilers issues diagnostics reading, in part, as follows (I've highlighted the type information we're after):

```
error: aggregate 'TD<int> xType' has incomplete type and
    cannot be defined
error: aggregate 'TD<const int *> yType' has incomplete type
    and cannot be defined
```

A different compiler provides the same information, but in a different form:

```
error: 'xType' uses undefined class 'TD<int>'
error: 'yType' uses undefined class 'TD<const int *>'
```

Formatting differences aside, almost all the compilers I've tested produce error messages with useful type information when this technique is employed.

Runtime Output

The printf approach to displaying type information (not that I'm recommending you use printf) can't be employed until runtime, but it offers full control over the formatting of the output. The challenge is to create a textual representation of the type you care about that is suitable for display. "No sweat," you're thinking, "it's typeid and std::type_info::name to the rescue." In our continuing quest to see the types deduced for x and y, you may figure we can write this:

```
std::cout << typeid(x).name() << '\n';     // display types for
std::cout << typeid(y).name() << '\n';     // x and y
```

This approach relies on the fact that invoking `typeid` on an object such as x or y yields a `std::type_info` object, and `std::type_info` has a member function, `name`, that produces a C-style string (i.e., a `const char*`) representation of the name of the type.

Calls to `std::type_info::name` are not guaranteed to return anything sensible, but implementations try to be helpful. The level of helpfulness varies. The GNU and Clang compilers report that the type of x is "i", and the type of y is "PKi", for example. These results make sense once you learn that, in output from these compilers, "i" means "int" and "PK" means "pointer to ~~konst~~ const." (Both compilers support a tool, `c++filt`, that decodes such "mangled" types.) Microsoft's compiler produces less cryptic output: "int" for x and "int const *" for y.

Because these results are correct for the types of x and y, you might be tempted to view the type-reporting problem as solved, but let's not be hasty. Consider a more complex example:

```
template<typename T>                    // template function to
void f(const T& param);                 // be called

std::vector<Widget> createVec();        // factory function

const auto vw = createVec();            // init vw w/factory return

if (!vw.empty()) {
  f(&vw[0]);                            // call f
  …
}
```

This code, which involves a user-defined type (`Widget`), an STL container (`std::vector`), and an `auto` variable (vw), is more representative of the situations where you might want some visibility into the types your compilers are deducing. For example, it'd be nice to know what types are inferred for the template type parameter T and the function parameter `param` in f.

Loosing `typeid` on the problem is straightforward. Just add some code to f to display the types you'd like to see:

```
template<typename T>
void f(const T& param)
{
  using std::cout;
```

```
    cout << "T =      " << typeid(T).name() << '\n';      // show T

    cout << "param = " << typeid(param).name() << '\n'; // show
    ...                                                  // param's
}                                                        // type
```

Executables produced by the GNU and Clang compilers produce this output:

```
T =     PK6Widget
param = PK6Widget
```

We already know that for these compilers, PK means "pointer to const," so the only mystery is the number 6. That's simply the number of characters in the class name that follows (Widget). So these compilers tell us that both T and param are of type const Widget*.

Microsoft's compiler concurs:

```
T =     class Widget const *
param = class Widget const *
```

Three independent compilers producing the same information suggests that the information is accurate. But look more closely. In the template f, param's declared type is const T&. That being the case, doesn't it seem odd that T and param have the same type? If T were int, for example, param's type should be const int&—not the same type at all.

Sadly, the results of std::type_info::name are not reliable. In this case, for example, the type that all three compilers report for param is incorrect. Furthermore, they're essentially *required* to be incorrect, because the specification for std::type_info::name mandates that the type be treated as if it had been passed to a template function as a by-value parameter. As Item 1 explains, that means that if the type is a reference, its reference-ness is ignored, and if the type after reference removal is const (or volatile), its constness (or volatileness) is also ignored. That's why param's type—which is const Widget * const &—is reported as const Widget*. First the type's reference-ness is removed, and then the constness of the resulting pointer is eliminated.

Equally sadly, the type information displayed by IDE editors is also not reliable—or at least not reliably useful. For this same example, one IDE editor I know reports T's type as (I am not making this up):

```
const
std::_Simple_types<std::_Wrap_alloc<std::_Vec_base_types<Widget,
std::allocator<Widget> >::_Alloc>::value_type>::value_type *
```

The same IDE editor shows param's type as:

```
const std::_Simple_types<...>::value_type *const &
```

That's less intimidating than the type for T, but the "..." in the middle is confusing until you realize that it's the IDE editor's way of saying "I'm omitting all that stuff that's part of T's type." With any luck, your development environment does a better job on code like this.

If you're more inclined to rely on libraries than luck, you'll be pleased to know that where `std::type_info::name` and IDEs may fail, the Boost TypeIndex library (often written as *Boost.TypeIndex*) is designed to succeed. The library isn't part of Standard C++, but neither are IDEs nor templates like TD. Furthermore, the fact that Boost libraries (available at *boost.org*) are cross-platform, open source, and available under a license designed to be palatable to even the most paranoid corporate legal team means that code using Boost libraries is nearly as portable as code relying on the Standard Library.

Here's how our function f can produce accurate type information using Boost.Type-Index:

```cpp
#include <boost/type_index.hpp>

template<typename T>
void f(const T& param)
{
  using std::cout;
  using boost::typeindex::type_id_with_cvr;

  // show T
  cout << "T =     "
       << type_id_with_cvr<T>().pretty_name()
       << '\n';

  // show param's type
  cout << "param = "
       << type_id_with_cvr<decltype(param)>().pretty_name()
       << '\n';
  ...
}
```

The way this works is that the function template `boost::typeindex::type_id_with_cvr` takes a type argument (the type about which we want information) and *doesn't* remove `const`, `volatile`, or reference qualifiers (hence the "with_cvr" in the template name). The result is a `boost::typeindex::type_index` object, whose `pretty_name` member function produces a `std::string` containing a human-friendly representation of the type.

With this implementation for `f`, consider again the call that yields incorrect type information for `param` when `typeid` is used:

```
std::vector<Widget> createVec();        // factory function

const auto vw = createVec();            // init vw w/factory return

if (!vw.empty()) {
  f(&vw[0]);                            // call f
  ...
}
```

Under compilers from GNU and Clang, Boost.TypeIndex produces this (accurate) output:

```
T =      Widget const*
param = Widget const* const&
```

Results under Microsoft's compiler are essentially the same:

```
T =      class Widget const *
param = class Widget const * const &
```

Such near-uniformity is nice, but it's important to remember that IDE editors, compiler error messages, and libraries like Boost.TypeIndex are merely tools you can use to help you figure out what types your compilers are deducing. All can be helpful, but at the end of the day, there's no substitute for understanding the type deduction information in Items 1–3.

Things to Remember

- Deduced types can often be seen using IDE editors, compiler error messages, and the Boost TypeIndex library.
- The results of some tools may be neither helpful nor accurate, so an understanding of C++'s type deduction rules remains essential.

---

auto

In concept, `auto` is as simple as simple can be, but it's more subtle than it looks. Using it saves typing, sure, but it also prevents correctness and performance issues that can bedevil manual type declarations. Furthermore, some of `auto`'s type deduction results, while dutifully conforming to the prescribed algorithm, are, from the perspective of a programmer, just wrong. When that's the case, it's important to know how to guide `auto` to the right answer, because falling back on manual type declarations is an alternative that's often best avoided.

This brief chapter covers all of `auto`'s ins and outs.

Item 5: Prefer `auto` to explicit type declarations.

Ah, the simple joy of

```
int x;
```

Wait. Damn. I forgot to initialize x, so its value is indeterminate. Maybe. It might actually be initialized to zero. Depends on the context. Sigh.

Never mind. Let's move on to the simple joy of declaring a local variable to be initialized by dereferencing an iterator:

```
template<typename It>      // algorithm to dwim ("do what I mean")
void dwim(It b, It e)      // for all elements in range from
{                          // b to e
  for (; b != e; ++b) {
    typename std::iterator_traits<It>::value_type
      currValue = *b;
    …
```

```
    }
  }
```

Ugh. "typename std::iterator_traits<It>::value_type" to express the type of the value pointed to by an iterator? Really? I must have blocked out the memory of how much fun that is. Damn. Wait—didn't I already say that?

Okay, simple joy (take three): the delight of declaring a local variable whose type is that of a closure. Oh, right. The type of a closure is known only to the compiler, hence can't be written out. Sigh. Damn.

Damn, damn, damn! Programming in C++ is not the joyous experience it should be!

Well, it didn't used to be. But as of C++11, all these issues go away, courtesy of auto. auto variables have their type deduced from their initializer, so they must be initialized. That means you can wave goodbye to a host of uninitialized variable problems as you speed by on the modern C++ superhighway:

```
int x1;                    // potentially uninitialized

auto x2;                   // error! initializer required

auto x3 = 0;               // fine, x3's value is well-defined
```

Said highway lacks the potholes associated with declaring a local variable whose value is that of a dereferenced iterator:

```
template<typename It>      // as before
void dwim(It b, It e)
{
  for (; b != e; ++b) {
    auto currValue = *b;

    …
  }
}
```

And because auto uses type deduction (see Item 2), it can represent types known only to compilers:

```
auto derefUPLess =                                // comparison func.
  [](const std::unique_ptr<Widget>& p1,           // for Widgets
     const std::unique_ptr<Widget>& p2)           // pointed to by
  { return *p1 < *p2; };                          // std::unique_ptrs
```

Very cool. In C++14, the temperature drops further, because parameters to lambda expressions may involve auto:

```
auto derefLess =                     // C++14 comparison
  [](const auto& p1,                 // function for
```

```
        const auto& p2)                        // values pointed
    { return *p1 < *p2; };                     // to by anything
                                               // pointer-like
```

Coolness notwithstanding, perhaps you're thinking we don't really need `auto` to declare a variable that holds a closure, because we can use a `std::function` object. It's true, we can, but possibly that's not what you were thinking. And maybe now you're thinking "What's a `std::function` object?" So let's clear that up.

`std::function` is a template in the C++11 Standard Library that generalizes the idea of a function pointer. Whereas function pointers can point only to functions, however, `std::function` objects can refer to any callable object, i.e., to anything that can be invoked like a function. Just as you must specify the type of function to point to when you create a function pointer (i.e., the signature of the functions you want to point to), you must specify the type of function to refer to when you create a `std::function` object. You do that through `std::function`'s template parameter. For example, to declare a `std::function` object named `func` that could refer to any callable object acting as if it had this signature,

```
bool(const std::unique_ptr<Widget>&,    // C++11 signature for
     const std::unique_ptr<Widget>&)    // std::unique_ptr<Widget>
                                        // comparison function
```

you'd write this:

```
std::function<bool(const std::unique_ptr<Widget>&,
                   const std::unique_ptr<Widget>&)> func;
```

Because lambda expressions yield callable objects, closures can be stored in `std::function` objects. That means we could declare the C++11 version of `deref-UPLess` without using `auto` as follows:

```
std::function<bool(const std::unique_ptr<Widget>&,
                   const std::unique_ptr<Widget>&)>
  derefUPLess = [](const std::unique_ptr<Widget>& p1,
                   const std::unique_ptr<Widget>& p2)
                { return *p1 < *p2; };
```

It's important to recognize that even setting aside the syntactic verbosity and need to repeat the parameter types, using `std::function` is not the same as using `auto`. An `auto`-declared variable holding a closure has the same type as the closure, and as such it uses only as much memory as the closure requires. The type of a `std::function`-declared variable holding a closure is an instantiation of the `std::function` template, and that has a fixed size for any given signature. This size may not be adequate for the closure it's asked to store, and when that's the case, the `std::function` constructor will allocate heap memory to store the closure. The result is that the std::function object typically uses more memory than the auto-declared object. And, thanks to implementation details that restrict inlining and yield indirect function calls, invoking a closure via a std::function object is almost certain to be slower than calling it via an auto-declared object. In other words, the std::function approach is generally bigger and slower than the auto approach, and it may yield out-of-memory exceptions, too. Plus, as you can see in the examples above, writing "auto" is a whole lot less work than writing the type of the std::function instantiation. In the competition between auto and std::function for holding a closure, it's pretty much game, set, and match for auto. (A similar argument can be made for auto over std::function for holding the result of calls to std::bind, but in Item 34, I do my best to convince you to use lambdas instead of std::bind, anyway.)

The advantages of auto extend beyond the avoidance of uninitialized variables, verbose variable declarations, and the ability to directly hold closures. One is the ability to avoid what I call problems related to "type shortcuts." Here's something you've probably seen—possibly even written:

```
std::vector<int> v;
…
unsigned sz = v.size();
```

The official return type of v.size() is std::vector<int>::size_type, but few developers are aware of that. std::vector<int>::size_type is specified to be an unsigned integral type, so a lot of programmers figure that unsigned is good enough and write code such as the above. This can have some interesting consequences. On 32-bit Windows, for example, both unsigned and std::vector<int>::size_type are the same size, but on 64-bit Windows, unsigned is 32 bits, while std::vector<int>::size_type is 64 bits. This means that code that works under 32-bit Windows may behave incorrectly under 64-bit Windows, and when porting your application from 32 to 64 bits, who wants to spend time on issues like that?

Using auto ensures that you don't have to:

```
auto sz = v.size();   // sz's type is std::vector<int>::size_type
```

Still unsure about the wisdom of using auto? Then consider this code:

```
std::unordered_map<std::string, int> m;
…

for (const std::pair<std::string, int>& p : m)
{
    …                     // do something with p
}
```

This looks perfectly reasonable, but there's a problem. Do you see it?

Recognizing what's amiss requires remembering that the key part of a `std::unordered_map` is const, so the type of `std::pair` in the hash table (which is what a `std::unordered_map` is) isn't `std::pair<std::string, int>`, it's `std::pair<const std::string, int>`. But that's not the type declared for the variable p in the loop above. As a result, compilers will strive to find a way to convert `std::pair<const std::string, int>` objects (i.e., what's in the hash table) to `std::pair<std::string, int>` objects (the declared type for p). They'll succeed by creating a temporary object of the type that p wants to bind to by copying each object in m, then binding the reference p to that temporary object. At the end of each loop iteration, the temporary object will be destroyed. If you wrote this loop, you'd likely be surprised by this behavior, because you'd almost certainly intend to simply bind the reference p to each element in m.

Such unintentional type mismatches can be autoed away:

```
for (const auto& p : m)
{
    …                              // as before
}
```

This is not only more efficient, it's also easier to type. Furthermore, this code has the very attractive characteristic that if you take p's address, you're sure to get a pointer to an element within m. In the code not using auto, you'd get a pointer to a temporary object—an object that would be destroyed at the end of the loop iteration.

The last two examples—writing unsigned when you should have written `std::vector<int>::size_type` and writing `std::pair<std::string, int>` when you should have written `std::pair<const std::string, int>`—demonstrate how explicitly specifying types can lead to implicit conversions that you neither want nor expect. If you use auto as the type of the target variable, you need not worry about mismatches between the type of variable you're declaring and the type of the expression used to initialize it.

There are thus several reasons to prefer auto over explicit type declarations. Yet auto isn't perfect. The type for each auto variable is deduced from its initializing expression, and some initializing expressions have types that are neither anticipated nor desired. The conditions under which such cases arise, and what you can do about them, are discussed in Items 2, 3, and 6, so I won't address them here. Instead, I'll turn my attention to a different concern you may have about using auto in place of traditional type declarations: the readability of the resulting source code.

First, take a deep breath and relax. `auto` is an option, not a mandate. If, in your professional judgment, your code will be clearer or more maintainable or in some other way better by using explicit type declarations, you're free to continue using them. But bear in mind that C++ breaks no new ground in adopting what is generally known in the programming languages world as *type inference*. Other statically typed procedural languages (e.g., C#, D, Scala, Visual Basic) have a more or less equivalent feature, to say nothing of a variety of statically typed functional languages (e.g., ML, Haskell, OCaml, F#, etc.). In part, this is due to the success of dynamically typed languages such as Perl, Python, and Ruby, where variables are rarely explicitly typed. The software development community has extensive experience with type inference, and it has demonstrated that there is nothing contradictory about such technology and the creation and maintenance of large, industrial-strength code bases.

Some developers are disturbed by the fact that using `auto` eliminates the ability to determine an object's type by a quick glance at the source code. However, IDEs' ability to show object types often mitigates this problem (even taking into account the IDE type-display issues mentioned in Item 4), and, in many cases, a somewhat abstract view of an object's type is just as useful as the exact type. It often suffices, for example, to know that an object is a container or a counter or a smart pointer, without knowing exactly what kind of container, counter, or smart pointer it is. Assuming well-chosen variable names, such abstract type information should almost always be at hand.

The fact of the matter is that writing types explicitly often does little more than introduce opportunities for subtle errors, either in correctness or efficiency or both. Furthermore, `auto` types automatically change if the type of their initializing expression changes, and that means that some refactorings are facilitated by the use of `auto`. For example, if a function is declared to return an `int`, but you later decide that a `long` would be better, the calling code automatically updates itself the next time you compile if the results of calling the function are stored in `auto` variables. If the results are stored in variables explicitly declared to be `int`, you'll need to find all the call sites so that you can revise them.

Things to Remember

- `auto` variables must be initialized, are generally immune to type mismatches that can lead to portability or efficiency problems, can ease the process of refactoring, and typically require less typing than variables with explicitly specified types.

- `auto`-typed variables are subject to the pitfalls described in Items 2 and 6.

Item 6: Use the explicitly typed initializer idiom when auto deduces undesired types.

Item 5 explains that using `auto` to declare variables offers a number of technical advantages over explicitly specifying types, but sometimes `auto`'s type deduction zigs when you want it to zag. For example, suppose I have a function that takes a `Widget` and returns a `std::vector<bool>`, where each `bool` indicates whether the `Widget` offers a particular feature:

```
std::vector<bool> features(const Widget& w);
```

Further suppose that bit 5 indicates whether the `Widget` has high priority. We can thus write code like this:

```
Widget w;
…

bool highPriority = features(w)[5];   // is w high priority?
…

processWidget(w, highPriority);        // process w in accord
                                       // with its priority
```

There's nothing wrong with this code. It'll work fine. But if we make the seemingly innocuous change of replacing the explicit type for `highPriority` with `auto`,

```
auto highPriority = features(w)[5];   // is w high priority?
```

the situation changes. All the code will continue to compile, but its behavior is no longer predictable:

```
processWidget(w, highPriority);        // undefined behavior!
```

As the comment indicates, the call to `processWidget` now has undefined behavior. But why? The answer is likely to be surprising. In the code using `auto`, the type of `highPriority` is no longer `bool`. Though `std::vector<bool>` conceptually holds `bool`s, `operator[]` for `std::vector<bool>` doesn't return a reference to an element of the container (which is what `std::vector::operator[]` returns for every type *except* `bool`). Instead, it returns an object of type `std::vector<bool>::reference` (a class nested inside `std::vector<bool>`).

`std::vector<bool>::reference` exists because `std::vector<bool>` is specified to represent its `bool`s in packed form, one bit per `bool`. That creates a problem for `std::vector<bool>`'s `operator[]`, because `operator[]` for `std::vector<T>` is supposed to return a `T&`, but C++ forbids references to bits. Not being able to return a bool&, operator[] for std::vector<bool> returns an object that *acts like* a bool&. For this act to succeed, std::vector<bool>::reference objects must be usable in essentially all contexts where bool&s can be. Among the features in std::vector<bool>::reference that make this work is an implicit conversion to bool. (Not to bool&, to *bool*. To explain the full set of techniques used by std::vector<bool>::reference to emulate the behavior of a bool& would take us too far afield, so I'll simply remark that this implicit conversion is only one stone in a larger mosaic.)

With this information in mind, look again at this part of the original code:

```
bool highPriority = features(w)[5];   // declare highPriority's
                                      // type explicitly
```

Here, features returns a std::vector<bool> object, on which operator[] is invoked. operator[] returns a std::vector<bool>::reference object, which is then implicitly converted to the bool that is needed to initialize highPriority. high-Priority thus ends up with the value of bit 5 in the std::vector<bool> returned by features, just like it's supposed to.

Contrast that with what happens in the auto-ized declaration for highPriority:

```
auto highPriority = features(w)[5];   // deduce highPriority's
                                      // type
```

Again, features returns a std::vector<bool> object, and, again, operator[] is invoked on it. operator[] continues to return a std::vector<bool>::reference object, but now there's a change, because auto deduces that as the type of high-Priority. highPriority doesn't have the value of bit 5 of the std::vector<bool> returned by features at all.

The value it does have depends on how std::vector<bool>::reference is implemented. One implementation is for such objects to contain a pointer to the machine word holding the referenced bit, plus the offset into that word for that bit. Consider what that means for the initialization of highPriority, assuming that such a std::vector<bool>::reference implementation is in place.

The call to features returns a temporary std::vector<bool> object. This object has no name, but for purposes of this discussion, I'll call it *temp*. operator[] is invoked on *temp*, and the std::vector<bool>::reference it returns contains a pointer to a word in the data structure holding the bits that are managed by *temp*, plus the offset into that word corresponding to bit 5. highPriority is a copy of this std::vector<bool>::reference object, so highPriority, too, contains a pointer to a word in *temp*, plus the offset corresponding to bit 5. At the end of the statement, *temp* is destroyed, because it's a temporary object. Therefore, `highPriority` contains a dangling pointer, and that's the cause of the undefined behavior in the call to `processWidget`:

```
processWidget(w, highPriority);    // undefined behavior!
                                   // highPriority contains
                                   // dangling pointer!
```

`std::vector<bool>::reference` is an example of a *proxy class*: a class that exists for the purpose of emulating and augmenting the behavior of some other type. Proxy classes are employed for a variety of purposes. `std::vector<bool>::reference` exists to offer the illusion that `operator[]` for `std::vector<bool>` returns a reference to a bit, for example, and the Standard Library's smart pointer types (see Chapter 4) are proxy classes that graft resource management onto raw pointers. The utility of proxy classes is well-established. In fact, the design pattern "Proxy" is one of the most longstanding members of the software design patterns pantheon.

Some proxy classes are designed to be apparent to clients. That's the case for `std::shared_ptr` and `std::unique_ptr`, for example. Other proxy classes are designed to act more or less invisibly. `std::vector<bool>::reference` is an example of such "invisible" proxies, as is its `std::bitset` compatriot, `std::bitset::reference`.

Also in that camp are some classes in C++ libraries employing a technique known as *expression templates*. Such libraries were originally developed to improve the efficiency of numeric code. Given a class `Matrix` and `Matrix` objects m1, m2, m3, and m4, for example, the expression

```
Matrix sum = m1 + m2 + m3 + m4;
```

can be computed much more efficiently if `operator+` for `Matrix` objects returns a proxy for the result instead of the result itself. That is, `operator+` for two `Matrix` objects would return an object of a proxy class such as Sum<Matrix, Matrix> instead of a `Matrix` object. As was the case with `std::vector<bool>::reference` and `bool`, there'd be an implicit conversion from the proxy class to `Matrix`, which would permit the initialization of sum from the proxy object produced by the expression on the right side of the "=". (The type of that object would traditionally encode the entire initialization expression, i.e., be something like Sum<Sum<Sum<Matrix, Matrix>, Matrix>, Matrix>. That's definitely a type from which clients should be shielded.)

As a general rule, "invisible" proxy classes don't play well with `auto`. Objects of such classes are often not designed to live longer than a single statement, so creating variables of those types tends to violate fundamental library design assumptions. That's the case with `std::vector<bool>::reference`, and we've seen that violating that assumption can lead to undefined behavior.

You therefore want to avoid code of this form:

```
auto someVar = expression of "invisible" proxy class type;
```

But how can you recognize when proxy objects are in use? The software employing them is unlikely to advertise their existence. They're supposed to be *invisible*, at least conceptually! And once you've found them, do you really have to abandon `auto` and the many advantages Item 5 demonstrates for it?

Let's take the how-do-you-find-them question first. Although "invisible" proxy classes are designed to fly beneath programmer radar in day-to-day use, libraries using them often document that they do so. The more you've familiarized yourself with the basic design decisions of the libraries you use, the less likely you are to be blindsided by proxy usage within those libraries.

Where documentation comes up short, header files fill the gap. It's rarely possible for source code to fully cloak proxy objects. They're typically returned from functions that clients are expected to call, so function signatures usually reflect their existence. Here's the spec for `std::vector<bool>::operator[]`, for example:

```
namespace std {                                    // from C++ Standards

    template <class Allocator>
    class vector<bool, Allocator> {
    public:
        …
        class reference { … };

        reference operator[](size_type n);
        …
    };
}
```

Assuming you know that `operator[]` for `std::vector<T>` normally returns a `T&`, the unconventional return type for `operator[]` in this case is a tip-off that a proxy class is in use. Paying careful attention to the interfaces you're using can often reveal the existence of proxy classes.

In practice, many developers discover the use of proxy classes only when they try to track down mystifying compilation problems or debug incorrect unit test results. Regardless of how you find them, once `auto` has been determined to be deducing the type of a proxy class instead of the type being proxied, the solution need not involve abandoning `auto`. `auto` itself isn't the problem. The problem is that `auto` isn't deducing the type you want it to deduce. The solution is to force a different type deduction. The way you do that is what I call *the explicitly typed initializer idiom*.

The explicitly typed initializer idiom involves declaring a variable with `auto`, but casting the initialization expression to the type you want `auto` to deduce. Here's how it can be used to force `highPriority` to be a `bool`, for example:

```
auto highPriority = static_cast<bool>(features(w)[5]);
```

Here, `features(w)[5]` continues to return a `std::vector<bool>::reference` object, just as it always has, but the cast changes the type of the expression to `bool`, which `auto` then deduces as the type for `highPriority`. At runtime, the `std::vector<bool>::reference` object returned from `std::vector<bool>::operator[]` executes the conversion to `bool` that it supports, and as part of that conversion, the still-valid pointer to the `std::vector<bool>` returned from `features` is dereferenced. That avoids the undefined behavior we ran into earlier. The index 5 is then applied to the bits pointed to by the pointer, and the `bool` value that emerges is used to initialize `highPriority`.

For the `Matrix` example, the explicitly typed initializer idiom would look like this:

```
auto sum = static_cast<Matrix>(m1 + m2 + m3 + m4);
```

Applications of the idiom aren't limited to initializers yielding proxy class types. It can also be useful to emphasize that you are deliberately creating a variable of a type that is different from that generated by the initializing expression. For example, suppose you have a function to calculate some tolerance value:

```
double calcEpsilon();                    // return tolerance value
```

`calcEpsilon` clearly returns a `double`, but suppose you know that for your application, the precision of a `float` is adequate, and you care about the difference in size between `float`s and `double`s. You could declare a `float` variable to store the result of `calcEpsilon`,

```
float ep = calcEpsilon();        // implicitly convert
                                 // double → float
```

but this hardly announces "I'm deliberately reducing the precision of the value returned by the function." A declaration using the explicitly typed initializer idiom, however, does:

```
auto ep = static_cast<float>(calcEpsilon());
```

Similar reasoning applies if you have a floating-point expression that you are deliberately storing as an integral value. Suppose you need to calculate the index of an element in a container with random access iterators (e.g., a `std::vector`, `std::deque`, or `std::array`), and you're given a `double` between `0.0` and `1.0` indicating how far from the beginning of the container the desired element is located. (`0.5` would indicate the middle of the container.) Further suppose that you're confident that the container isn't empty and that the resulting index will fit in an `int`. If the container is `c` and the double is `d`, you could calculate the index this way,

```
int idx = d * c.size();
if (idx == c.size()) --idx;        // keep idx valid when d == 1.0
```

but this obscures the fact that you're intentionally converting the `double` resulting from `d * c.size()` to an `int`. The explicitly typed initializer idiom makes things transparent:

```
auto idx = static_cast<int>(d * c.size());
if (idx == c.size()) --idx;        // keep idx valid when d == 1.0
```

Things to Remember

- "Invisible" proxy types can cause `auto` to deduce the "wrong" type for an initializing expression.

- The explicitly typed initializer idiom forces `auto` to deduce the type you want it to have.

CHAPTER 3

Moving to Modern C++

When it comes to big-name features, C++11 and C++14 have a lot to boast of. `auto`, smart pointers, move semantics, lambdas, concurrency—each is so important, I devote a chapter to it. It's essential to master those features, but becoming an effective modern C++ programmer requires a series of smaller steps, too. Each step answers specific questions that arise during the journey from C++98 to modern C++. When should you use braces instead of parentheses for object creation? Why are alias declarations better than `typedef`s? How does `constexpr` differ from `const`? What's the relationship between `const` member functions and thread safety? The list goes on and on. And one by one, this chapter provides the answers.

Item 7: Distinguish between ( ) and { } when creating objects.

Depending on your perspective, syntax choices for object initialization in C++11 embody either an embarrassment of riches or a confusing mess. As a general rule, initialization values may be specified with parentheses, an equals sign, or braces:

```
int x(0);          // initializer is in parentheses

int y = 0;         // initializer follows "="

int z{ 0 };        // initializer is in braces
```

In many cases, it's also possible to use an equals sign and braces together:

```
int z = { 0 };     // initializer uses "=" and braces
```

For the remainder of this Item, I'll generally ignore the equals-sign-plus-braces syntax, because C++ usually treats it the same as the braces-only version.

The "confusing mess" lobby points out that the use of an equals sign for initialization often misleads C++ newbies into thinking that an assignment is taking place, even though it's not. For built-in types like int, the difference is academic, but for user-defined types, it's important to distinguish initialization from assignment, because different function calls are involved:

```
Widget w1;              // call default constructor

Widget w2 = w1;         // not an assignment; calls copy ctor

w1 = w2;                // an assignment; calls copy operator=
```

Even with several initialization syntaxes, there were some situations where C++98 had no way to express a desired initialization. For example, it wasn't possible to directly indicate that an STL container should be created holding a particular set of values (e.g., 1, 3, and 5).

To address the confusion of multiple initialization syntaxes, as well as the fact that they don't cover all initialization scenarios, C++11 introduces *uniform initialization*: a single initialization syntax that can, at least in concept, be used anywhere and express everything. It's based on braces, and for that reason I prefer the term *braced initialization*. "Uniform initialization" is an idea. "Braced initialization" is a syntactic construct.

Braced initialization lets you express the formerly inexpressible. Using braces, specifying the initial contents of a container is easy:

```
std::vector<int> v{ 1, 3, 5 }; // v's initial content is 1, 3, 5
```

Braces can also be used to specify default initialization values for non-static data members. This capability—new to C++11—is shared with the "=" initialization syntax, but not with parentheses:

```
class Widget {
  …

private:
  int x{ 0 };           // fine, x's default value is 0
  int y = 0;            // also fine
  int z(0);             // error!
};
```

On the other hand, uncopyable objects (e.g., std::atomics—see Item 40) may be initialized using braces or parentheses, but not using "=":

```
std::atomic<int> ai1{ 0 };      // fine
```

```
std::atomic<int> ai2(0);        // fine
```

```
std::atomic<int> ai3 = 0;       // error!
```

It's thus easy to understand why braced initialization is called "uniform." Of C++'s three ways to designate an initializing expression, only braces can be used everywhere.

A novel feature of braced initialization is that it prohibits implicit *narrowing conversions* among built-in types. If the value of an expression in a braced initializer isn't guaranteed to be expressible by the type of the object being initialized, compilers are required to complain:

```
double x, y, z;

...

int sum1{ x + y + z };          // error! sum of doubles may
                                // not be expressible as int
```

Initialization using parentheses and "=" doesn't check for narrowing conversions, because that could break too much legacy code:

```
int sum2(x + y + z);            // okay (value of expression
                                // truncated to an int)
```

```
int sum3 = x + y + z;           // ditto
```

Another noteworthy characteristic of braced initialization is its immunity to C++'s *most vexing parse*. A side effect of C++'s rule that anything that can be parsed as a declaration must be interpreted as one, the most vexing parse most frequently afflicts developers when they want to default-construct an object, but inadvertently end up declaring a function instead. The root of the problem is that if you want to call a constructor with an argument, you can do it like this,

```
Widget w1(10);        // call Widget ctor with argument 10
```

but if you try to call a Widget constructor with zero arguments using the analogous syntax, you declare a function instead of an object:

```
Widget w2();          // most vexing parse! declares a function
                      // named w2 that returns a Widget!
```

Functions can't be declared using braces for the parameter list, so default-constructing an object using braces doesn't have this problem:

```
Widget w3{};          // calls Widget ctor with no args
```

There's thus a lot to be said for braced initialization. It's the syntax that can be used in the widest variety of contexts, it prevents implicit narrowing conversions, and it's immune to C++'s most vexing parse. A trifecta of goodness! So why isn't this Item entitled something like "Prefer braced initialization syntax"?

The drawback to braced initialization is the sometimes-surprising behavior that accompanies it. Such behavior grows out of the unusually tangled relationship among braced initializers, `std::initializer_lists`, and constructor overload resolution. Their interactions can lead to code that seems like it should do one thing, but actually does another. For example, Item 2 explains that when an `auto`-declared variable has a braced initializer, the type deduced is `std::initializer_list`, even though other ways of declaring a variable with the same initializer would yield a more intuitive type. As a result, the more you like `auto`, the less enthusiastic you're likely to be about braced initialization.

In constructor calls, parentheses and braces have the same meaning as long as `std::initializer_list` parameters are not involved:

```
class Widget {
public:
  Widget(int i, bool b);        // ctors not declaring
  Widget(int i, double d);      // std::initializer_list params
  ...
};

Widget w1(10, true);           // calls first ctor

Widget w2{10, true};           // also calls first ctor

Widget w3(10, 5.0);            // calls second ctor

Widget w4{10, 5.0};            // also calls second ctor
```

If, however, one or more constructors declare a parameter of type `std::initializer_list`, calls using the braced initialization syntax strongly prefer the overloads taking `std::initializer_lists`. *Strongly.* If there's *any way* for compilers to construe a call using a braced initializer to be to a constructor taking a `std::initializer_list`, compilers will employ that interpretation. If the `Widget` class above is augmented with a constructor taking a `std::initializer_list<long double>`, for example,

```
class Widget {
public:
  Widget(int i, bool b);                      // as before
  Widget(int i, double d);                    // as before
```

```
    Widget(std::initializer_list<long double> il);    // added

    …
};
```

Widgets w2 and w4 will be constructed using the new constructor, even though the type of the `std::initializer_list` elements (`long double`) is, compared to the non-`std::initializer_list` constructors, a worse match for both arguments! Look:

```
Widget w1(10, true);      // uses parens and, as before,
                          // calls first ctor

Widget w2{10, true};      // uses braces, but now calls
                          // std::initializer_list ctor
                          // (10 and true convert to long double)

Widget w3(10, 5.0);       // uses parens and, as before,
                          // calls second ctor

Widget w4{10, 5.0};       // uses braces, but now calls
                          // std::initializer_list ctor
                          // (10 and 5.0 convert to long double)
```

Even what would normally be copy and move construction can be hijacked by `std::initializer_list` constructors:

```
class Widget {
public:
  Widget(int i, bool b);                          // as before
  Widget(int i, double d);                        // as before
  Widget(std::initializer_list<long double> il);  // as before

  operator float() const;                         // convert
  …                                               // to float

};

Widget w5(w4);            // uses parens, calls copy ctor

Widget w6{w4};            // uses braces, calls
                          // std::initializer_list ctor
                          // (w4 converts to float, and float
                          // converts to long double)
```

```
    Widget w7(std::move(w4));     // uses parens, calls move ctor

    Widget w8{std::move(w4)};     // uses braces, calls
                                  // std::initializer_list ctor
                                  // (for same reason as w6)
```

Compilers' determination to match braced initializers with constructors taking
std::initializer_lists is so strong, it prevails even if the best-match std::ini-
tializer_list constructor can't be called. For example:

```
    class Widget {
    public:
      Widget(int i, bool b);                      // as before
      Widget(int i, double d);                    // as before

      Widget(std::initializer_list<bool> il);     // element type is
                                                  // now bool


      …                                           // no implicit
    };                                            // conversion funcs
```

```
    Widget w{10, 5.0};        // error! requires narrowing conversions
```

Here, compilers will ignore the first two constructors (the second of which offers an
exact match on both argument types) and try to call the constructor taking a
std::initializer_list<bool>. Calling that constructor would require converting
an int (10) and a double (5.0) to bools. Both conversions would be narrowing
(bool can't exactly represent either value), and narrowing conversions are prohibited
inside braced initializers, so the call is invalid, and the code is rejected.

Only if there's no way to convert the types of the arguments in a braced initializer to
the type in a std::initializer_list do compilers fall back on normal overload
resolution. For example, if we replace the std::initializer_list<bool> constructor with one taking a std::initializer_list<std::string>, the non-
std::initializer_list constructors become candidates again, because there is no
way to convert ints and bools to std::strings:

```
    class Widget {
    public:
      Widget(int i, bool b);                    // as before
      Widget(int i, double d);                  // as before

      // std::initializer_list element type is now std::string
      Widget(std::initializer_list<std::string> il);
      …                                         // no implicit
    };                                          // conversion funcs
```

```
Widget w1(10, true);      // uses parens, still calls first ctor

Widget w2{10, true};      // uses braces, now calls first ctor

Widget w3(10, 5.0);       // uses parens, still calls second ctor

Widget w4{10, 5.0};       // uses braces, now calls second ctor
```

This brings us near the end of our examination of braced initializers and constructor overloading, but there's an interesting edge case that needs to be addressed. Suppose you use an empty set of braces to construct an object that supports default construction and also supports `std::initializer_list` construction. What do your empty braces mean? If they mean "no arguments," you get default construction, but if they mean "empty `std::initializer_list`," you get construction from a `std::initializer_list` with no elements.

The rule is that you get default construction. Empty braces mean no arguments, not an empty `std::initializer_list`:

```
class Widget {
public:
  Widget();                                 // default ctor

  Widget(std::initializer_list<int> il);    // std::initializer
                                            // _list ctor

                                            // no implicit
  ...                                       // conversion funcs
};

Widget w1;          // calls default ctor

Widget w2{};        // also calls default ctor

Widget w3();            // most vexing parse! declares a function!
```

If you *want* to call a `std::initializer_list` constructor with an empty `std::initializer_list`, you do it by making the empty braces a constructor argument—by putting the empty braces inside the parentheses demarcating what you're passing:[1]

```
Widget w4({});          // calls std::initializer_list ctor
                        // with empty list
```

---

1 If you use braces instead of parentheses to demarcate the constructor argument,

```
    Widget w5{{}};
```

you may not get what you expect. For details, consult my 21 November 2016 blog post at *The View From Aristeia*, "Help me sort out the meaning of "{}" as a constructor argument" (*http://scottmeyers.blogspot.com/2016/11/help-me-sort-out-meaning-of-as.html*).

At this point, with seemingly arcane rules about braced initializers, `std::initializer_lists`, and constructor overloading burbling about in your brain, you may be wondering how much of this information matters in day-to-day programming. More than you might think, because one of the classes directly affected is `std::vector`. `std::vector` has a non-`std::initializer_list` constructor that allows you to specify the initial size of the container and a value each of the initial elements should have, but it also has a constructor taking a `std::initializer_list` that permits you to specify the initial values in the container. If you create a `std::vector` of a numeric type (e.g., a `std::vector<int>`) and you pass two arguments to the constructor, whether you enclose those arguments in parentheses or braces makes a tremendous difference:

```
std::vector<int> v1(10, 20);  // use non-std::initializer_list
                              // ctor: create 10-element
                              // std::vector, all elements have
                              // value of 20

std::vector<int> v2{10, 20};  // use std::initializer_list ctor:
                              // create 2-element std::vector,
                              // element values are 10 and 20
```

But let's step back from `std::vector` and also from the details of parentheses, braces, and constructor overloading resolution rules. There are two primary takeaways from this discussion. First, as a class author, you need to be aware that if your set of overloaded constructors includes one or more functions taking a `std::initializer_list`, client code using braced initialization may see only the `std::initializer_list` overloads. As a result, it's best to design your constructors so that the overload called isn't affected by whether clients use parentheses or braces. In other words, learn from what is now viewed as an error in the design of the `std::vector` interface, and design your classes to avoid it.

An implication is that if you have a class with no `std::initializer_list` constructor, and you add one, client code using braced initialization may find that calls that used to resolve to non-`std::initializer_list` constructors now resolve to the new function. Of course, this kind of thing can happen any time you add a new function to a set of overloads: calls that used to resolve to one of the old overloads might start calling the new one. The difference with `std::initializer_list` constructor overloads is that a `std::initializer_list` overload doesn't just compete with other overloads, it overshadows them to the point where the other overloads may hardly be considered. So add such overloads only with great deliberation.

The second lesson is that as a class client, you must choose carefully between parentheses and braces when creating objects. Most developers end up choosing one kind of delimiter as a default, using the other only when they have to. Braces-by-default folks are attracted by their unrivaled breadth of applicability, their prohibition of narrowing conversions, and their immunity to C++'s most vexing parse. Such folks understand that in some cases (e.g., creation of a `std::vector` with a given size and initial element value), parentheses are required. On the other hand, the go-parentheses-go crowd embraces parentheses as their default argument delimiter. They're attracted to its consistency with the C++98 syntactic tradition, its avoidance of the `auto`-deduced-a-`std::initializer_list` problem, and the knowledge that their object creation calls won't be inadvertently waylaid by `std::initializer_list` constructors. They concede that sometimes only braces will do (e.g., when creating a container with particular values). There's no consensus that either approach is better than the other, so my advice is to pick one and apply it consistently.

If you're a template author, the tension between parentheses and braces for object creation can be especially frustrating, because, in general, it's not possible to know which should be used. For example, suppose you'd like to create an object of an arbitrary type from an arbitrary number of arguments. A variadic template makes this conceptually straightforward:

```
template<typename T,              // type of object to create
         typename... Ts>          // types of arguments to use
void doSomeWork(Ts&&... params)
{

    create local T object from params...
    …

}
```

There are two ways to turn the line of pseudocode into real code (see Item 25 for information about `std::forward`):

```
T localObject(std::forward<Ts>(params)...);    // using parens

T localObject{std::forward<Ts>(params)...};    // using braces
```

So consider this calling code:

```
std::vector<int> v;
…
doSomeWork<std::vector<int>>(10, 20);
```

If `doSomeWork` uses parentheses when creating `localObject`, the result is a `std::vector` with 10 elements. If `doSomeWork` uses braces, the result is a `std::vector` with 2 elements. Which is correct? The author of `doSomeWork` can't know. Only the caller can.

This is precisely the problem faced by the Standard Library functions `std::make_unique` and `std::make_shared` (see Item 21). These functions resolve the problem by internally using parentheses and by documenting this decision as part of their interfaces.[2]

Things to Remember

- Braced initialization is the most widely usable initialization syntax, it prevents narrowing conversions, and it's immune to C++'s most vexing parse.
- During constructor overload resolution, braced initializers are matched to `std::initializer_list` parameters if at all possible, even if other constructors offer seemingly better matches.
- An example of where the choice between parentheses and braces can make a significant difference is creating a `std::vector<numeric type>` with two arguments.
- Choosing between parentheses and braces for object creation inside templates can be challenging.

Item 8: Prefer `nullptr` to 0 and NULL.

So here's the deal: the literal 0 is an `int`, not a pointer. If C++ finds itself looking at 0 in a context where only a pointer can be used, it'll grudgingly interpret 0 as a null pointer, but that's a fallback position. C++'s primary policy is that 0 is an `int`, not a pointer.

Practically speaking, the same is true of NULL. There is some uncertainty in the details in NULL's case, because implementations are allowed to give NULL an integral type other than `int` (e.g., `long`). That's not common, but it doesn't really matter, because the issue here isn't the exact type of NULL, it's that neither 0 nor NULL has a pointer type.

---

2 More flexible designs—ones that permit callers to determine whether parentheses or braces should be used in functions generated from a template—are possible. For details, see the 5 June 2013 entry of *Andrzej's C++ blog*, "Intuitive interface — Part I."

In C++98, the primary implication of this was that overloading on pointer and integral types could lead to surprises. Passing 0 or NULL to such overloads never called a pointer overload:

```
void f(int);        // three overloads of f
void f(bool);
void f(void*);

f(0);               // calls f(int), not f(void*)

f(NULL);            // might not compile, but typically calls
                    // f(int). Never calls f(void*)
```

The uncertainty regarding the behavior of f(NULL) is a reflection of the leeway granted to implementations regarding the type of NULL. If NULL is defined to be, say, 0L (i.e., 0 as a long), the call is ambiguous, because conversion from long to int, long to bool, and 0L to void* are considered equally good. The interesting thing about that call is the contradiction between the *apparent* meaning of the source code ("I'm calling f with NULL—the null pointer") and its *actual* meaning ("I'm calling f with some kind of integer—not the null pointer"). This counterintuitive behavior is what led to the guideline for C++98 programmers to avoid overloading on pointer and integral types. That guideline remains valid in C++11, because, the advice of this Item notwithstanding, it's likely that some developers will continue to use 0 and NULL, even though nullptr is a better choice.

nullptr's advantage is that it doesn't have an integral type. To be honest, it doesn't have a pointer type, either, but you can think of it as a pointer of *all* types. nullptr's actual type is std::nullptr_t, and, in a wonderfully circular definition, std::nullptr_t is defined to be the type of nullptr. The type std::nullptr_t implicitly converts to all raw pointer types, and that's what makes nullptr act as if it were a pointer of all types.

Calling the overloaded function f with nullptr calls the void* overload (i.e., the pointer overload), because nullptr can't be viewed as anything integral:

```
f(nullptr);         // calls f(void*) overload
```

Using nullptr instead of 0 or NULL thus avoids overload resolution surprises, but that's not its only advantage. It can also improve code clarity, especially when auto variables are involved. For example, suppose you encounter this in a code base:

```
auto result = findRecord( /* arguments */ );

if (result == 0) {
```

```
    ...
}
```

If you don't happen to know (or can't easily find out) what `findRecord` returns, it may not be clear whether `result` is a pointer type or an integral type. After all, 0 (what `result` is tested against) could go either way. If you see the following, on the other hand,

```
auto result = findRecord( /* arguments */ );

if (result == nullptr) {
    ...
}
```

there's no ambiguity: `result` must be a pointer type.

`nullptr` shines especially brightly when templates enter the picture. Suppose you have some functions that should be called only when the appropriate mutex has been locked. Each function takes a different kind of pointer:

```
int    f1(std::shared_ptr<Widget> spw);   // call these only when
double f2(std::unique_ptr<Widget> upw);   // the appropriate
bool   f3(Widget* pw);                     // mutex is locked
```

Calling code that wants to pass null pointers could look like this:

```
std::mutex f1m, f2m, f3m;           // mutexes for f1, f2, and f3

using MuxGuard =                     // C++11 typedef; see Item 9
  std::lock_guard<std::mutex>;
...

{
  MuxGuard g(f1m);                   // lock mutex for f1
  auto result = f1(0);               // pass 0 as null ptr to f1
}                                    // unlock mutex

...

{
  MuxGuard g(f2m);                   // lock mutex for f2
  auto result = f2(NULL);            // pass NULL as null ptr to f2
}                                    // unlock mutex

...

{
```

```
      MuxGuard g(f3m);             // lock mutex for f3
      auto result = f3(nullptr);   // pass nullptr as null ptr to f3
}                                  // unlock mutex
```

The failure to use nullptr in the first two calls in this code is sad, but the code works, and that counts for something. However, the repeated pattern in the calling code—lock mutex, call function, unlock mutex—is more than sad. It's disturbing. This kind of source code duplication is one of the things that templates are designed to avoid, so let's templatize the pattern:

```
template<typename FuncType,
         typename MuxType,
         typename PtrType>
auto lockAndCall(FuncType func,
                 MuxType& mutex,
                 PtrType ptr) -> decltype(func(ptr))
{
  using MuxGuard = std::lock_guard<MuxType>;

  MuxGuard g(mutex);
  return func(ptr);
}
```

If the return type of this function (auto ... -> decltype(func(ptr)) has you scratching your head, do your head a favor and navigate to Item 3, which explains what's going on. There you'll see that in C++14, the return type could be reduced to a simple decltype(auto):

```
template<typename FuncType,
         typename MuxType,
         typename PtrType>
decltype(auto) lockAndCall(FuncType func,          // C++14
                           MuxType& mutex,
                           PtrType ptr)
{
  using MuxGuard = std::lock_guard<MuxType>;

  MuxGuard g(mutex);
  return func(ptr);
}
```

Given the lockAndCall template (either version), callers can write code like this:

```
auto result1 = lockAndCall(f1, f1m, 0);          // error!

...
```

```
auto result2 = lockAndCall(f2, f2m, NULL);        // error!
```

```
...
```

```
auto result3 = lockAndCall(f3, f3m, nullptr);     // fine
```

Well, they can write it, but, as the comments indicate, in two of the three cases, the code won't compile. The problem in the first call is that when 0 is passed to lockAnd-Call, template type deduction kicks in to figure out its type. The type of 0 is, was, and always will be int, so that's the type of the parameter ptr inside the instantiation of this call to lockAndCall. Unfortunately, this means that in the call to func inside lockAndCall, an int is being passed, and that's not compatible with the std::shared_ptr<Widget> parameter that f1 expects. The 0 passed in the call to lockAndCall was intended to represent a null pointer, but what actually got passed was a run-of-the-mill int. Trying to pass this int to f1 as a std::shared_ptr <Widget> is a type error. The call to lockAndCall with 0 fails because inside the template, an int is being passed to a function that requires a std:: shared_ptr<Widget>.

The analysis for the call involving NULL is essentially the same. When NULL is passed to lockAndCall, an integral type is deduced for the parameter ptr, and a type error occurs when ptr—an int or int-like type—is passed to f2, which expects to get a std::unique_ptr<Widget>.

In contrast, the call involving nullptr has no trouble. When nullptr is passed to lockAndCall, the type for ptr is deduced to be std::nullptr_t. When ptr is passed to f3, there's an implicit conversion from std::nullptr_t to Widget*, because std::nullptr_t implicitly converts to all pointer types.

The fact that template type deduction deduces the "wrong" types for 0 and NULL (i.e., their true types, rather than their fallback meaning as a representation for a null pointer) is the most compelling reason to use nullptr instead of 0 or NULL when you want to refer to a null pointer. With nullptr, templates pose no special challenge. Combined with the fact that nullptr doesn't suffer from the overload resolution surprises that 0 and NULL are susceptible to, the case is ironclad. When you want to refer to a null pointer, use nullptr, not 0 or NULL.

Things to Remember

- Prefer nullptr to 0 and NULL.
- Avoid overloading on integral and pointer types.

Item 9: Prefer alias declarations to `typedef`s.

I'm confident we can agree that using STL containers is a good idea, and I hope that Item 18 convinces you that using `std::unique_ptr` is a good idea, but my guess is that neither of us is fond of writing types like "`std::unique_ptr<std::unordered_map<std::string, std::string>>`" more than once. Just thinking about it probably increases the risk of carpal tunnel syndrome.

Avoiding such medical tragedies is easy. Introduce a `typedef`:

```
typedef
  std::unique_ptr<std::unordered_map<std::string, std::string>>
  UPtrMapSS;
```

But `typedef`s are soooo C++98. They work in C++11, sure, but C++11 also offers *alias declarations*:

```
using UPtrMapSS =
  std::unique_ptr<std::unordered_map<std::string, std::string>>;
```

Given that the `typedef` and the alias declaration do exactly the same thing, it's reasonable to wonder whether there is a solid technical reason for preferring one over the other.

There is, but before I get to it, I want to mention that many people find the alias declaration easier to swallow when dealing with types involving function pointers:

```
// FP is a synonym for a pointer to a function taking an int and
// a const std::string& and returning nothing
typedef void (*FP)(int, const std::string&);       // typedef

// same meaning as above
using FP = void (*)(int, const std::string&);       // alias
                                                     // declaration
```

Of course, neither form is particularly easy to choke down, and few people spend much time dealing with synonyms for function pointer types, anyway, so this is hardly a compelling reason to choose alias declarations over `typedef`s.

But a compelling reason does exist: templates. In particular, alias declarations may be templatized (in which case they're called *alias templates*), while `typedef`s cannot. This gives C++11 programmers a straightforward mechanism for expressing things that in C++98 had to be hacked together with `typedef`s nested inside templatized `struct`s. For example, consider defining a synonym for a linked list that uses a custom allocator, `MyAlloc`. With an alias template, it's a piece of cake:

```
template<typename T>                                // MyAllocList<T>
using MyAllocList = std::list<T, MyAlloc<T>>;       // is synonym for
                                                    // std::list<T,
                                                    //    MyAlloc<T>>

MyAllocList<Widget> lw;                             // client code
```

With a `typedef`, you pretty much have to create the cake from scratch:

```
template<typename T>                                // MyAllocList<T>::type
struct MyAllocList {                                // is synonym for
  typedef std::list<T, MyAlloc<T>> type;            // std::list<T,
};                                                  //    MyAlloc<T>>

MyAllocList<Widget>::type lw;                       // client code
```

It gets worse. If you want to use the `typedef` inside a template for the purpose of creating a linked list holding objects of a type specified by a template parameter, you have to precede the `typedef` name with `typename`:

```
template<typename T>
class Widget {                                      // Widget<T> contains
private:                                            // a MyAllocList<T>
  typename MyAllocList<T>::type list;               // as a data member
  ...
};
```

Here, `MyAllocList<T>::type` refers to a type that's dependent on a template type parameter (T). `MyAllocList<T>::type` is thus a *dependent type*, and one of C++'s many endearing rules is that the names of dependent types must be preceded by `typename`.

If `MyAllocList` is defined as an alias template, this need for `typename` vanishes (as does the cumbersome ":: type" suffix):

```
template<typename T>
using MyAllocList = std::list<T, MyAlloc<T>>;       // as before

template<typename T>
class Widget {
private:
  MyAllocList<T> list;                                        // no "typename",
  ...                                                         // no "::type"
};
```

To you, `MyAllocList<T>` (i.e., use of the alias template) may look just as dependent on the template parameter T as `MyAllocList<T>::type` (i.e., use of the nested typedef), but you're not a compiler. When compilers process the Widget template and encounter the use of MyAllocList<T> (i.e., use of the alias template), they know that MyAllocList<T> is the name of a type, because MyAllocList is an alias template: it *must* name a type. MyAllocList<T> is thus a *non-dependent type*, and a typename specifier is neither required nor permitted.

When compilers see MyAllocList<T>::type (i.e., use of the nested typedef) in the Widget template, on the other hand, they can't know for sure that it names a type, because there might be a specialization of MyAllocList that they haven't yet seen where MyAllocList<T>::type refers to something other than a type. That sounds crazy, but don't blame compilers for this possibility. It's the humans who have been known to produce such code.

For example, some misguided soul may have concocted something like this:

```
class Wine { … };

template<>                      // MyAllocList specialization
class MyAllocList<Wine> {       // for when T is Wine
private:
  enum class WineType           // see Item 10 for info on
  { White, Red, Rose };         // "enum class"

  WineType type;                // in this class, type is
  …                             // a data member!
};
```

As you can see, MyAllocList<Wine>::type doesn't refer to a type. If Widget were to be instantiated with Wine, MyAllocList<T>::type inside the Widget template would refer to a data member, not a type. Inside the Widget template, then, whether MyAllocList<T>::type refers to a type is honestly dependent on what T is, and that's why compilers insist on your asserting that it is a type by preceding it with typename.

If you've done any template metaprogramming (TMP), you've almost certainly bumped up against the need to take template type parameters and create revised types from them. For example, given some type T, you might want to strip off any const- or reference-qualifiers that T contains, e.g., you might want to turn const std::string& into std::string. Or you might want to add const to a type or turn it into an lvalue reference, e.g., turn Widget into const Widget or into Widget&. (If you haven't done any TMP, that's too bad, because if you want to be a truly effective C++ programmer, you need to be familiar with at least the basics of this facet of C++. You can see examples of TMP in action, including the kinds of type transformations I just mentioned, in Items 23 and 27.)

C++11 gives you the tools to perform these kinds of transformations in the form of *type traits*, an assortment of templates inside the header `<type_traits>`. There are dozens of type traits in that header, and not all of them perform type transformations, but the ones that do offer a predictable interface. Given a type T to which you'd like to apply a transformation, the resulting type is std::*transformation* <T>::type. For example:

```
std::remove_const<T>::type              // yields T from const T

std::remove_reference<T>::type          // yields T from T& and T&&

std::add_lvalue_reference<T>::type      // yields T& from T
```

The comments merely summarize what these transformations do, so don't take them too literally. Before using them on a project, you'd look up the precise specifications, I know.

My motivation here isn't to give you a tutorial on type traits, anyway. Rather, note that application of these transformations entails writing "::type" at the end of each use. If you apply them to a type parameter inside a template (which is virtually always how you employ them in real code), you'd also have to precede each use with type-name. The reason for both of these syntactic speed bumps is that the C++11 type traits are implemented as nested typedefs inside templatized structs. That's right, they're implemented using the type synonym technology I've been trying to convince you is inferior to alias templates!

There's a historical reason for that, but we'll skip over it (it's dull, I promise), because the Standardization Committee belatedly recognized that alias templates are the better way to go, and they included such templates in C++14 for all the C++11 type transformations. The aliases have a common form: for each C++11 transformation std::*transformation*<T>::type, there's a corresponding C++14 alias template named std::*transformation*_t. Examples will clarify what I mean:

```
std::remove_const<T>::type          // C++11: const T → T
std::remove_const_t<T>              // C++14 equivalent

std::remove_reference<T>::type      // C++11: T&/T&& → T
std::remove_reference_t<T>          // C++14 equivalent

std::add_lvalue_reference<T>::type  // C++11: T → T&
std::add_lvalue_reference_t<T>      // C++14 equivalent
```

The C++11 constructs remain valid in C++14, but I don't know why you'd want to use them. Even if you don't have access to C++14, writing the alias templates yourself is child's play. Only C++11 language features are required, and even children can mimic a pattern, right? If you happen to have access to an electronic copy of the C++14 Standard, it's easier still, because all that's required is some copying and pasting. Here, I'll get you started:

```
template <class T>
using remove_const_t = typename remove_const<T>::type;

template <class T>
using remove_reference_t = typename remove_reference<T>::type;

template <class T>
using add_lvalue_reference_t =
  typename add_lvalue_reference<T>::type;
```

See? Couldn't be easier.

Things to Remember

- typedefs don't support templatization, but alias declarations do.
- Alias templates avoid the "::type" suffix and, in templates, the "typename" prefix often required to refer to typedefs.
- C++14 offers alias templates for all the C++11 type traits transformations.

Item 10: Prefer scoped enums to unscoped enums.

As a general rule, declaring a name inside curly braces limits the visibility of that name to the scope defined by the braces. Not so for the enumerators declared in C++98-style enums. The names of such enumerators belong to the scope containing the enum, and that means that nothing else in that scope may have the same name:

```
enum Color { black, white, red };    // black, white, red are
                                      // in same scope as Color

auto white = false;                   // error! white already
                                      // declared in this scope
```

The fact that these enumerator names leak into the scope containing their enum definition gives rise to the official term for this kind of enum: *unscoped*. Their new C++11 counterparts, *scoped enums*, don't leak names in this way:

```
enum class Color { black, white, red };    // black, white, red
                                           // are scoped to Color

auto white = false;         // fine, no other
```

```cpp
                                        // "white" in scope

Color c = white;                        // error! no enumerator named
                                        // "white" is in this scope

Color c = Color::white;                 // fine

auto c = Color::white;                  // also fine (and in accord
                                        // with Item 5's advice)
```

Because scoped enums are declared via "enum class", they're sometimes referred to as *enum classes*.

The reduction in namespace pollution offered by scoped enums is reason enough to prefer them over their unscoped siblings, but scoped enums have a second compelling advantage: their enumerators are much more strongly typed. Enumerators for unscoped enums implicitly convert to integral types (and, from there, to floating-point types). Semantic travesties such as the following are therefore completely valid:

```cpp
enum Color { black, white, red };       // unscoped enum

std::vector<std::size_t>                // func. returning
  primeFactors(std::size_t x);          // prime factors of x

Color c = red;
...

if (c < 14.5) {                         // compare Color to double (!)

    auto factors =                      // compute prime factors
      primeFactors(c);                  // of a Color (!)
    ...
}
```

Throw a simple "class" after "enum", however, thus transforming an unscoped enum into a scoped one, and it's a very different story. There are no implicit conversions from enumerators in a scoped enum to any other type:

```cpp
enum class Color { black, white, red }; // enum is now scoped

Color c = Color::red;                   // as before, but
...                                     // with scope qualifier

if (c < 14.5) {                         // error! can't compare
                                        // Color and double
```

```
    auto factors =                    // error! can't pass Color to
      primeFactors(c);                // function expecting std::size_t
    ...
}
```

If you honestly want to perform a conversion from Color to a different type, do what you always do to twist the type system to your wanton desires—use a cast:

```
if (static_cast<double>(c) < 14.5) {    // odd code, but
                                        // it's valid

    auto factors =                                  // suspect, but
      primeFactors(static_cast<std::size_t>(c));    // it compiles
    ...
}
```

It may seem that scoped enums have a third advantage over unscoped enums, because scoped enums may be forward-declared, i.e., their names may be declared without specifying their enumerators:

```
enum Color;             // error!

enum class Color;       // fine
```

This is misleading. In C++11, unscoped enums may also be forward-declared, but only after a bit of additional work. The work grows out of the fact that every enum in C++ has an integral *underlying type* that is determined by compilers. For an unscoped enum like Color,

```
enum Color { black, white, red };
```

compilers might choose char as the underlying type, because there are only three values to represent. However, some enums have a range of values that is much larger, e.g.:

```
enum Status { good = 0,
              failed = 1,
              incomplete = 100,
              corrupt = 200,
              indeterminate = 0xFFFFFFFF
            };
```

Here the values to be represented range from 0 to 0xFFFFFFFF. Except on unusual machines (where a char consists of at least 32 bits), compilers will have to select an integral type larger than char for the representation of Status values.

To make efficient use of memory, compilers often want to choose the smallest under-lying type for an enum that's sufficient to represent its range of enumerator values. In some cases, compilers will optimize for speed instead of size, and in that case, they may not choose the smallest permissible underlying type, but they certainly want to be *able* to optimize for size. To make that possible, C++98 supports only enum defini-tions (where all enumerators are listed); enum declarations are not allowed. That makes it possible for compilers to select an underlying type for each enum prior to the enum being used.

But the inability to forward-declare enums has drawbacks. The most notable is proba-bly the increase in compilation dependencies. Consider again the Status enum:

```
enum Status { good = 0,
              failed = 1,
              incomplete = 100,
              corrupt = 200,
              indeterminate = 0xFFFFFFFF
            };
```

This is the kind of enum that's likely to be used throughout a system, hence included in a header file that every part of the system is dependent on. If a new status value is then introduced,

```
enum Status { good = 0,
              failed = 1,
              incomplete = 100,
              corrupt = 200,
              audited = 500,
              indeterminate = 0xFFFFFFFF
            };
```

it's likely that the entire system will have to be recompiled, even if only a single sub-system—possibly only a single function!—uses the new enumerator. This is the kind of thing that people *hate*. And it's the kind of thing that the ability to forward-declare enums in C++11 eliminates. For example, here's a perfectly valid declaration of a scoped enum and a function that takes one as a parameter:

```
enum class Status;                       // forward declaration

void continueProcessing(Status s);    // use of fwd-declared enum
```

The header containing these declarations requires no recompilation if Status's definition is revised. Furthermore, if Status is modified (e.g., to add the audited enumerator), but continueProcessing's behavior is unaffected (e.g., because continueProcessing doesn't use audited), continueProcessing's implementation need not be recompiled, either.

But if compilers need to know the size of an enum before it's used, how can C++11's enums get away with forward declarations when C++98's enums can't? The answer is simple: there's a default underlying type for scoped enums, and for both kinds of enums, you can specify the underlying type if you want to.

By default, the underlying type for scoped enums is int:

```
enum class Status;                // underlying type is int
```

If the default doesn't suit you, you can override it:

```
enum class Status: std::uint32_t;  // underlying type for
                                   // Status is std::uint32_t
                                   // (from <cstdint>)
```

Either way, compilers know the size of the enumerators in a scoped enum.

To specify the underlying type for an unscoped enum, you do the same thing as for a scoped enum, and the result may be forward-declared:

```
enum Color: std::uint8_t;          // fwd decl for unscoped enum;
                                   // underlying type is
                                   // std::uint8_t
```

Underlying type specifications can also go on an enum's definition:

```
enum class Status: std::uint32_t { good = 0,
                                   failed = 1,
                                   incomplete = 100,
                                   corrupt = 200,
                                   audited = 500,
                                   indeterminate = 0xFFFFFFFF
                                 };
```

In view of the fact that scoped enums avoid namespace pollution and aren't susceptible to nonsensical implicit type conversions, it may surprise you to hear that there's at least one situation where unscoped enums may be useful. That's when referring to fields within C++11's std::tuples. For example, suppose we have a tuple holding values for the name, email address, and reputation value for a user at a social networking website:

```
using UserInfo =                   // type alias; see Item 9
    std::tuple<std::string,        // name
```

```
                std::string,          // email
                std::size_t> ;        // reputation
```

Though the comments indicate what each field of the tuple represents, that's probably not very helpful when you encounter code like this in a separate source file:

```
UserInfo uInfo;                       // object of tuple type

...

auto val = std::get<1>(uInfo);        // get value of field 1
```

As a programmer, you have a lot of stuff to keep track of. Should you really be expected to remember that field 1 corresponds to the user's email address? I think not. Using an unscoped enum to associate names with field numbers avoids the need to:

```
enum UserInfoFields { uiName, uiEmail, uiReputation };

UserInfo uInfo;                                   // as before

...

auto val = std::get<uiEmail>(uInfo);   // ah, get value of
                                       // email field
```

What makes this work is the implicit conversion from `UserInfoFields` to `std::size_t`, which is the type that `std::get` requires.

The corresponding code with scoped enums is substantially more verbose:

```
enum class UserInfoFields { uiName, uiEmail, uiReputation };

UserInfo uInfo;                                   // as before

...

auto val =
  std::get<static_cast<std::size_t>(UserInfoFields::uiEmail)>
    (uInfo);
```

The verbosity can be reduced by writing a function that takes an enumerator and returns its corresponding `std::size_t` value, but it's a bit tricky. `std::get` is a template, and the value you provide is a template argument (notice the use of angle brackets, not parentheses), so the function that transforms an enumerator into a `std::size_t` has to produce its result *during compilation*. As Item 15 explains, that means it must be a `constexpr` function.

In fact, it should really be a `constexpr` function template, because it should work with any kind of enum. And if we're going to make that generalization, we should generalize the return type, too. Rather than returning `std::size_t`, we'll return the enum's underlying type. It's available via the `std::underlying_type` type trait. (See Item 9 for information on type traits.) Finally, we'll declare it `noexcept` (see Item 14), because we know it will never yield an exception. The result is a function template `toUType` that takes an arbitrary enumerator and can return its value as a compile-time constant:

```
template<typename E>
constexpr typename std::underlying_type<E>::type
  toUType(E enumerator) noexcept
{
  return
    static_cast<typename
               std::underlying_type<E>::type>(enumerator);
}
```

In C++14, `toUType` can be simplified by replacing `typename std::underlying_type<E>::type` with the sleeker `std::underlying_type_t` (see Item 9):

```
template<typename E>                                    // C++14
constexpr std::underlying_type_t<E>
  toUType(E enumerator) noexcept
{
  return static_cast<std::underlying_type_t<E>>(enumerator);
}
```

The even-sleeker `auto` return type (see Item 3) is also valid in C++14:

```
template<typename E>                                    // C++14
constexpr auto
  toUType(E enumerator) noexcept
{
  return static_cast<std::underlying_type_t<E>>(enumerator);
}
```

Regardless of how it's written, `toUType` permits us to access a field of the tuple like this:

```
auto val = std::get<toUType(UserInfoFields::uiEmail)>(uInfo);
```

It's still more to write than use of the unscoped `enum`, but it also avoids namespace pollution and inadvertent conversions involving enumerators. In many cases, you may decide that typing a few extra characters is a reasonable price to pay for the ability to avoid the pitfalls of an enum technology that dates to a time when the state of the art in digital telecommunications was the 2400-baud modem.

- C++98-style enums are now known as unscoped enums.

- Enumerators of scoped enums are visible only within the enum. They convert to other types only with a cast.

- Both scoped and unscoped enums support specification of the underlying type. The default underlying type for scoped enums is int. Unscoped enums have no default underlying type.

- Scoped enums may always be forward-declared. Unscoped enums may be forward-declared only if their declaration specifies an underlying type.

Item 11: Prefer deleted functions to private undefined ones.

If you're providing code to other developers, and you want to prevent them from calling a particular function, you generally just don't declare the function. No function declaration, no function to call. Easy, peasy. But sometimes C++ declares functions for you, and if you want to prevent clients from calling those functions, the peasy isn't quite so easy any more.

The situation arises only for the "special member functions," i.e., the member functions that C++ automatically generates when they're needed. Item 17 discusses these functions in detail, but for now, we'll worry only about the copy constructor and the copy assignment operator. This chapter is largely devoted to common practices in C++98 that have been superseded by better practices in C++11, and in C++98, if you want to suppress use of a member function, it's almost always the copy constructor, the assignment operator, or both.

The C++98 approach to preventing use of these functions is to declare them private and not define them. For example, near the base of the iostreams hierarchy in the C++ Standard Library is the class template basic_ios. All istream and ostream classes inherit (possibly indirectly) from this class. Copying istreams and ostreams is undesirable, because it's not really clear what such operations should do. An istream object, for example, represents a stream of input values, some of which may have already been read, and some of which will potentially be read later. If an istream were to be copied, would that entail copying all the values that had already been read as well as all the values that would be read in the future? The easiest way to deal with such questions is to define them out of existence. Prohibiting the copying of streams does just that.

To render istream and ostream classes uncopyable, `basic_ios` is specified in C++98 as follows (including the comments):

```
template <class charT, class traits = char_traits<charT> >
class basic_ios : public ios_base {
public:

  ...

private:
  basic_ios(const basic_ios& );           // not defined
  basic_ios& operator=(const basic_ios&); // not defined
};
```

Declaring these functions `private` prevents clients from calling them. Deliberately failing to define them means that if code that still has access to them (i.e., member functions or `friend`s of the class) uses them, linking will fail due to missing function definitions.

In C++11, there's a better way to achieve essentially the same end: use "= `delete`" to mark the copy constructor and the copy assignment operator as *deleted functions*. Here's the same part of `basic_ios` as it's specified in C++11:

```
template <class charT, class traits = char_traits<charT> >
class basic_ios : public ios_base {
public:

  ...
  basic_ios(const basic_ios& ) = delete;
  basic_ios& operator=(const basic_ios&) = delete;

  ...
};
```

The difference between deleting these functions and declaring them `private` may seem more a matter of fashion than anything else, but there's greater substance here than you might think. Deleted functions may not be used in any way, so even code that's in member and `friend` functions will fail to compile if it tries to copy `basic_ios` objects. That's an improvement over the C++98 behavior, where such improper usage wouldn't be diagnosed until link-time.

By convention, deleted functions are declared `public`, not `private`. There's a reason for that. When client code tries to use a member function, C++ checks accessibility before deleted status. When client code tries to use a deleted `private` function, some compilers complain only about the function being `private`, even though the function's accessibility doesn't really affect whether it can be used. It's worth bearing this in mind when revising legacy code to replace `private`-and-not-defined member functions with deleted ones, because making the new functions `public` will generally result in better error messages.

An important advantage of deleted functions is that *any* function may be deleted, while only member functions may be `private`. For example, suppose we have a non-member function that takes an integer and returns whether it's a lucky number:

```
bool isLucky(int number);
```

C++'s C heritage means that pretty much any type that can be viewed as vaguely numerical will implicitly convert to `int`, but some calls that would compile might not make sense:

```
if (isLucky('a')) …        // is 'a' a lucky number?

if (isLucky(true)) …       // is "true"?

if (isLucky(3.5)) …        // should we truncate to 3
                           // before checking for luckiness?
```

If lucky numbers must really be integers, we'd like to prevent calls such as these from compiling.

One way to accomplish that is to create deleted overloads for the types we want to filter out:

```
bool isLucky(int number);          // original function

bool isLucky(char) = delete;       // reject chars

bool isLucky(bool) = delete;       // reject bools

bool isLucky(double) = delete;     // reject doubles and
                                   // floats
```

(The comment on the `double` overload that says that both doubles and `floats` will be rejected may surprise you, but your surprise will dissipate once you recall that, given a choice between converting a `float` to an `int` or to a `double`, C++ prefers the conversion to `double`. Calling `isLucky` with a `float` will therefore call the `double` overload, not the `int` one. Well, it'll try to. The fact that that overload is deleted will prevent the call from compiling.)

Although deleted functions can't be used, they are part of your program. As such, they are taken into account during overload resolution. That's why, with the deleted function declarations above, the undesirable calls to `isLucky` will be rejected:

```
if (isLucky('a')) …        // error! call to deleted function
```

```
if (isLucky(true)) …             // error!

if (isLucky(3.5f)) …             // error!
```

Another trick that deleted functions can perform (and that `private` member functions can't) is to prevent use of template instantiations that should be disabled. For
example, suppose you need a template that works with built-in pointers (Chapter 4's
advice to prefer smart pointers to raw pointers notwithstanding):

```
template<typename T>
void processPointer(T* ptr);
```

There are two special cases in the world of pointers. One is `void*` pointers, because
there is no way to dereference them, to increment or decrement them, etc. The other
is `char*` pointers, because they typically represent pointers to C-style strings, not
pointers to individual characters. These special cases often call for special handling,
and, in the case of the `processPointer` template, let's assume the proper handling is
to reject calls using those types. That is, it should not be possible to call `process-
Pointer` with `void*` or `char*` pointers.

That's easily enforced. Just delete those instantiations:

```
template<>
void processPointer<void>(void*) = delete;

template<>
void processPointer<char>(char*) = delete;
```

Now, if calling `processPointer` with a `void*` or a `char*` is invalid, it's probably also
invalid to call it with a `const void*` or a `const char*`, so those instantiations will
typically need to be deleted, too:

```
template<>
void processPointer<const void>(const void*) = delete;

template<>
void processPointer<const char>(const char*) = delete;
```

And if you really want to be thorough, you'll also delete the `volatile void*`, volatile `char*`, `const volatile void*` and `const volatile char*` overloads, and then
you'll get to work on the overloads for pointers to the other standard character types:
`wchar_t`, `char16_t`, and `char32_t`.

Interestingly, if you have a function template inside a class, and you'd like to disable
some instantiations by declaring them `private` (à la classic C++98 convention), you
can't, because it's not possible to give a member function template specialization a

different access level from that of the main template. If processPointer were a member function template inside Widget, for example, and you wanted to disable calls for void* pointers, this would be the C++98 approach, though it would not compile:

```
class Widget {
public:
    …
    template<typename T>
    void processPointer(T* ptr)
    { … }

private:
    template<>                                    // error!
    void processPointer<void>(void*);

};
```

The problem is that template specializations must be written at namespace scope, not class scope. This issue doesn't arise for deleted functions, because they don't need a different access level. They can be deleted outside the class (hence at namespace scope):

```
class Widget {
public:
    …
    template<typename T>
    void processPointer(T* ptr)
    { … }
    …

};
```

```
template<>                                              // still
void Widget::processPointer<void>(void*) = delete;      // public,
                                                        // but
                                                        // deleted
```

The truth is that the C++98 practice of declaring functions private and not defining them was really an attempt to achieve what C++11's deleted functions actually accomplish. As an emulation, the C++98 approach is not as good as the real thing. It doesn't work outside classes, it doesn't always work inside classes, and when it does work, it may not work until link-time. So stick to deleted functions.

Item 12: Declare overriding functions override.

The world of object-oriented programming in C++ revolves around classes, inheritance, and virtual functions. Among the most fundamental ideas in this world is that virtual function implementations in derived classes *override* the implementations of their base class counterparts. It's disheartening, then, to realize just how easily virtual function overriding can go wrong. It's almost as if this part of the language were designed with the idea that Murphy's Law wasn't just to be obeyed, it was to be honored.

Because "overriding" sounds a lot like "overloading," yet is completely unrelated, let me make clear that virtual function overriding is what makes it possible to invoke a derived class function through a base class interface:

```cpp
class Base {
public:
  virtual void doWork();        // base class virtual function

  …
};

class Derived: public Base {
public:
  virtual void doWork();        // overrides Base::doWork
                                // ("virtual" is optional
  …                             // here)
};

std::unique_ptr<Base> upb =     // create base class pointer
  std::make_unique<Derived>();  // to derived class object;
                                // see Item 21 for info on
  …                             // std::make_unique

upb->doWork();                  // call doWork through base
                                // class ptr; derived class
                                // function is invoked
```

For overriding to occur, several requirements must be met:

- The base class function must be virtual.
- The base and derived function names must be identical (except in the case of destructors).
- The parameter types of the base and derived functions must be identical.
- The `const`ness of the base and derived functions must be identical.
- The return types and exception specifications of the base and derived functions must be compatible.

To these constraints, which were also part of C++98, C++11 adds one more:

- The functions' *reference qualifiers* must be identical. Member function reference qualifiers are one of C++11's less-publicized features, so don't be surprised if you've never heard of them. They make it possible to limit use of a member function to lvalues only or to rvalues only. Member functions need not be virtual to use them:

```
class Widget {
public:
    …
    void doWork() &;        // this version of doWork applies
                            // only when *this is an lvalue

    void doWork() &&;       // this version of doWork applies
};                          // only when *this is an rvalue

    …

    Widget makeWidget();    // factory function (returns rvalue)

    Widget w;               // normal object (an lvalue)

    …

    w.doWork();             // calls Widget::doWork for lvalues
                            // (i.e., Widget::doWork &)

    makeWidget().doWork();  // calls Widget::doWork for rvalues
                            // (i.e., Widget::doWork &&)
```

I'll say more about member functions with reference qualifiers later, but for now, simply note that if a virtual function in a base class has a reference qualifier, derived class overrides of that function must have exactly the same reference qualifier. If they don't, the declared functions will still exist in the derived class, but they won't override anything in the base class.

All these requirements for overriding mean that small mistakes can make a big difference. Code containing overriding errors is typically valid, but its meaning isn't what you intended. You therefore can't rely on compilers notifying you if you do something wrong. For example, the following code is completely legal and, at first sight, looks reasonable, but it contains no virtual function overrides—not a single derived class function that is tied to a base class function. Can you identify the problem in each case, i.e., why each derived class function doesn't override the base class function with the same name?

```
class Base {
public:
  virtual void mf1() const;
  virtual void mf2(int x);
  virtual void mf3() &;
  void mf4() const;
};

class Derived: public Base {
public:
  virtual void mf1();
  virtual void mf2(unsigned int x);
  virtual void mf3() &&;
  virtual void mf4() const;
};
```

Need some help?

- mf1 is declared const in Base, but not in Derived.
- mf2 takes an int in Base, but an unsigned int in Derived.
- mf3 is lvalue-qualified in Base, but rvalue-qualified in Derived.
- mf4 isn't declared virtual in Base.

You may think, "Hey, in practice, these things will elicit compiler warnings, so I don't need to worry." Maybe that's true. But maybe it's not. With one compiler I checked, the code was accepted without complaint, and that was with all warnings enabled. (Other compilers provided warnings about some of the issues, but not all of them.)

Because declaring derived class overrides is important to get right, but easy to get wrong, C++11 gives you a way to make explicit that a derived class function is supposed to override a base class version: declare it `override`. Applying this to the example above would yield this derived class:

```cpp
class Derived: public Base {
public:
  virtual void mf1() override;
  virtual void mf2(unsigned int x) override;
  virtual void mf3() && override;
  virtual void mf4() const override;
};
```

This won't compile, of course, because when written this way, compilers will kvetch about all the overriding-related problems. That's exactly what you want, and it's why you should declare all your overriding functions `override`.

The code using `override` that does compile looks as follows (assuming that the goal is for all functions in `Derived` to override virtuals in `Base`):

```cpp
class Base {
public:
  virtual void mf1() const;
  virtual void mf2(int x);
  virtual void mf3() &;
  virtual void mf4() const;
};

class Derived: public Base {
public:
  virtual void mf1() const override;
  virtual void mf2(int x) override;
  virtual void mf3() & override;
  virtual void mf4() const override;
};
```

Note that in this example, part of getting things to work involves declaring mf4 virtual in `Base`. Most overriding-related errors occur in derived classes, but it's possible for things to be incorrect in base classes, too.

A policy of using `override` on all your derived class overrides can do more than just enable compilers to tell you when would-be overrides aren't overriding anything. It can also help you gauge the ramifications if you're contemplating changing the signature of a virtual function in a base class. If derived classes use `override` everywhere, you can just change the signature, recompile your system, see how much damage you've caused (i.e., how many derived classes fail to compile), then decide whether the signature change is worth the trouble. Without `override`, you'd have to hope you have comprehensive unit tests in place, because, as we've seen, derived class virtuals that are supposed to override base class functions, but don't, need not elicit compiler diagnostics.

C++ has always had keywords, but C++11 introduces two *contextual keywords*, override and final.[3] These keywords have the characteristic that they are reserved, but only in certain contexts. In the case of override, it has a reserved meaning only when it occurs at the end of a member function declaration. That means that if you have legacy code that already uses the name override, you don't need to change it for C++11:

```
class Warning {            // potential legacy class from C++98
public:

    ...
    void override();       // legal in both C++98 and C++11
                           // (with the same meaning)
    ...
};
```

That's all there is to say about override, but it's not all there is to say about member function reference qualifiers. I promised I'd provide more information on them later, and now it's later.

If we want to write a function that accepts only lvalue arguments, we declare a non-const lvalue reference parameter:

```
void doSomething(Widget& w);       // accepts only lvalue Widgets
```

If we want to write a function that accepts only rvalue arguments, we declare an rvalue reference parameter:

```
void doSomething(Widget&& w);      // accepts only rvalue Widgets
```

Member function reference qualifiers simply make it possible to draw the same distinction for the object on which a member function is invoked, i.e., *this. It's precisely analogous to the const at the end of a member function declaration, which indicates that the object on which the member function is invoked (i.e., *this) is const.

The need for reference-qualified member functions is not common, but it can arise. For example, suppose our Widget class has a std::vector data member, and we offer an accessor function that gives clients direct access to it:

```
class Widget {
public:
```

---

3 Applying final to a virtual function prevents the function from being overridden in derived classes. final may also be applied to a class, in which case the class is prohibited from being used as a base class.

```
using DataType = std::vector<double>;       // see Item 9 for
...                                          // info on "using"

DataType& data() { return values; }
...

private:
  DataType values;
};
```

This is hardly the most encapsulated design that's seen the light of day, but set that aside and consider what happens in this client code:

```
Widget w;
...

auto vals1 = w.data();                  // copy w.values into vals1
```

The return type of `Widget::data` is an lvalue reference (a `std::vector<double>&`, to be precise), and because lvalue references are defined to be lvalues, we're initializing `vals1` from an lvalue. `vals1` is thus copy constructed from `w.values`, just as the comment says.

Now suppose we have a factory function that creates `Widget`s,

```
Widget makeWidget();
```

and we want to initialize a variable with the `std::vector` inside the `Widget` returned from `makeWidget`:

```
auto vals2 = makeWidget().data();    // copy values inside the
                                     // Widget into vals2
```

Again, `Widgets::data` returns an lvalue reference, and, again, the lvalue reference is an lvalue, so, again, our new object (`vals2`) is copy constructed from `values` inside the `Widget`. This time, though, the `Widget` is the temporary object returned from `makeWidget` (i.e., an rvalue), so copying the `std::vector` inside it is a waste of time. It'd be preferable to move it, but, because `data` is returning an lvalue reference, the rules of C++ require that compilers generate code for a copy. (There's some wiggle room for optimization through what is known as the "as if rule," but you'd be foolish to rely on your compilers finding a way to take advantage of it.)

What's needed is a way to specify that when `data` is invoked on an rvalue `Widget`, the result should also be an rvalue. Using reference qualifiers to overload `data` for lvalue and rvalue `Widget`s makes that possible:

```
class Widget {
public:
  using DataType = std::vector<double>;
  …

  DataType& data() &                    // for lvalue Widgets,
  { return values; }                    // return lvalue

  DataType&& data() &&                  // for rvalue Widgets,
  { return std::move(values); }         // return rvalue
  …

private:
  DataType values;
};
```

Notice the differing return types from the `data` overloads. The lvalue reference overload returns an lvalue reference (i.e., an lvalue), and the rvalue reference overload returns an rvalue reference (which, as a function return type, is an rvalue). This means that client code now behaves as we'd like:

```
auto vals1 = w.data();                // calls lvalue overload for
                                      // Widget::data, copy-
                                      // constructs vals1

auto vals2 = makeWidget().data();     // calls rvalue overload for
                                      // Widget::data, move-
                                      // constructs vals2
```

This is certainly nice, but don't let the warm glow of this happy ending distract you from the true point of this Item. That point is that whenever you declare a function in a derived class that's meant to override a virtual function in a base class, be sure to declare that function `override`.

By the way, if a member function is reference qualified, all overloads of that function must be reference qualified. That's because a non-reference-qualified overload may be invoked on both lvalue and rvalue objects. Such an overload would compete with reference-qualified overloads, and all calls to the function would be ambiguous.

Things to Remember

- Declare overriding functions `override`.
- Member function reference qualifiers make it possible to treat lvalue and rvalue objects (`*this`) differently.

Item 13: Prefer `const_iterators` to `iterators`.

`const_iterators` are the STL equivalent of pointers-to-const. They point to values that may not be modified. The standard practice of using `const` whenever possible dictates that you should use `const_iterators` any time you need an iterator, yet have no need to modify what the iterator points to.

That's as true for C++98 as for C++11, but in C++98, `const_iterators` had only halfhearted support. It wasn't that easy to create them, and once you had one, the ways you could use it were limited. For example, suppose you want to search a `std::vector<int>` for the first occurrence of 1983 (the year "C++" replaced "C with Classes" as the name of the programming language), then insert the value 1998 (the year the first ISO C++ Standard was adopted) at that location. If there's no 1983 in the vector, the insertion should go at the end of the vector. Using `iterators` in C++98, that was easy:

```
std::vector<int> values;

...

std::vector<int>::iterator it =
  std::find(values.begin(), values.end(), 1983);
values.insert(it, 1998);
```

But `iterators` aren't really the proper choice here, because this code never modifies what an `iterator` points to. Revising the code to use `const_iterators` should be trivial, but in C++98, it was anything but. Here's one approach that's conceptually sound, though still not correct:

```
typedef std::vector<int>::iterator IterT;           // type-
typedef std::vector<int>::const_iterator ConstIterT;  // defs

std::vector<int> values;

...

ConstIterT ci =
  std::find(static_cast<ConstIterT>(values.begin()),  // cast
            static_cast<ConstIterT>(values.end()),    // cast
            1983);

values.insert(static_cast<IterT>(ci), 1998);  // may not
                                              // compile; see
                                              // below
```

The typedefs aren't required, of course, but they make the casts in the code easier to write. (If you're wondering why I'm showing typedefs instead of following the advice of Item 9 to use alias declarations, it's because this example shows C++98 code, and alias declarations are a feature new to C++11.)

The casts in the call to std::find are present because values is a non-const container and in C++98, there was no simple way to get a const_iterator from a non-const container. The casts aren't strictly necessary, because it was possible to get const_iterators in other ways (e.g., you could bind values to a reference-to-const variable, then use that variable in place of values in your code), but one way or another, the process of getting const_iterators to elements of a non-const container involved some amount of contorting.

Once you had the const_iterators, matters often got worse, because in C++98, locations for insertions (and erasures) could be specified only by iterators. const_iterators weren't acceptable. That's why, in the code above, I cast the const_iterator (that I was so careful to get from std::find) into an iterator: passing a const_iterator to insert wouldn't compile.

To be honest, the code I've shown might not compile, either, because there's no portable conversion from a const_iterator to an iterator, not even with a static_cast. Even the semantic sledgehammer known as reinterpret_cast can't do the job. (That's not a C++98 restriction. It's true in C++11, too. const_iterators simply don't convert to iterators, no matter how much it might seem like they should.) There are some portable ways to generate iterators that point where const_iterators do, but they're not obvious, not universally applicable, and not worth discussing in this book. Besides, I hope that by now my point is clear: const_iterators were so much trouble in C++98, they were rarely worth the bother. At the end of the day, developers don't use const whenever *possible*, they use it whenever *practical*, and in C++98, const_iterators just weren't very practical.

All that changed in C++11. Now const_iterators are both easy to get and easy to use. The container member functions cbegin and cend produce const_iterators, even for non-const containers, and STL member functions that use iterators to identify positions (e.g., insert and erase) actually use const_iterators. Revising the original C++98 code that uses iterators to use const_iterators in C++11 is truly trivial:

```
std::vector<int> values;                          // as before

...

auto it =                                          // use cbegin
```

```
std::find(values.cbegin(), values.cend(), 1983); // and cend

values.insert(it, 1998);
```

Now *that's* code using `const_iterators` that's practical!

About the only situation in which C++11's support for `const_iterators` comes up a bit short is when you want to write maximally generic library code. Such code takes into account that some containers and container-like data structures offer `begin` and `end` (plus `cbegin`, `cend`, `rbegin`, etc.) as *non-member* functions, rather than members. This is the case for built-in arrays, for example, and it's also the case for some third-party libraries with interfaces consisting only of free functions. Maximally generic code thus uses non-member functions rather than assuming the existence of member versions.

For example, we could generalize the code we've been working with into a `findAnd Insert` template as follows:

```
template<typename C, typename V>
void findAndInsert(C& container,          // in container, find
                   const V& targetVal,    // first occurrence
                   const V& insertVal)    // of targetVal, then
{                                         // insert insertVal
  using std::cbegin;                      // there
  using std::cend;

  auto it = std::find(cbegin(container),  // non-member cbegin
                      cend(container),     // non-member cend
                      targetVal);

  container.insert(it, insertVal);
}
```

This works fine in C++14, but, sadly, not in C++11. Through an oversight during standardization, C++11 added the non-member functions `begin` and `end`, but it failed to add `cbegin`, `cend`, `rbegin`, `rend`, `crbegin`, and `crend`. C++14 rectifies that oversight.

If you're using C++11, you want to write maximally generic code, and none of the libraries you're using provides the missing templates for non-member `cbegin` and friends, you can throw your own implementations together with ease. For example, here's an implementation of non-member `cbegin`:

```
template <class C>
auto cbegin(const C& container) -> decltype(std::begin(container))
{
```

```
    return std::begin(container);       // see explanation below
}
```

You're surprised to see that non-member `cbegin` doesn't call member `cbegin`, aren't you? So was I. But follow the logic. This `cbegin` template accepts any type of argument representing a container-like data structure, C, and it accesses this argument through its reference-to-const parameter, `container`. If C is a conventional container type (e.g., a `std::vector<int>`), `container` will be a reference to a `const` version of that container (e.g., a `const std::vector<int>&`). Invoking the non-member `begin` function (provided by C++11) on a `const` container yields a `const_iterator`, and that iterator is what this template returns. The advantage of implementing things this way is that it works even for containers that offer a `begin` member function (which, for containers, is what C++11's non-member `begin` calls), but fail to offer a `cbegin` member. You can thus use this non-member `cbegin` on containers that directly support only `begin`.

This template also works if C is a built-in array type. In that case, `container` becomes a reference to a `const` array. C++11 provides a specialized version of non-member `begin` for arrays that returns a pointer to the array's first element. The elements of a `const` array are `const`, so the pointer that non-member `begin` returns for a `const` array is a pointer-to-`const`, and a pointer-to-`const` is, in fact, a `const_iterator` for an array. (For insight into how a template can be specialized for built-in arrays, consult Item 1's discussion of type deduction in templates that take reference parameters to arrays.)

But back to basics. The point of this Item is to encourage you to use `const_iterators` whenever you can. The fundamental motivation—using `const` whenever it's meaningful—predates C++11, but in C++98, it simply wasn't practical when working with iterators. In C++11, it's eminently practical, and C++14 tidies up the few bits of unfinished business that C++11 left behind.

Things to Remember

- Prefer `const_iterators` to `iterators`.
- In maximally generic code, prefer non-member versions of `begin`, `end`, `rbegin`, etc., over their member function counterparts.

Item 14: Declare functions noexcept if they won't emit exceptions.

In C++98, exception specifications were rather temperamental beasts. You had to summarize the exception types a function might emit, so if the function's implementation was modified, the exception specification might require revision, too. Changing an exception specification could break client code, because callers might be dependent on the original exception specification. Compilers typically offered no help in maintaining consistency among function implementations, exception specifications, and client code. Most programmers ultimately decided that C++98 exception specifications weren't worth the trouble.

During work on C++11, a consensus emerged that the truly meaningful information about a function's exception-emitting behavior was whether it had any. Black or white, either a function might emit an exception or it guaranteed that it wouldn't. This maybe-or-never dichotomy forms the basis of C++11's exception specifications, which essentially replace C++98's. (C++98-style exception specifications remain valid, but they're deprecated.) In C++11, unconditional noexcept is for functions that guarantee they won't emit exceptions.

Whether a function should be so declared is a matter of interface design. The exception-emitting behavior of a function is of key interest to clients. Callers can query a function's noexcept status, and the results of such a query can affect the exception safety or efficiency of the calling code. As such, whether a function is noexcept is as important a piece of information as whether a member function is const. Failure to declare a function noexcept when you know that it won't emit an exception is simply poor interface specification.

But there's an additional incentive to apply noexcept to functions that won't produce exceptions: it permits compilers to generate better object code. To understand why, it helps to examine the difference between the C++98 and C++11 ways of saying that a function won't emit exceptions. Consider a function f that promises callers they'll never receive an exception. The two ways of expressing that are:

```
int f(int x) throw();      // no exceptions from f: C++98 style

int f(int x) noexcept;     // no exceptions from f: C++11 style
```

If, at runtime, an exception leaves f, f's exception specification is violated. With the C++98 exception specification, the call stack is unwound to f's caller, and, after some actions not relevant here, program execution is terminated. With the C++11 exception specification, runtime behavior is slightly different: the stack is only *possibly* unwound before program execution is terminated.

The difference between unwinding the call stack and *possibly* unwinding it has a surprisingly large impact on code generation. In a `noexcept` function, optimizers need not keep the runtime stack in an unwindable state if an exception would propagate out of the function, nor must they ensure that objects in a `noexcept` function are destroyed in the inverse order of construction should an exception leave the function. Functions with "`throw()`" exception specifications lack such optimization flexibility, as do functions with no exception specification at all. The situation can be summarized this way:

```
RetType function(params) noexcept;      // most optimizable

RetType function(params) throw();       // less optimizable

RetType function(params);               // less optimizable
```

This alone is sufficient reason to declare functions `noexcept` whenever you know they won't produce exceptions.

For some functions, the case is even stronger. The move operations are the preeminent example. Suppose you have a C++98 code base making use of a `std::vector<Widget>`. Widgets are added to the `std::vector` from time to time via `push_back`:

```
std::vector<Widget> vw;

…

Widget w;

…                        // work with w

vw.push_back(w);         // add w to vw

…
```

Assume this code works fine, and you have no interest in modifying it for C++11. However, you do want to take advantage of the fact that C++11's move semantics can improve the performance of legacy code when move-enabled types are involved. You therefore ensure that `Widget` has move operations, either by writing them yourself or by seeing to it that the conditions for their automatic generation are fulfilled (see Item 17).

When a new element is added to a `std::vector`, it's possible that the `std::vector` lacks space for it, i.e., that the `std::vector`'s size is equal to its capacity. When that happens, the `std::vector` allocates a new, larger, chunk of memory to hold its elements, and it transfers the elements from the existing chunk of memory to the new one. In C++98, the transfer was accomplished by copying each element from the old memory to the new memory, then destroying the objects in the old memory. This approach enabled `push_back` to offer the strong exception safety guarantee: if an exception was thrown during the copying of the elements, the state of the `std::vector` remained unchanged, because none of the elements in the old memory were destroyed until all elements had been successfully copied into the new memory.

In C++11, a natural optimization would be to replace the copying of `std::vector` elements with moves. Unfortunately, doing this runs the risk of violating `push_back`'s exception safety guarantee. If *n* elements have been moved from the old memory and an exception is thrown moving element *n+1*, the `push_back` operation can't run to completion. But the original `std::vector` has been modified: *n* of its elements have been moved from. Restoring their original state may not be possible, because attempting to move each object back into the original memory may itself yield an exception.

This is a serious problem, because the behavior of legacy code could depend on `push_back`'s strong exception safety guarantee. Therefore, C++11 implementations can't silently replace copy operations inside `push_back` with moves unless it's known that the move operations won't emit exceptions. In that case, having moves replace copies would be safe, and the only side effect would be improved performance.

`std::vector::push_back` takes advantage of this "move if you can, but copy if you must" strategy, and it's not the only function in the Standard Library that does. Other functions sporting the strong exception safety guarantee in C++98 (e.g., `std::vector::reserve`, `std::deque::insert`, etc.) behave the same way. All these functions replace calls to copy operations in C++98 with calls to move operations in C++11 only if the move operations are known to not emit exceptions. But how can a function know if a move operation won't produce an exception? The answer is obvious: it checks to see if the operation is declared `noexcept`.[4]

`swap` functions comprise another case where `noexcept` is particularly desirable. `swap` is a key component of many STL algorithm implementations, and it's commonly employed in copy assignment operators, too. Its widespread use renders the optimizations that `noexcept` affords especially worthwhile. Interestingly, whether `swap`s in the Standard Library are `noexcept` is sometimes dependent on whether user-

---

4 The checking is typically rather roundabout. Functions like `std::vector::push_back` call `std::move_if_noexcept`, a variation of `std::move` that conditionally casts to an rvalue (see Item 23), depending on whether the type's move constructor is `noexcept`. In turn, `std::move_if_noexcept` consults `std::is_nothrow_move_constructible`, and the value of this type trait (see Item 9) is set by compilers, based on whether the move constructor has a `noexcept` (or `throw()`) designation.

defined swaps are noexcept. For example, the declarations for the Standard Library's swaps for arrays and std::pair are:

```
template <class T, size_t N>
void swap(T (&a)[N],                                           // see
         T (&b)[N]) noexcept(noexcept(swap(*a, *b)));          // below

template <class T1, class T2>
struct pair {

    ...
    void swap(pair& p) noexcept(noexcept(swap(first, p.first)) &&
                                noexcept(swap(second, p.second)));

    ...
};
```

These functions are *conditionally noexcept*: whether they are noexcept depends on whether the expressions inside the noexcept clauses are noexcept. Given two arrays of Widget, for example, swapping them is noexcept only if swapping individual elements in the arrays is noexcept, i.e., if swap for Widget is noexcept. The author of Widget's swap thus determines whether swapping arrays of Widget is noexcept. That, in turn, determines whether other swaps, such as the one for arrays of arrays of Widget, are noexcept. Similarly, whether swapping two std::pair objects containing Widgets is noexcept depends on whether swap for Widgets is noexcept. The fact that swapping higher-level data structures can generally be noexcept only if swapping their lower-level constituents is noexcept should motivate you to offer noexcept swap functions whenever you can.

By now, I hope you're excited about the optimization opportunities that noexcept affords. Alas, I must temper your enthusiasm. Optimization is important, but correctness is more important. I noted at the beginning of this Item that noexcept is part of a function's interface, so you should declare a function noexcept only if you are willing to commit to a noexcept implementation over the long term. If you declare a function noexcept and later regret that decision, your options are bleak. You can remove noexcept from the function's declaration (i.e., change its interface), thus running the risk of breaking client code. You can change the implementation such that an exception could escape, yet keep the original (now incorrect) exception specification. If you do that, your program will be terminated if an exception tries to leave the function. Or you can resign yourself to your existing implementation, abandoning whatever kindled your desire to change the implementation in the first place. None of these options is appealing.

The fact of the matter is that most functions are *exception-neutral*. Such functions throw no exceptions themselves, but functions they call might emit one. When that happens, the exception-neutral function allows the emitted exception to pass through on its way to a handler further up the call chain. Exception-neutral functions are never noexcept, because they may emit such "just passing through" exceptions. Most functions, therefore, quite properly lack the noexcept designation.

Some functions, however, have natural implementations that emit no exceptions, and for a few more—notably the move operations and swap—being noexcept can have such a significant payoff, it's worth implementing them in a noexcept manner if at all possible.[5] When you can honestly say that a function should never emit exceptions, you should definitely declare it noexcept.

Please note that I said some functions have *natural* noexcept implementations. Twisting a function's implementation to permit a noexcept declaration is the tail wagging the dog. Is putting the cart before the horse. Is not seeing the forest for the trees. Is...choose your favorite metaphor. If a straightforward function implementation might yield exceptions (e.g., by invoking a function that might throw), the hoops you'll jump through to hide that from callers (e.g., catching all exceptions and replacing them with status codes or special return values) will not only complicate your function's implementation, it will typically complicate code at call sites, too. For example, callers may have to check for status codes or special return values. The runtime cost of those complications (e.g., extra branches, larger functions that put more pressure on instruction caches, etc.) could exceed any speedup you'd hope to achieve via noexcept, plus you'd be saddled with source code that's more difficult to comprehend and maintain. That'd be poor software engineering.

For some functions, being noexcept is so important, they're that way by default. In C++98, it was considered bad style to permit the memory deallocation functions (i.e., operator delete and operator delete[]) and destructors to emit exceptions, and in C++11, this style rule has been all but upgraded to a language rule. By default, all memory deallocation functions and all destructors—both user-defined and compiler-generated—are implicitly noexcept. There's thus no need to declare them noexcept. (Doing so doesn't hurt anything, it's just unconventional.) The only time a destructor is not implicitly noexcept is when a data member of the class (including inherited members and those contained inside other data members) is of a type that expressly states that its destructor may emit exceptions (e.g., declares it "noexcept(false)"). Such destructors are uncommon. There are none in the Standard Library, and if the

---

5 The interface specifications for move operations on containers in the Standard Library lack noexcept. However, implementers are permitted to strengthen exception specifications for Standard Library functions, and, in practice, it is common for at least some container move operations to be declared noexcept. That practice exemplifies this Item's advice. Having found that it's possible to write container move operations such that exceptions aren't thrown, implementers often declare the operations noexcept, even though the Standard does not require them to do so.

destructor for an object being used by the Standard Library (e.g., because it's in a container or was passed to an algorithm) emits an exception, the behavior of the program is undefined.

It's worth noting that some library interface designers distinguish functions with *wide contracts* from those with *narrow contracts*. A function with a wide contract has no preconditions. Such a function may be called regardless of the state of the program, and it imposes no constraints on the arguments that callers pass it.[6] Functions with wide contracts never exhibit undefined behavior.

Functions without wide contracts have narrow contracts. For such functions, if a precondition is violated, results are undefined.

If you're writing a function with a wide contract and you know it won't emit exceptions, following the advice of this Item and declaring it noexcept is easy. For functions with narrow contracts, the situation is trickier. For example, suppose you're writing a function f taking a std::string parameter, and suppose f's natural implementation never yields an exception. That suggests that f should be declared noexcept.

Now suppose that f has a precondition: the length of its std::string parameter doesn't exceed 32 characters. If f were to be called with a std::string whose length is greater than 32, behavior would be undefined, because a precondition violation *by definition* results in undefined behavior. f is under no obligation to check this precondition, because functions may assume that their preconditions are satisfied. (Callers are responsible for ensuring that such assumptions are valid.) Even with a precondition, then, declaring f noexcept seems appropriate:

```
void f(const std::string& s) noexcept;    // precondition:
                                           // s.length() <= 32
```

But suppose that f's implementer chooses to check for precondition violations. Checking isn't required, but it's also not forbidden, and checking the precondition could be useful, e.g., during system testing. Debugging an exception that's been thrown is generally easier than trying to track down the cause of undefined behavior. But how should a precondition violation be reported such that a test harness or a client error handler could detect it? A straightforward approach would be to throw a "precondition was violated" exception, but if f is declared noexcept, that would be impossible; throwing an exception would lead to program termination. For this rea-

---

6 "Regardless of the state of the program" and "no constraints" doesn't legitimize programs whose behavior is already undefined. For example, std::vector::size has a wide contract, but that doesn't require that it behave reasonably if you invoke it on a random chunk of memory that you've cast to a std::vector. The result of the cast is undefined, so there are no behavioral guarantees for the program containing the cast.

son, library designers who distinguish wide from narrow contracts generally reserve noexcept for functions with wide contracts.

As a final point, let me elaborate on my earlier observation that compilers typically offer no help in identifying inconsistencies between function implementations and their exception specifications. Consider this code, which is perfectly legal:

```
void setup();            // functions defined elsewhere
void cleanup();

void doWork() noexcept
{
  setup();               // set up work to be done

  …                      // do the actual work

  cleanup();             // perform cleanup actions
}
```

Here, doWork is declared noexcept, even though it calls the non-noexcept functions setup and cleanup. This seems contradictory, but it could be that setup and cleanup document that they never emit exceptions, even though they're not declared that way. There could be good reasons for their non-noexcept declarations. For example, they might be part of a library written in C. (Even functions from the C Standard Library that have been moved into the std namespace lack exception specifications, e.g., std::strlen isn't declared noexcept.) Or they could be part of a C++98 library that decided not to use C++98 exception specifications and hasn't yet been revised for C++11.

Because there are legitimate reasons for noexcept functions to rely on code lacking the noexcept guarantee, C++ permits such code, and compilers generally don't issue warnings about it.

Things to Remember

- noexcept is part of a function's interface, and that means that callers may depend on it.
- noexcept functions are more optimizable than non-noexcept functions.
- noexcept is particularly valuable for the move operations, swap, memory deallocation functions, and destructors.
- Most functions are exception-neutral rather than noexcept.

Item 15: Use `constexpr` whenever possible.

If there were an award for the most confusing new word in C++11, `constexpr` would probably win it. When applied to objects, it's essentially a beefed-up form of `const`, but when applied to functions, it has a quite different meaning. Cutting through the confusion is worth the trouble, because when `constexpr` corresponds to what you want to express, you definitely want to use it.

Conceptually, `constexpr` indicates a value that's not only constant, it's known during compilation. The concept is only part of the story, though, because when `constexpr` is applied to functions, things are more nuanced than this suggests. Lest I ruin the surprise ending, for now I'll just say that you can't assume that the results of `constexpr` functions are `const`, nor can you take for granted that their values are known during compilation. Perhaps most intriguingly, these things are *features*. It's *good* that `constexpr` functions need not produce results that are `const` or known during compilation!

But let's begin with `constexpr` objects. Such objects are, in fact, `const`, and they do, in fact, have values that are known at compile time. (Technically, their values are determined during *translation*, and translation consists not just of compilation but also of linking. Unless you write compilers or linkers for C++, however, this has no effect on you, so you can blithely program as if the values of `constexpr` objects were determined during compilation.)

Values known during compilation are privileged. They may be placed in read-only memory, for example, and, especially for developers of embedded systems, this can be a feature of considerable importance. Of broader applicability is that integral values that are constant and known during compilation can be used in contexts where C++ requires an *integral constant expression*. Such contexts include specification of array sizes, integral template arguments (including lengths of `std::array` objects), enumerator values, alignment specifiers, and more. If you want to use a variable for these kinds of things, you certainly want to declare it `constexpr`, because then compilers will ensure that it has a compile-time value:

```
    int sz;                              // non-constexpr variable

    …

    constexpr auto arraySize1 = sz;      // error! sz's value not
                                         // known at compilation

    std::array<int, sz> data1;           // error! same problem

    constexpr auto arraySize2 = 10;      // fine, 10 is a
```

```
                                           // compile-time constant

    std::array<int, arraySize2> data2;     // fine, arraySize2
                                           // is constexpr
```

Note that `const` doesn't offer the same guarantee as `constexpr`, because `const` objects need not be initialized with values known during compilation:

```
    int sz;                                // as before

    ...

    const auto arraySize = sz;             // fine, arraySize is
                                           // const copy of sz

    std::array<int, arraySize> data;       // error! arraySize's value
                                           // not known at compilation
```

Simply put, all `constexpr` objects are `const`, but not all `const` objects are `constexpr`. If you want compilers to guarantee that a variable has a value that can be used in contexts requiring compile-time constants, the tool to reach for is `constexpr`, not `const`.

Usage scenarios for `constexpr` objects become more interesting when `constexpr` functions are involved. Such functions produce compile-time constants *when they are called with compile-time constants*. If they're called with values not known until runtime, they produce runtime values. This may sound as if you don't know what they'll do, but that's the wrong way to think about it. The right way to view it is this:

- `constexpr` functions can be used in contexts that demand compile-time constants. If the values of the arguments you pass to a `constexpr` function in such a context are known during compilation, the result will be computed during compilation. If any of the arguments' values is not known during compilation, your code will be rejected.

- When a `constexpr` function is called with one or more values that are not known during compilation, it acts like a normal function, computing its result at runtime. This means you don't need two functions to perform the same operation, one for compile-time constants and one for all other values. The `constexpr` function does it all.

Suppose we need a data structure to hold the results of an experiment that can be run in a variety of ways. For example, the lighting level can be high, low, or off during the course of the experiment, as can the fan speed and the temperature, etc. If there are n environmental conditions relevant to the experiment, each of which has three possible states, the number of combinations is 3^n. Storing experimental results for all combinations of conditions thus requires a data structure with enough room for 3^n values. Assuming each result is an int and that n is known (or can be computed) during compilation, a std::array could be a reasonable data structure choice. But we'd need a way to compute 3^n during compilation. The C++ Standard Library provides std::pow, which is the mathematical functionality we need, but, for our purposes, there are two problems with it. First, std::pow works on floating-point types, and we need an integral result. Second, std::pow isn't constexpr (i.e., isn't guaranteed to return a compile-time result when called with compile-time values), so we can't use it to specify a std::array's size.

Fortunately, we can write the pow we need. I'll show how to do that in a moment, but first let's look at how it could be declared and used:

```
constexpr                              // pow's a constexpr func
int pow(int base, unsigned exp) noexcept    // that never throws
{
  …                                    // impl is below
}

constexpr auto numConds = 5;           // # of conditions

std::array<int, pow(3, numConds)> results;  // results has
                                       // 3^numConds
                                       // elements
```

Recall that the constexpr in front of pow doesn't say that pow returns a const value, it says that if base and exp are compile-time constants, pow's result may be used as a compile-time constant. If base and/or exp are not compile-time constants, pow's result will be computed at runtime. That means that pow can not only be called to do things like compile-time-compute the size of a std::array, it can also be called in runtime contexts such as this:

```
auto base = readFromDB("base");        // get these values
auto exp = readFromDB("exponent");     // at runtime

auto baseToExp = pow(base, exp);       // call pow function
                                       // at runtime
```

Because constexpr functions must be able to return compile-time results when called with compile-time values, restrictions are imposed on their implementations. The restrictions differ between C++11 and C++14.

In C++11, constexpr functions may contain no more than a single executable statement: a return. That sounds more limiting than it is, because two tricks can be used to extend the expressiveness of constexpr functions beyond what you might think. First, the conditional "?:" operator can be used in place of if-else statements, and second, recursion can be used instead of loops. pow can therefore be implemented like this:

```
constexpr int pow(int base, unsigned exp) noexcept
{
    return (exp == 0 ? 1 : base * pow(base, exp - 1));
}
```

This works, but it's hard to imagine that anybody except a hard-core functional programmer would consider it pretty. In C++14, the restrictions on constexpr functions are substantially looser, so the following implementation becomes possible:

```
constexpr int pow(int base, unsigned exp) noexcept      // C++14
{
    auto result = 1;
    for (unsigned i = 0; i < exp; ++i) result *= base;

    return result;
}
```

constexpr functions are limited to taking and returning *literal types*, which essentially means types that can have values determined during compilation. In C++11, all built-in types except void qualify, but user-defined types may be literal, too, because constructors and other member functions may be constexpr:

```
class Point {
public:
    constexpr Point(double xVal = 0, double yVal = 0) noexcept
    : x(xVal), y(yVal)
    {}

    constexpr double xValue() const noexcept { return x; }
    constexpr double yValue() const noexcept { return y; }

    void setX(double newX) noexcept { x = newX; }
    void setY(double newY) noexcept { y = newY; }

private:
    double x, y;
};
```

Here, the Point constructor can be declared constexpr, because if the arguments passed to it are known during compilation, the value of the data members of the constructed `Point` can also be known during compilation. `Point`s so initialized could thus be `constexpr`:

```
constexpr Point p1(9.4, 27.7);      // fine, "runs" constexpr
                                    // ctor during compilation

constexpr Point p2(28.8, 5.3);      // also fine
```

Similarly, the getters `xValue` and `yValue` can be `constexpr`, because if they're invoked on a `Point` object with a value known during compilation (e.g., a `constexpr` `Point` object), the values of the data members `x` and `y` can be known during compilation. That makes it possible to write `constexpr` functions that call `Point`'s getters and to initialize `constexpr` objects with the results of such functions:

```
constexpr
Point midpoint(const Point& p1, const Point& p2) noexcept
{
  return { (p1.xValue() + p2.xValue()) / 2,    // call constexpr
           (p1.yValue() + p2.yValue()) / 2 };  // member funcs
}

constexpr auto mid = midpoint(p1, p2);    // init constexpr
                                          // object w/result of
                                          // constexpr function
```

This is very exciting. It means that the object `mid`, though its initialization involves calls to constructors, getters, and a non-member function, can be created in read-only memory! It means you could use an expression like `mid.xValue() * 10` in an argument to a template or in an expression specifying the value of an enumerator![7] It means that the traditionally fairly strict line between work done during compilation and work done at runtime begins to blur, and some computations traditionally done at runtime can migrate to compile time. The more code taking part in the migration, the faster your software will run. (Compilation may take longer, however.)

In C++11, two restrictions prevent `Point`'s member functions `setX` and `setY` from being declared `constexpr`. First, they modify the object they operate on, and in C++11, `constexpr` member functions are implicitly `const`. Second, they have `void` return types, and `void` isn't a literal type in C++11. Both these restrictions are lifted in C++14, so in C++14, even `Point`'s setters can be `constexpr`:

---

7 Because `Point::xValue` returns `double`, the type of `mid.xValue() * 10` is also `double`. Floating-point types can't be used to instantiate templates or to specify enumerator values, but they can be used as part of larger expressions that yield integral types. For example, `static_cast<int>(mid.xValue() * 10)` could be used to instantiate a template or to specify an enumerator value.

```
class Point {
public:

    ...

    constexpr void setX(double newX) noexcept        // C++14
    { x = newX; }

    constexpr void setY(double newY) noexcept        // C++14
    { y = newY; }

    ...

};
```

That makes it possible to write functions like this:

```
// return reflection of p with respect to the origin (C++14)
constexpr Point reflection(const Point& p) noexcept
{
    Point result;                      // create non-const Point

    result.setX(-p.xValue());          // set its x and y values
    result.setY(-p.yValue());

    return result;                     // return copy of it
}
```

Client code could look like this:

```
constexpr Point p1(9.4, 27.7);         // as above
constexpr Point p2(28.8, 5.3);
constexpr auto mid = midpoint(p1, p2);

constexpr auto reflectedMid =          // reflectedMid's value is
    reflection(mid);                   // (-19.1 -16.5) and known
                                       // during compilation
```

The advice of this Item is to use constexpr whenever possible, and by now I hope it's clear why: both constexpr objects and constexpr functions can be employed in a wider range of contexts than non-constexpr objects and functions. By using constexpr whenever possible, you maximize the range of situations in which your objects and functions may be used.

It's important to note that constexpr is part of an object's or function's interface. constexpr proclaims "I can be used in a context where C++ requires a constant expression." If you declare an object or function constexpr, clients may use it in such contexts. If you later decide that your use of `constexpr` was a mistake and you remove it, you may cause arbitrarily large amounts of client code to stop compiling. (The simple act of adding I/O to a function for debugging or performance tuning could lead to such a problem, because I/O statements are generally not permitted in `constexpr` functions.) Part of "whenever possible" in "Use `constexpr` whenever possible" is your willingness to make a long-term commitment to the constraints it imposes on the objects and functions you apply it to.

Things to Remember

- `constexpr` objects are `const` and are initialized with values known during compilation.
- `constexpr` functions can produce compile-time results when called with arguments whose values are known during compilation.
- `constexpr` objects and functions may be used in a wider range of contexts than non-`constexpr` objects and functions.
- `constexpr` is part of an object's or function's interface.

Item 16: Make `const` member functions thread safe.

If we're working in a mathematical domain, we might find it convenient to have a class representing polynomials. Within this class, it would probably be useful to have a function to compute the root(s) of a polynomial, i.e., values where the polynomial evaluates to zero. Such a function would not modify the polynomial, so it'd be natural to declare it `const`:

```
class Polynomial {
public:
  using RootsType =          // data structure holding values
    std::vector<double>;     // where polynomial evals to zero
                             // (see Item 9 for info on "using")
  ...

  RootsType roots() const;

  ...

};
```

Computing the roots of a polynomial can be expensive, so we don't want to do it if we don't have to. And if we do have to do it, we certainly don't want to do it more than once. We'll thus cache the root(s) of the polynomial if we have to compute them, and we'll implement `roots` to return the cached value. Here's the basic approach:

```
class Polynomial {
public:
  using RootsType = std::vector<double>;

  RootsType roots() const
  {
    if (!rootsAreValid) {          // if cache not valid

      ...                          // compute roots,
                                   // store them in rootVals
      rootsAreValid = true;
    }

    return rootVals;
  }

private:
  mutable bool rootsAreValid{ false };    // see Item 7 for info
  mutable RootsType rootVals{};           // on initializers
};
```

Conceptually, `roots` doesn't change the `Polynomial` object on which it operates, but, as part of its caching activity, it may need to modify `rootVals` and `rootsAreValid`. That's a classic use case for `mutable`, and that's why it's part of the declarations for these data members.

Imagine now that two threads simultaneously call `roots` on a `Polynomial` object:

```
Polynomial p;

...
```

```
/*----- Thread 1 ----- */      /*------- Thread 2 ------- */

auto rootsOfP = p.roots();      auto valsGivingZero = p.roots();
```

This client code is perfectly reasonable. `roots` is a `const` member function, and that means it represents a read operation. Having multiple threads perform a read operation without synchronization is safe. At least it's supposed to be. In this case, it's not, because inside `roots`, one or both of these threads might try to modify the data members `rootsAreValid` and `rootVals`. That means that this code could have different threads reading and writing the same memory without synchronization, and that's the definition of a data race. This code has undefined behavior.

The problem is that roots is declared const, but it's not thread safe. The const declaration is as correct in C++11 as it would be in C++98 (retrieving the roots of a polynomial doesn't change the value of the polynomial), so what requires rectification is the lack of thread safety.

The easiest way to address the issue is the usual one: employ a mutex:

```
class Polynomial {
public:
  using RootsType = std::vector<double>;

  RootsType roots() const
  {
    std::lock_guard<std::mutex> g(m);      // lock mutex

    if (!rootsAreValid) {                  // if cache not valid

      ...                                  // compute/store roots

      rootsAreValid = true;
    }

    return rootVals;
  }                                        // unlock mutex

private:
  mutable std::mutex m;
  mutable bool rootsAreValid{ false };
  mutable RootsType rootVals{};
};
```

The std::mutex m is declared mutable, because locking and unlocking it are non-const member functions, and within roots (a const member function), m would otherwise be considered a const object.

It's worth noting that because std::mutex can be neither copied nor moved, a side effect of adding m to Polynomial is that Polynomial loses the ability to be copied and moved.

In some situations, a mutex is overkill. For example, if all you're doing is counting how many times a member function is called, a std::atomic counter (i.e., one where other threads are guaranteed to see its operations occur indivisibly—see Item 40) will often be a less expensive way to go. (Whether it actually is less expensive depends on the hardware you're running on and the implementation of mutexes in your Standard Library.) Here's how you can employ a `std::atomic` to count calls:

```
class Point {                                        // 2D point
public:
  …

  double distanceFromOrigin() const noexcept    // see Item 14
  {                                              // for noexcept

    ++callCount;                                 // atomic increment

    return std::hypot(x, y);                     // std::hypot is
  }                                              // new in C++11

private:
  mutable std::atomic<unsigned> callCount{ 0 };
  double x, y;
};
```

Like `std::mutex`es, `std::atomic`s are uncopyable and unmovable, so the existence of `callCount` in `Point` means that `Point` is also neither copyable nor movable.

Because operations on `std::atomic` variables are often less expensive than mutex acquisition and release, you may be tempted to lean on `std::atomic`s more heavily than you should. For example, in a class caching an expensive-to-compute `int`, you might try to use a pair of `std::atomic` variables instead of a mutex:

```
class Widget {
public:
  …

  int magicValue() const
  {
    if (cacheValid) return cachedValue;
    else {
      auto val1 = expensiveComputation1();
      auto val2 = expensiveComputation2();
      cachedValue = val1 + val2;                 // uh oh, part 1
      cacheValid = true;                         // uh oh, part 2
      return cachedValue;
    }
  }

private:
```

```
    mutable std::atomic<bool> cacheValid{ false };
    mutable std::atomic<int> cachedValue;
};
```

This will work, but sometimes it will work a lot harder than it should. Consider:

- A thread calls Widget::magicValue, sees cacheValid as false, performs the two expensive computations, and assigns their sum to cachedValue.

- At that point, a second thread calls Widget::magicValue, also sees cacheValid as false, and thus carries out the same expensive computations that the first thread has just finished. (This "second thread" may in fact be *several* other threads.)

To eliminate this problem, you might consider reversing the order of the assignments to cachedValue and cacheValid, but you'd soon realize that (1) multiple threads could still compute val1 and val2 before cacheValid is set to true, thus defeating the point of the exercise, and (2) it would actually make things worse. Consider:

```
class Widget {
public:
  …

  int magicValue() const
  {
    if (cacheValid) return cachedValue;
    else {
      auto val1 = expensiveComputation1();
      auto val2 = expensiveComputation2();
      cacheValid = true;                     // uh oh, part 1
      return cachedValue = val1 + val2;      // uh oh, part 2
    }
  }

  …

};
```

Imagine that cacheValid is false, and then:

- One thread calls Widget::magicValue and executes through the point where cacheValid is set to true.

- At that moment, a second thread calls Widget::magicValue and checks cache-Valid. Seeing it true, the thread returns cachedValue, even though the first

```
```

thread has not yet made an assignment to it. The returned value is therefore incorrect.

There's a lesson here. For a single variable or memory location requiring synchronization, use of a `std::atomic` is adequate, but once you get to two or more variables or memory locations that require manipulation as a unit, you should reach for a mutex. For `Widget::magicValue`, that would look like this:

```
class Widget {
public:
    …

    int magicValue() const
    {
        std::lock_guard<std::mutex> guard(m);    // lock m

        if (cacheValid) return cachedValue;
        else {
            auto val1 = expensiveComputation1();
            auto val2 = expensiveComputation2();
            cachedValue = val1 + val2;
            cacheValid = true;
            return cachedValue;
        }
    }                                            // unlock m
    …

private:
    mutable std::mutex m;
    mutable int cachedValue;                     // no longer atomic
    mutable bool cacheValid{ false };            // no longer atomic
};
```

Now, this Item is predicated on the assumption that multiple threads may simultaneously execute a `const` member function on an object. If you're writing a `const` member function where that's not the case—where you can *guarantee* that there will never be more than one thread executing that member function on an object—the thread safety of the function is immaterial. For example, it's unimportant whether member functions of classes designed for exclusively single-threaded use are thread safe. In such cases, you can avoid the costs associated with mutexes and `std::atomics`, as well as the side effect of their rendering the classes containing them uncopyable and unmovable. However, such threading-free scenarios are increasingly uncommon, and they're likely to become rarer still. The safe bet is that `const` member functions will be subject to concurrent execution, and that's why you should ensure that your const member functions are thread safe.

Things to Remember

- Make const member functions thread safe unless you're *certain* they'll never be used in a concurrent context.
- Use of std::atomic variables may offer better performance than a mutex, but they're suited for manipulation of only a single variable or memory location.

Item 17: Understand special member function generation.

In official C++ parlance, the *special member functions* are the ones that C++ is willing to generate on its own. C++98 has four such functions: the default constructor, the destructor, the copy constructor, and the copy assignment operator. There's fine print, of course. These functions are generated only if they're needed, i.e., if some code uses them without their being expressly declared in the class. A default constructor is generated only if the class declares no constructors at all. (This prevents compilers from creating a default constructor for a class where you've specified that constructor arguments are required.) Generated special member functions are implicitly public and inline, and they're nonvirtual unless the function in question is a destructor in a derived class inheriting from a base class with a virtual destructor. In that case, the compiler-generated destructor for the derived class is also virtual.

But you already know these things. Yes, yes, ancient history: Mesopotamia, the Shang dynasty, FORTRAN, C++98. But times have changed, and the rules for special member function generation in C++ have changed with them. It's important to be aware of the new rules, because few things are as central to effective C++ programming as knowing when compilers silently insert member functions into your classes.

As of C++11, the special member functions club has two more inductees: the move constructor and the move assignment operator. Their signatures are:

```
class Widget {
public:
  …
  Widget(Widget&& rhs);              // move constructor

  Widget& operator=(Widget&& rhs);   // move assignment operator

  …
};
```

The rules governing their generation and behavior are analogous to those for their copying siblings. The move operations are generated only if they're needed, and if they are generated, they perform "memberwise moves" on the non-static data members of the class. That means that the move constructor move-constructs each non-static data member of the class from the corresponding member of its parameter `rhs`, and the move assignment operator move-assigns each non-static data member from its parameter. The move constructor also move-constructs its base class parts (if there are any), and the move assignment operator move-assigns its base class parts.

Now, when I refer to a move operation move-constructing or move-assigning a data member or base class, there is no guarantee that a move will actually take place. "Memberwise moves" are, in reality, more like memberwise move *requests*, because types that aren't *move-enabled* (i.e., that offer no special support for move operations, e.g., most C++98 legacy classes) will be "moved" via their copy operations. The heart of each memberwise "move" is application of `std::move` to the object to be moved from, and the result is used during function overload resolution to determine whether a move or a copy should be performed. Item 23 covers this process in detail. For this Item, simply remember that a memberwise move consists of move operations on data members and base classes that support move operations, but a copy operation for those that don't.

As is the case with the copy operations, the move operations aren't generated if you declare them yourself. However, the precise conditions under which they are generated differ a bit from those for the copy operations.

The two copy operations are independent: declaring one doesn't prevent compilers from generating the other. So if you declare a copy constructor, but no copy assignment operator, then write code that requires copy assignment, compilers will generate the copy assignment operator for you. Similarly, if you declare a copy assignment operator, but no copy constructor, yet your code requires copy construction, compilers will generate the copy constructor for you. That was true in C++98, and it's still true in C++11.

The two move operations are not independent. If you declare either, that prevents compilers from generating the other. The rationale is that if you declare, say, a move constructor for your class, you're indicating that there's something about how move construction should be implemented that's different from the default memberwise move that compilers would generate. And if there's something wrong with memberwise move construction, there'd probably be something wrong with memberwise move assignment, too. So declaring a move constructor prevents a move assignment operator from being generated, and declaring a move assignment operator prevents compilers from generating a move constructor.

Furthermore, move operations won't be generated for any class that explicitly declares a copy operation. The justification is that declaring a copy operation (construction or assignment) indicates that the normal approach to copying an object (memberwise copy) isn't appropriate for the class, and compilers figure that if memberwise copy isn't appropriate for the copy operations, memberwise move probably isn't appropriate for the move operations.

This goes in the other direction, too. Declaring a move operation (construction or assignment) in a class causes compilers to disable the copy operations. (The copy operations are disabled by deleting them—see Item 11). After all, if memberwise move isn't the proper way to move an object, there's no reason to expect that memberwise copy is the proper way to copy it. This may sound like it could break C++98 code, because the conditions under which the copy operations are enabled are more constrained in C++11 than in C++98, but this is not the case. C++98 code can't have move operations, because there was no such thing as "moving" objects in C++98. The only way a legacy class can have user-declared move operations is if they were added for C++11, and classes that are modified to take advantage of move semantics have to play by the C++11 rules for special member function generation.

Perhaps you've heard of a guideline known as the *Rule of Three*. The Rule of Three states that if you declare any of a copy constructor, copy assignment operator, or destructor, you should declare all three. It grew out of the observation that the need to take over the meaning of a copy operation almost always stemmed from the class performing some kind of resource management, and that almost always implied that (1) whatever resource management was being done in one copy operation probably needed to be done in the other copy operation and (2) the class destructor would also be participating in management of the resource (usually releasing it). The classic resource to be managed was memory, and this is why all Standard Library classes that manage memory (e.g., the STL containers that perform dynamic memory management) all declare "the big three": both copy operations and a destructor.

A consequence of the Rule of Three is that the presence of a user-declared destructor indicates that simple memberwise copy is unlikely to be appropriate for the copying operations in the class. That, in turn, suggests that if a class declares a destructor, the copy operations probably shouldn't be automatically generated, because they wouldn't do the right thing. At the time C++98 was adopted, the significance of this line of reasoning was not fully appreciated, so in C++98, the existence of a user-declared destructor had no impact on compilers' willingness to generate copy operations. That continues to be the case in C++11, but only because restricting the conditions under which the copy operations are generated would break too much legacy code.

The reasoning behind the Rule of Three remains valid, however, and that, combined with the observation that declaration of a copy operation precludes the implicit generation of the move operations, motivates the fact that C++11 does *not* generate move operations for a class with a user-declared destructor.

So move operations are generated for classes (when needed) only if these three things are true:

- No copy operations are declared in the class.
- No move operations are declared in the class.
- No destructor is declared in the class.

At some point, analogous rules may be extended to the copy operations, because C++11 deprecates the automatic generation of copy operations for classes declaring copy operations or a destructor. This means that if you have code that depends on the generation of copy operations in classes declaring a destructor or one of the copy operations, you should consider upgrading these classes to eliminate the dependence. Provided the behavior of the compiler-generated functions is correct (i.e., if member-wise copying of the class's non-static data members is what you want), your job is easy, because C++11's "= default" lets you say that explicitly:

```
class Widget {
public:
    …
    ~Widget();                               // user-declared dtor

    …                                        // default copy ctor
    Widget(const Widget&) = default;         // behavior is OK

    Widget&                                  // default copy assign
        operator=(const Widget&) = default;  // behavior is OK
    …
};
```

This approach is often useful in polymorphic base classes, i.e., classes defining interfaces through which derived class objects are manipulated. Polymorphic base classes normally have virtual destructors, because if they don't, some operations (e.g., the use of delete or typeid on a derived class object through a base class pointer or reference) yield undefined or misleading results. Unless a class inherits a destructor that's already virtual, the only way to make a destructor virtual is to explicitly declare it that way. Often, the default implementation would be correct, and "= default" is a good way to express that. However, a user-declared destructor suppresses generation of the move operations, so if movability is to be supported, "= default" often finds a second application. Declaring the move operations disables the copy operations, so if copyability is also desired, one more round of "= default" does the job:

```
class Base {
public:
    virtual ~Base() = default;               // make dtor virtual
```

```
  Base(Base&&) = default;                 // support moving
  Base& operator=(Base&&) = default;

  Base(const Base&) = default;            // support copying
  Base& operator=(const Base&) = default;

  …

};
```

In fact, even if you have a class where compilers are willing to generate the copy and move operations and where the generated functions would behave as you want, you may choose to adopt a policy of declaring them yourself and using "= default" for their definitions. It's more work, but it makes your intentions clearer, and it can help you sidestep some fairly subtle bugs. For example, suppose you have a class representing a string table, i.e., a data structure that permits fast lookups of string values via an integer ID:

```
class StringTable {
public:
  StringTable() {}
    …                 // functions for insertion, erasure, lookup,
                      // etc., but no copy/move/dtor functionality

private:
  std::map<int, std::string> values;
};
```

Assuming that the class declares no copy operations, no move operations, and no destructor, compilers will automatically generate these functions if they are used. That's very convenient.

But suppose that sometime later, it's decided that logging the default construction and the destruction of such objects would be useful. Adding that functionality is easy:

```
class StringTable {
public:
  StringTable()
  { makeLogEntry("Creating StringTable object"); }      // added

  ~StringTable()                                         // also
  { makeLogEntry("Destroying StringTable object"); }     // added

                                        // other funcs as before
    …
```

```
private:
    std::map<int, std::string> values;   // as before
};
```

This looks reasonable, but declaring a destructor has a potentially significant side effect: it prevents the move operations from being generated. However, creation of the class's copy operations is unaffected. The code is therefore likely to compile, run, and pass its functional testing. That includes testing its move functionality, because even though this class is no longer move-enabled, requests to move it will compile and run. Such requests will, as noted earlier in this Item, cause copies to be made. Which means that code "moving" StringTable objects actually copies them, i.e., copies the underlying std::map<int, std::string> objects. And copying a std::map<int, std::string> is likely to be *orders of magnitude* slower than moving it. The simple act of adding a destructor to the class could thereby have introduced a significant performance problem! Had the copy and move operations been explicitly defined using "= default", the problem would not have arisen.

Now, having endured my endless blathering about the rules governing the copy and move operations in C++11, you may wonder when I'll turn my attention to the two other special member functions, the default constructor and the destructor. That time is now, but only for this sentence, because almost nothing has changed for these member functions: the rules in C++11 are nearly the same as in C++98.

The C++11 rules governing the special member functions are thus:

- **Default constructor**: Same rules as C++98. Generated only if the class contains no user-declared constructors.

- **Destructor**: Essentially same rules as C++98; sole difference is that destructors are noexcept by default (see Item 14). As in C++98, virtual only if a base class destructor is virtual.

- **Copy constructor**: Same runtime behavior as C++98: memberwise copy construction of non-static data members. Generated only if the class lacks a user-declared copy constructor. Deleted if the class declares a move operation. Generation of this function in a class with a user-declared copy assignment operator or destructor is deprecated.

- **Copy assignment operator**: Same runtime behavior as C++98: memberwise copy assignment of non-static data members. Generated only if the class lacks a user-declared copy assignment operator. Deleted if the class declares a move operation. Generation of this function in a class with a user-declared copy constructor or destructor is deprecated.

- **Move constructor** and **move assignment operator**: Each performs memberwise moving of non-static data members. Generated only if the class lacks user-declared copy operations, move operations, and destructor.

Note that there's nothing in the rules about the existence of a member function *template* preventing compilers from generating the special member functions. That means that if Widget looks like this,

```
class Widget {
    …
    template<typename T>              // construct Widget
    Widget(const T& rhs);             // from anything

    template<typename T>              // assign Widget
    Widget& operator=(const T& rhs);  // from anything
    …
};
```

compilers will still generate copy and move operations for Widget (assuming the usual conditions governing their generation are fulfilled), even though these templates could be instantiated to produce the signatures for the copy constructor and copy assignment operator. (That would be the case when T is Widget.) In all likelihood, this will strike you as an edge case barely worth acknowledging, but there's a reason I'm mentioning it. Item 26 demonstrates that it can have important consequences.

Things to Remember

- The special member functions are those compilers may generate on their own: default constructor, destructor, copy operations, and move operations.
- Move operations are generated only for classes lacking explicitly declared move operations, copy operations, and a destructor.
- The copy constructor is generated only for classes lacking an explicitly declared copy constructor, and it's deleted if a move operation is declared. The copy assignment operator is generated only for classes lacking an explicitly declared copy assignment operator, and it's deleted if a move operation is declared. Generation of the copy operations in classes with an explicitly declared copy operation or destructor is deprecated.
- Member function templates never suppress generation of special member functions.

CHAPTER 4

Smart Pointers

Poets and songwriters have a thing about love. And sometimes about counting. Occasionally both. Inspired by the rather different takes on love and counting by Elizabeth Barrett Browning ("How do I love thee? Let me count the ways.") and Paul Simon ("There must be 50 ways to leave your lover."), we might try to enumerate the reasons why a raw pointer is hard to love:

1. Its declaration doesn't indicate whether it points to a single object or to an array.

2. Its declaration reveals nothing about whether you should destroy what it points to when you're done using it, i.e., if the pointer *owns* the thing it points to.

3. If you determine that you should destroy what the pointer points to, there's no way to tell how. Should you use `delete`, or is there a different destruction mechanism (e.g., a dedicated destruction function the pointer should be passed to)?

4. If you manage to find out that `delete` is the way to go, Reason 1 means it may not be possible to know whether to use the single-object form ("`delete`") or the array form ("`delete []`"). If you use the wrong form, results are undefined.

5. Assuming you ascertain that the pointer owns what it points to and you discover how to destroy it, it's difficult to ensure that you perform the destruction *exactly once* along every path in your code (including those due to exceptions). Missing a path leads to resource leaks, and doing the destruction more than once leads to undefined behavior.

6. There's typically no way to tell if the pointer dangles, i.e., points to memory that no longer holds the object the pointer is supposed to point to. Dangling pointers arise when objects are destroyed while pointers still point to them.

Raw pointers are powerful tools, to be sure, but decades of experience have demonstrated that with only the slightest lapse in concentration or discipline, these tools can turn on their ostensible masters.

Smart pointers are one way to address these issues. Smart pointers are wrappers around raw pointers that act much like the raw pointers they wrap, but that avoid many of their pitfalls. You should therefore prefer smart pointers to raw pointers. Smart pointers can do virtually everything raw pointers can, but with far fewer opportunities for error.

There are four smart pointers in C++11: `std::auto_ptr`, `std::unique_ptr`, `std::shared_ptr`, and `std::weak_ptr`. All are designed to help manage the lifetimes of dynamically allocated objects, i.e., to avoid resource leaks by ensuring that such objects are destroyed in the appropriate manner at the appropriate time (including in the event of exceptions).

`std::auto_ptr` is a deprecated leftover from C++98. It was an attempt to standardize what later became C++11's `std::unique_ptr`. Doing the job right required move semantics, but C++98 didn't have them. As a workaround, `std::auto_ptr` co-opted its copy operations for moves. This led to surprising code (copying a `std::auto_ptr` sets it to null!) and frustrating usage restrictions (e.g., it wasn't possible to store `std::auto_ptr`s in containers).

`std::unique_ptr` does everything `std::auto_ptr` does, plus more. It does it as efficiently, and it does it without warping what it means to copy an object. It's better than `std::auto_ptr` in every way. The only legitimate use case for `std::auto_ptr` is a need to compile code with C++98 compilers. Unless you have that constraint, you should replace `std::auto_ptr` with `std::unique_ptr` and never look back.

The smart pointer APIs are remarkably varied. About the only functionality common to all is default construction. Because comprehensive references for these APIs are widely available, I'll focus my discussions on information that's often missing from API overviews, e.g., noteworthy use cases, runtime cost analyses, etc. Mastering such information can be the difference between merely using these smart pointers and using them *effectively*.

Item 18: Use `std::unique_ptr` for exclusive-ownership resource management.

When you reach for a smart pointer, `std::unique_ptr` should generally be the one closest at hand. It's reasonable to assume that, by default, `std::unique_ptr`s are the same size as raw pointers, and for most operations (including dereferencing), they execute exactly the same instructions. This means you can use them even in situations where memory and cycles are tight. If a raw pointer is small enough and fast enough for you, a `std::unique_ptr` almost certainly is, too.

`std::unique_ptr` embodies *exclusive ownership* semantics. A non-null `std::unique_ptr` always owns what it points to. Moving a `std::unique_ptr` transfers ownership from the source pointer to the destination pointer. (The source pointer is set to null.) Copying a `std::unique_ptr` isn't allowed, because if you could copy a `std::unique_ptr`, you'd end up with two `std::unique_ptr`s to the same resource, each thinking it owned (and should therefore destroy) that resource. `std::unique_ptr` is thus a *move-only type*. Upon destruction, a non-null `std::unique_ptr` destroys its resource. By default, resource destruction is accomplished by applying `delete` to the raw pointer inside the `std::unique_ptr`.

A common use for `std::unique_ptr` is as a factory function return type for objects in a hierarchy. Suppose we have a hierarchy for types of investments (e.g., stocks, bonds, real estate, etc.) with a base class `Investment`.

```
class Investment { … };

class Stock:
  public Investment { … };

class Bond:
  public Investment { … };

class RealEstate:
  public Investment { … };
```

A factory function for such a hierarchy typically allocates an object on the heap and returns a pointer to it, with the caller being responsible for deleting the object when it's no longer needed. That's a perfect match for `std::unique_ptr`, because the caller acquires responsibility for the resource returned by the factory (i.e., exclusive ownership of it), and the `std::unique_ptr` automatically deletes what it points to when the `std::unique_ptr` is destroyed. A factory function for the `Investment` hierarchy could be declared like this:

```
template<typename... Ts>          // return std::unique_ptr
std::unique_ptr<Investment>       // to an object created
makeInvestment(Ts&&... params);   // from the given args
```

Callers could use the returned `std::unique_ptr` in a single scope as follows,

```
{
    …
```

```
auto pInvestment =                      // pInvestment is of type
    makeInvestment( arguments );        // std::unique_ptr<Investment>

    …

}                                       // destroy *pInvestment
```

but they could also use it in ownership-migration scenarios, such as when the `std::unique_ptr` returned from the factory is moved into a container, the container element is subsequently moved into a data member of an object, and that object is later destroyed. When that happens, the object's `std::unique_ptr` data member would also be destroyed, and its destruction would cause the resource returned from the factory to be destroyed. If the ownership chain got interrupted due to an exception or other atypical control flow (e.g., early function return or `break` from a loop), the `std::unique_ptr` owning the managed resource would eventually have its destructor called,[1] and the resource it was managing would thereby be destroyed.

By default, that destruction would take place via `delete`, but, during construction, `std::unique_ptr` objects can be configured to use *custom deleters*: arbitrary functions (or function objects, including those arising from lambda expressions) to be invoked when it's time for their resources to be destroyed. If the object created by `makeInvestment` shouldn't be directly `deleted`, but instead should first have a log entry written, `makeInvestment` could be implemented as follows. (An explanation follows the code, so don't worry if you see something whose motivation is less than obvious.)

```
auto delInvmt = [](Investment* pInvestment)     // custom
                {                               // deleter
                    makeLogEntry(pInvestment);  // (a lambda
                    delete pInvestment;         // expression)
                };

template<typename... Ts>                        // revised
std::unique_ptr<Investment, decltype(delInvmt)> // return type
makeInvestment(Ts&&... params)
{
    std::unique_ptr<Investment, decltype(delInvmt)> // ptr to be
        pInv(nullptr, delInvmt);                    // returned
```

---

1 There are a few exceptions to this rule. Most stem from abnormal program termination. If an exception propagates out of a thread's primary function (e.g., `main`, for the program's initial thread) or if a `noexcept` specification is violated (see Item 14), local objects may not be destroyed, and if `std::abort` or an exit function (i.e., `std::_Exit`, `std::exit`, or `std::quick_exit`) is called, they definitely won't be.

```
if ( /* a Stock object should be created */ )
{
  pInv.reset(new Stock(std::forward<Ts>(params)...));
}
else if ( /* a Bond object should be created */ )
{
  pInv.reset(new Bond(std::forward<Ts>(params)...));
}
else if ( /* a RealEstate object should be created */ )
{
  pInv.reset(new RealEstate(std::forward<Ts>(params)...));
}

return pInv;
}
```

In a moment, I'll explain how this works, but first consider how things look if you're a caller. Assuming you store the result of the `makeInvestment` call in an `auto` variable, you frolic in blissful ignorance of the fact that the resource you're using requires special treatment during deletion. In fact, you veritably bathe in bliss, because the use of `std::unique_ptr` means you need not concern yourself with when the resource should be destroyed, much less ensure that the destruction happens exactly once along every path through the program. `std::unique_ptr` takes care of all those things automatically. From a client's perspective, `makeInvestment`'s interface is sweet.

The implementation is pretty nice, too, once you understand the following:

- `delInvmt` is the custom deleter for the object returned from `makeInvestment`. All custom deletion functions accept a raw pointer to the object to be destroyed, then do what is necessary to destroy that object. In this case, the action is to call `makeLogEntry` and then apply `delete`. Using a lambda expression to create `delInvmt` is convenient, but, as we'll see shortly, it's also more efficient than writing a conventional function.

- When a custom deleter is to be used, its type must be specified as the second type argument to `std::unique_ptr`. In this case, that's the type of `delInvmt`, and that's why the return type of `makeInvestment` is `std::unique_ptr<Investment, decltype(delInvmt)>`. (For information about `decltype`, see Item 3.)

- The basic strategy of `makeInvestment` is to create a null `std::unique_ptr`, make it point to an object of the appropriate type, and then return it. To associate the custom deleter `delInvmt` with `pInv`, we pass that as its second constructor argument.

- Attempting to assign a raw pointer (e.g., from new) to a `std::unique_ptr` won't compile, because it would constitute an implicit conversion from a raw to a smart pointer. Such implicit conversions can be problematic, so C++11's smart pointers prohibit them. That's why `reset` is used to have pInv assume ownership of the object created via new.

- With each use of new, we use `std::forward` to perfect-forward the arguments passed to `makeInvestment` (see Item 25). This makes all the information provided by callers available to the constructors of the objects being created.

- The custom deleter takes a parameter of type `Investment*`. Regardless of the actual type of object created inside `makeInvestment` (i.e., Stock, Bond, or RealEstate), it will ultimately be `deleted` inside the lambda expression as an `Investment*` object. This means we'll be deleting a derived class object via a base class pointer. For that to work, the base class—`Investment`—must have a virtual destructor:

```
class Investment {
public:
    …                                         // essential
    virtual ~Investment();                    // design
    …                                         // component!
};
```

In C++14, the existence of function return type deduction (see Item 3) means that `makeInvestment` could be implemented in this simpler and more encapsulated fashion:

```
template<typename... Ts>
auto makeInvestment(Ts&&... params)           // C++14
{
    auto delInvmt = [](Investment* pInvestment)   // this is now
                    {                             // inside
                        makeLogEntry(pInvestment);  // make-
                        delete pInvestment;         // Investment
                    };

    std::unique_ptr<Investment, decltype(delInvmt)>   // as
        pInv(nullptr, delInvmt);                      // before

    if ( … )                                      // as before
    {
        pInv.reset(new Stock(std::forward<Ts>(params)...));
    }
    else if ( … )                                 // as before
```

```
  {
    pInv.reset(new Bond(std::forward<Ts>(params)...));
  }
  else if ( … )                                          // as before
  {
    pInv.reset(new RealEstate(std::forward<Ts>(params)...));
  }
  return pInv;                                           // as before
}
```

I remarked earlier that, when using the default deleter (i.e., `delete`), you can reasonably assume that `std::unique_ptr` objects are the same size as raw pointers. When custom deleters enter the picture, this may no longer be the case. Deleters that are function pointers generally cause the size of a `std::unique_ptr` to grow from one word to two. For deleters that are function objects, the change in size depends on how much state is stored in the function object. Stateless function objects (e.g., from lambda expressions with no captures) typically incur no size penalty when used as deleters, and this means that when a custom deleter can be implemented as either a function or a captureless lambda expression, the lambda is preferable:

```
auto delInvmt1 = [](Investment* pInvestment)           // custom
                 {                                      // deleter
                     makeLogEntry(pInvestment);         // as
                     delete pInvestment;                // stateless
                 };                                     // lambda

template<typename... Ts>                                // return type
std::unique_ptr<Investment, decltype(delInvmt1)>        // has size of
makeInvestment(Ts&&... args);                           // Investment*

void delInvmt2(Investment* pInvestment)                 // custom
{                                                       // deleter
  makeLogEntry(pInvestment);                            // as function
  delete pInvestment;
}

template<typename... Ts>                                // return type has
std::unique_ptr<Investment,                             // size of Investment*
                void (*)(Investment*)>                  // plus at least size
makeInvestment(Ts&&... params);                         // of function pointer!
```

Function object deleters with extensive state can yield `std::unique_ptr` objects of significant size. If you find that a custom deleter makes your `std::unique_ptrs` unacceptably large, you probably need to change your design.

Factory functions are not the only common use case for `std::unique_ptrs`. They're even more popular as a mechanism for implementing the Pimpl Idiom. The code for that isn't complicated, but in some cases it's less than straightforward, so I'll refer you to Item 22, which is dedicated to the topic.

`std::unique_ptr` comes in two forms, one for individual objects (`std::unique_ptr<T>`) and one for arrays (`std::unique_ptr<T[]>`). As a result, there's never any ambiguity about what kind of entity a `std::unique_ptr` points to. The `std::unique_ptr` API is designed to match the form you're using. For example, there's no indexing operator (`operator[]`) for the single-object form, while the array form lacks dereferencing operators (`operator*` and `operator->`).

The existence of `std::unique_ptr` for arrays should be of only intellectual interest to you, because `std::array`, `std::vector`, and `std::string` are virtually always better data structure choices than raw arrays. About the only situation I can conceive of when a `std::unique_ptr<T[]>` would make sense would be when you're using a C-like API that returns a raw pointer to a heap array that you assume ownership of.

`std::unique_ptr` is the C++11 way to express exclusive ownership, but one of its most attractive features is that it easily and efficiently converts to a `std::shared_ptr`:

```
std::shared_ptr<Investment> sp =      // converts std::unique_ptr
    makeInvestment( arguments );      // to std::shared_ptr
```

This is a key part of why `std::unique_ptr` is so well suited as a factory function return type. Factory functions can't know whether callers will want to use exclusive-ownership semantics for the object they return or whether shared ownership (i.e., `std::shared_ptr`) would be more appropriate. By returning a `std::unique_ptr`, factories provide callers with the most efficient smart pointer, but they don't hinder callers from replacing it with its more flexible sibling. (For information about `std::shared_ptr`, proceed to Item 19.)

Things to Remember

- `std::unique_ptr` is a small, fast, move-only smart pointer for managing resources with exclusive-ownership semantics.

- By default, resource destruction takes place via `delete`, but custom deleters can be specified. Stateful deleters and function pointers as deleters increase the size of `std::unique_ptr` objects.

- Converting a `std::unique_ptr` to a `std::shared_ptr` is easy.

Item 19: Use `std::shared_ptr` for shared-ownership resource management.

Programmers using languages with garbage collection point and laugh at what C++ programmers go through to prevent resource leaks. "How primitive!" they jeer. "Didn't you get the memo from Lisp in the 1960s? Machines should manage resource lifetimes, not humans." C++ developers roll their eyes. "You mean the memo where the only resource is memory and the timing of resource reclamation is nondeterministic? We prefer the generality and predictability of destructors, thank you." But our bravado is part bluster. Garbage collection really is convenient, and manual lifetime management really can seem akin to constructing a mnemonic memory circuit using stone knives and bear skins. Why can't we have the best of both worlds: a system that works automatically (like garbage collection), yet applies to all resources and has predictable timing (like destructors)?

`std::shared_ptr` is the C++11 way of binding these worlds together. An object accessed via `std::shared_ptrs` has its lifetime managed by those pointers through *shared ownership*. No specific `std::shared_ptr` owns the object. Instead, all `std::shared_ptrs` pointing to it collaborate to ensure its destruction at the point where it's no longer needed. When the last `std::shared_ptr` pointing to an object stops pointing there (e.g., because the `std::shared_ptr` is destroyed or made to point to a different object), that `std::shared_ptr` destroys the object it points to. As with garbage collection, clients need not concern themselves with managing the lifetime of pointed-to objects, but as with destructors, the timing of the objects' destruction is deterministic.

A `std::shared_ptr` can tell whether it's the last one pointing to a resource by consulting the resource's *reference count*, a value associated with the resource that keeps track of how many `std::shared_ptrs` point to it. `std::shared_ptr` constructors increment this count (usually—see below), `std::shared_ptr` destructors decrement it, and copy assignment operators do both. (If `sp1` and `sp2` are `std::shared_ptrs` to different objects, the assignment "`sp1 = sp2;`" modifies `sp1` such that it points to the object pointed to by `sp2`. The net effect of the assignment is that the reference count for the object originally pointed to by `sp1` is decremented, while that for the object pointed to by `sp2` is incremented.) If a `std::shared_ptr` sees a reference count of zero after performing a decrement, no more `std::shared_ptrs` point to the resource, so the `std::shared_ptr` destroys it.

The existence of the reference count has performance implications:

- **std::shared_ptrs are twice the size of a raw pointer**, because they internally contain a raw pointer to the resource as well as a raw pointer to the resource's reference count.[2]

- **Memory for the reference count must be dynamically allocated**. Conceptually, the reference count is associated with the object being pointed to, but pointed-to objects know nothing about this. They thus have no place to store a reference count. (A pleasant implication is that any object—even those of built-in types—may be managed by std::shared_ptrs.) Item 21 explains that the cost of the dynamic allocation is avoided when the std::shared_ptr is created by std::make_shared, but there are situations where std::make_shared can't be used. Either way, the reference count is stored as dynamically allocated data.

- **Increments and decrements of the reference count must be atomic**, because there can be simultaneous readers and writers in different threads. For example, a std::shared_ptr pointing to a resource in one thread could be executing its destructor (hence decrementing the reference count for the resource it points to), while, in a different thread, a std::shared_ptr to the same object could be copied (and therefore incrementing the same reference count). Atomic operations are typically slower than non-atomic operations, so even though reference counts are usually only a word in size, you should assume that reading and writing them is comparatively costly.

Did I pique your curiosity when I wrote that std::shared_ptr constructors only "usually" increment the reference count for the object they point to? Creating a std::shared_ptr pointing to an object always yields one more std::shared_ptr pointing to that object, so why mustn't we *always* increment the reference count?

Move construction, that's why. Move-constructing a std::shared_ptr from another std::shared_ptr sets the source std::shared_ptr to null, and that means that the old std::shared_ptr stops pointing to the resource at the moment the new std::shared_ptr starts. As a result, no reference count manipulation is required. Moving std::shared_ptrs is therefore faster than copying them: copying requires incrementing the reference count, but moving doesn't. This is as true for assignment as for construction, so move construction is faster than copy construction, and move assignment is faster than copy assignment.

Like std::unique_ptr (see Item 18), std::shared_ptr uses delete as its default resource-destruction mechanism, but it also supports custom deleters. The design of this support differs from that for std::unique_ptr, however. For

---

2 This implementation is not required by the Standard, but every Standard Library implementation I'm familiar with employs it.

`std::unique_ptr`, the type of the deleter is part of the type of the smart pointer. For `std::shared_ptr`, it's not:

```
auto loggingDel = [](Widget *pw)        // custom deleter
                   {                      // (as in Item 18)
                       makeLogEntry(pw);
                       delete pw;
                   };

std::unique_ptr<                         // deleter type is
  Widget, decltype(loggingDel)           // part of ptr type
  > upw(new Widget, loggingDel);

std::shared_ptr<Widget>                  // deleter type is not
  spw(new Widget, loggingDel);           // part of ptr type
```

The `std::shared_ptr` design is more flexible. Consider two `std::shared_ptr<Widget>`s, each with a custom deleter of a different type (e.g., because the custom deleters are specified via lambda expressions):

```
auto customDeleter1 = [](Widget *pw) { … };  // custom deleters,
auto customDeleter2 = [](Widget *pw) { … };  // each with a
                                              // different type

std::shared_ptr<Widget> pw1(new Widget, customDeleter1);
std::shared_ptr<Widget> pw2(new Widget, customDeleter2);
```

Because `pw1` and `pw2` have the same type, they can be placed in a container of objects of that type:

```
std::vector<std::shared_ptr<Widget>> vpw{ pw1, pw2 };
```

They could also be assigned to one another, and they could each be passed to a function taking a parameter of type `std::shared_ptr<Widget>`. None of these things can be done with `std::unique_ptr`s that differ in the types of their custom deleters, because the type of the custom deleter would affect the type of the `std::unique_ptr`.

In another difference from `std::unique_ptr`, specifying a custom deleter doesn't change the size of a `std::shared_ptr` object. Regardless of deleter, a `std::shared_ptr` object is two pointers in size. That's great news, but it should make you vaguely uneasy. Custom deleters can be function objects, and function objects can contain arbitrary amounts of data. That means they can be arbitrarily large. How can a `std::shared_ptr` refer to a deleter of arbitrary size without using any more memory?

It can't. It may have to use more memory. However, that memory isn't part of the `std::shared_ptr` object. It's on the heap or, if the creator of the `std::shared_ptr` took advantage of `std::shared_ptr` support for custom allocators, it's wherever the memory managed by the allocator is located. I remarked earlier that a `std::shared_ptr` object contains a pointer to the reference count for the object it points to. That's true, but it's a bit misleading, because the reference count is part of a larger data structure known as the *control block*. There's a control block for each object managed by `std::shared_ptr`s. The control block contains, in addition to the reference count, a copy of the custom deleter, if one has been specified. If a custom allocator was specified, the control block contains a copy of that, too. The control block contains additional data, including, as Item 21 explains, a secondary reference count known as the weak count, but we'll largely ignore such data in this Item. We can envision the memory associated with a `std::shared_ptr<T>` object as looking like this:

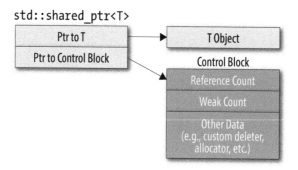

An object's control block is set up by the function creating the first `std::shared_ptr` to the object. At least that's what's supposed to happen. In general, it's impossible for a function creating a `std::shared_ptr` to an object to know whether some other `std::shared_ptr` already points to that object, so the following rules for control block creation are used:

- **`std::make_shared` (see Item 21) always creates a control block.** It manufactures a new object to point to, so there is certainly no control block for that object at the time `std::make_shared` is called.

- **A control block is created when a `std::shared_ptr` is constructed from a unique-ownership pointer (i.e., a `std::unique_ptr` or `std::auto_ptr`).** Unique-ownership pointers don't use control blocks, so there should be no control block for the pointed-to object. (As part of its construction, the `std::shared_ptr` assumes ownership of the pointed-to object, so the unique-ownership pointer is set to null.)

- **When a `std::shared_ptr` constructor is called with a raw pointer, it creates a control block.** If you wanted to create a `std::shared_ptr` from an object that already had a control block, you'd presumably pass a `std::shared_ptr` or a `std::weak_ptr` (see Item 20) as a constructor argument, not a raw pointer. `std::shared_ptr` constructors taking `std::shared_ptrs` or `std::weak_ptrs` as constructor arguments don't create new control blocks, because they can rely on the smart pointers passed to them to point to any necessary control blocks.

A consequence of these rules is that constructing more than one `std::shared_ptr` from a single raw pointer gives you a complimentary ride on the particle accelerator of undefined behavior, because the pointed-to object will have multiple control blocks. Multiple control blocks means multiple reference counts, and multiple reference counts means the object will be destroyed multiple times (once for each reference count). That means that code like this is bad, bad, bad:

```
auto pw = new Widget;                          // pw is raw ptr

...

std::shared_ptr<Widget> spw1(pw, loggingDel);  // create control
                                               // block for *pw

...

std::shared_ptr<Widget> spw2(pw, loggingDel);  // create 2nd
                                               // control block
                                               // for *pw!
```

The creation of the raw pointer pw to a dynamically allocated object is bad, because it runs contrary to the advice behind this entire chapter: to prefer smart pointers to raw pointers. (If you've forgotten the motivation for that advice, refresh your memory on page 117.) But set that aside. The line creating pw is a stylistic abomination, but at least it doesn't cause undefined program behavior.

Now, the constructor for spw1 is called with a raw pointer, so it creates a control block (and thereby a reference count) for what's pointed to. In this case, that's *pw (i.e., the object pointed to by pw). In and of itself, that's okay, but the constructor for spw2 is called with the same raw pointer, so it also creates a control block (hence a reference count) for *pw. *pw thus has two reference counts, each of which will eventually become zero, and that will ultimately lead to an attempt to destroy *pw twice. The second destruction is responsible for the undefined behavior.

There are at least two lessons regarding `std::shared_ptr` use here. First, try to avoid passing raw pointers to a `std::shared_ptr` constructor. The usual alternative is to use `std::make_shared` (see Item 21), but in the example above, we're using custom deleters, and that's not possible with `std::make_shared`. Second, if you must pass a raw pointer to a `std::shared_ptr` constructor, pass the result of new directly instead of going through a raw pointer variable. If the first part of the code above were rewritten like this,

```
std::shared_ptr<Widget> spw1(new Widget,      // direct use of new
                             loggingDel);
```

it'd be a lot less tempting to create a second `std::shared_ptr` from the same raw pointer. Instead, the author of the code creating `spw2` would naturally use `spw1` as an initialization argument (i.e., would call the `std::shared_ptr` copy constructor), and that would pose no problem whatsoever:

```
std::shared_ptr<Widget> spw2(spw1);      // spw2 uses same
                                         // control block as spw1
```

An especially surprising way that using raw pointer variables as `std::shared_ptr` constructor arguments can lead to multiple control blocks involves the `this` pointer. Suppose our program uses `std::shared_ptrs` to manage `Widget` objects, and we have a data structure that keeps track of `Widgets` that have been processed:

```
std::vector<std::shared_ptr<Widget>> processedWidgets;
```

Further suppose that `Widget` has a member function that does the processing:

```
class Widget {
public:
  …
  void process();
  …
};
```

Here's a reasonable-looking approach for `Widget::process`:

```
void Widget::process()
{
  …                                             // process the Widget

  processedWidgets.emplace_back(this);      // add it to list of
}                                           // processed Widgets;
                                            // this is wrong!
```

The comment about this being wrong says it all—or at least most of it. (The part that's wrong is the passing of `this`, not the use of `emplace_back`. If you're not familiar with `emplace_back`, see Item 42.) This code will compile, but it's passing a raw pointer (`this`) to a container of `std::shared_ptrs`. The `std::shared_ptr` thus constructed will create a new control block for the pointed-to `Widget` (`*this`). That doesn't sound harmful until you realize that if there are `std::shared_ptrs` outside the member function that already point to that `Widget`, it's game, set, and match for undefined behavior.

The `std::shared_ptr` API includes a facility for just this kind of situation. It has probably the oddest of all names in the Standard C++ Library: `std::enable_shared_from_this`. That's a template for a base class you inherit from if you want a class managed by `std::shared_ptrs` to be able to safely create a `std::shared_ptr` from a `this` pointer. In our example, `Widget` would inherit from `std::enable_shared_from_this` as follows:

```
class Widget: public std::enable_shared_from_this<Widget> {
public:
    …
    void process();
    …
};
```

As I said, `std::enable_shared_from_this` is a base class template. Its type parameter is always the name of the class being derived, so `Widget` inherits from `std::enable_shared_from_this<Widget>`. If the idea of a derived class inheriting from a base class templatized on the derived class makes your head hurt, try not to think about it. The code is completely legal, and the design pattern behind it is so well established, it has a standard name, albeit one that's almost as odd as `std::enable_shared_from_this`. The name is *The Curiously Recurring Template Pattern (CRTP)*. If you'd like to learn more about it, unleash your search engine, because here we need to get back to `std::enable_shared_from_this`.

`std::enable_shared_from_this` defines a member function that creates a `std::shared_ptr` to the current object, but it does it without duplicating control blocks. The member function is `shared_from_this`, and you use it in member functions whenever you want a `std::shared_ptr` that points to the same object as the `this` pointer. Here's a safe implementation of `Widget::process`:

```
void Widget::process()
{
    // as before, process the Widget
    …

    // add std::shared_ptr to current object to processedWidgets
    processedWidgets.emplace_back(shared_from_this());
}
```

Internally, `shared_from_this` looks up the control block for the current object, and it creates a new `std::shared_ptr` that refers to that control block. The design relies on the current object having an associated control block. For that to be the case, there must be an existing `std::shared_ptr` (e.g., one outside the member function calling `shared_from_this`) that points to the current object. If no such `std::shared_ptr` exists (i.e., if the current object has no associated control block), behavior is undefined, although `shared_from_this` typically throws an exception.

To prevent clients from calling member functions that invoke `shared_from_this` before a `std::shared_ptr` points to the object, classes inheriting from `std::enable_shared_from_this` often declare their constructors `private` and have clients create objects by calling factory functions that return `std::shared_ptrs`. Widget, for example, could look like this:

```
class Widget: public std::enable_shared_from_this<Widget> {
public:
  // factory function that perfect-forwards args
  // to a private ctor
  template<typename... Ts>
  static std::shared_ptr<Widget> create(Ts&&... params);

  ...
  void process();                 // as before
  ...

private:
  ...                             // ctors
};
```

By now, you may only dimly recall that our discussion of control blocks was motivated by a desire to understand the costs associated with `std::shared_ptrs`. Now that we understand how to avoid creating too many control blocks, let's return to the original topic.

A control block is typically only a few words in size, although custom deleters and allocators may make it larger. The usual control block implementation is more sophisticated than you might expect. It makes use of inheritance, and there's even a virtual function. (It's used to ensure that the pointed-to object is properly destroyed.) That means that using `std::shared_ptrs` also incurs the cost of the machinery for the virtual function used by the control block.

Having read about dynamically allocated control blocks, arbitrarily large deleters and allocators, virtual function machinery, and atomic reference count manipulations, your enthusiasm for `std::shared_ptrs` may have waned somewhat. That's fine.

They're not the best solution to every resource management problem. But for the functionality they provide, std::shared_ptrs exact a very reasonable cost. Under typical conditions, where the default deleter and default allocator are used and where the std::shared_ptr is created by std::make_shared, the control block is only about three words in size, and its allocation is essentially free. (It's incorporated into the memory allocation for the object being pointed to. For details, see Item 21.) Dereferencing a std::shared_ptr is no more expensive than dereferencing a raw pointer. Performing an operation requiring a reference count manipulation (e.g., copy construction, assignment, destruction) entails one or two atomic operations, but these operations typically map to individual machine instructions, so although they may be expensive compared to non-atomic instructions, they're still just single instructions. The virtual function machinery in the control block is generally used only once per object managed by std::shared_ptrs: when the object is destroyed.

In exchange for these rather modest costs, you get automatic lifetime management of dynamically allocated resources. Most of the time, using std::shared_ptr is vastly preferable to trying to manage the lifetime of an object with shared ownership by hand. If you find yourself doubting whether you can afford use of std::shared_ptr, reconsider whether you really need shared ownership. If exclusive ownership will do or even *may* do, std::unique_ptr is a better choice. Its performance profile is close to that for raw pointers, and "upgrading" from std::unique_ptr to std::shared_ptr is easy, because a std::shared_ptr can be created from a std::unique_ptr.

The reverse is not true. Once you've turned lifetime management of a resource over to a std::shared_ptr, there's no changing your mind. Even if the reference count is one, you can't reclaim ownership of the resource in order to, say, have a std::unique_ptr manage it. The ownership contract between a resource and the std::shared_ptrs that point to it is of the 'til-death-do-us-part variety. No divorce, no annulment, no dispensations.

Something else std::shared_ptrs can't do is work with arrays. In yet another difference from std::unique_ptr, std::shared_ptr has an API that's designed only for pointers to single objects. There's no std::shared_ptr<T[]>. From time to time, "clever" programmers stumble on the idea of using a std::shared_ptr<T> to point to an array, specifying a custom deleter to perform an array delete (i.e., delete []). This can be made to compile, but it's a horrible idea. For one thing, std::shared_ptr offers no operator[], so indexing into the array requires awkward expressions based on pointer arithmetic. For another, std::shared_ptr supports derived-to-base pointer conversions that make sense for single objects, but that open holes in the type system when applied to arrays. (For this reason, the `std::unique_ptr<T[]>` API prohibits such conversions.) Most importantly, given the variety of C++11 alternatives to built-in arrays (e.g., `std::array`, `std::vector`, `std::string`), declaring a smart pointer to a dumb array is almost always a sign of bad design.

Things to Remember

- `std::shared_ptr`s offer convenience approaching that of garbage collection for the shared lifetime management of arbitrary resources.

- Compared to `std::unique_ptr`, `std::shared_ptr` objects are typically twice as big, incur overhead for control blocks, and require atomic reference count manipulations.

- Default resource destruction is via `delete`, but custom deleters are supported. The type of the deleter has no effect on the type of the `std::shared_ptr`.

- Avoid creating `std::shared_ptr`s from variables of raw pointer type.

Item 20: Use `std::weak_ptr` for `std::shared_ptr`-like pointers that can dangle.

Paradoxically, it can be convenient to have a smart pointer that acts like a `std::shared_ptr` (see Item 19), but that doesn't participate in the shared ownership of the pointed-to resource. In other words, a pointer like `std::shared_ptr` that doesn't affect an object's reference count. This kind of smart pointer has to contend with a problem unknown to `std::shared_ptr`s: the possibility that what it points to has been destroyed. A truly smart pointer would deal with this problem by tracking when it *dangles*, i.e., when the object it is supposed to point to no longer exists. That's precisely the kind of smart pointer `std::weak_ptr` is.

You may be wondering how a `std::weak_ptr` could be useful. You'll probably wonder even more when you examine the `std::weak_ptr` API. It looks anything but smart. `std::weak_ptr`s can't be dereferenced, nor can they be tested for nullness. That's because `std::weak_ptr` isn't a standalone smart pointer. It's an augmentation of `std::shared_ptr`.

The relationship begins at birth. `std::weak_ptr`s are typically created from `std::shared_ptr`s. They point to the same place as the `std::shared_ptr`s initializing them, but they don't affect the reference count of the object they point to:

```
auto spw =                      // after spw is constructed,
    std::make_shared<Widget>(); // the pointed-to Widget's
```

```
                                     // ref count (RC) is 1. (See
                                     // Item 21 for info on
                                     // std::make_shared.)
...

std::weak_ptr<Widget> wpw(spw);      // wpw points to same Widget
                                     // as spw. RC remains 1
...

spw = nullptr;                       // RC goes to 0, and the
                                     // Widget is destroyed.
                                     // wpw now dangles
```

std::weak_ptrs that dangle are said to have *expired*. You can test for this directly,

```
if (wpw.expired()) ...               // if wpw doesn't point
                                     // to an object...
```

but often what you desire is a check to see if a std::weak_ptr has expired and, if it hasn't (i.e., if it's not dangling), to access the object it points to. This is easier desired than done. Because std::weak_ptrs lack dereferencing operations, there's no way to write the code. Even if there were, separating the check and the dereference would introduce a race condition: between the call to expired and the dereferencing action, another thread might reassign or destroy the last std::shared_ptr pointing to the object, thus causing that object to be destroyed. In that case, your dereference would yield undefined behavior.

What you need is an atomic operation that checks to see if the std::weak_ptr has expired and, if not, gives you access to the object it points to. This is done by creating a std::shared_ptr from the std::weak_ptr. The operation comes in two forms, depending on what you'd like to have happen if the std::weak_ptr has expired when you try to create a std::shared_ptr from it. One form is std::weak_ptr::lock, which returns a std::shared_ptr. The std::shared_ptr is null if the std::weak_ptr has expired:

```
std::shared_ptr<Widget> spw1 = wpw.lock();  // if wpw's expired,
                                            // spw1 is null

auto spw2 = wpw.lock();                     // same as above,
                                            // but uses auto
```

The other form is the std::shared_ptr constructor taking a std::weak_ptr as an argument. In this case, if the std::weak_ptr has expired, an exception is thrown:

```
std::shared_ptr<Widget> spw3(wpw);   // if wpw's expired,
                                     // throw std::bad_weak_ptr
```

But you're probably still wondering about how `std::weak_ptrs` can be useful. Consider a factory function that produces smart pointers to read-only objects based on a unique ID. In accord with Item 18's advice regarding factory function return types, it returns a `std::unique_ptr`:

```
std::unique_ptr<const Widget> loadWidget(WidgetID id);
```

If `loadWidget` is an expensive call (e.g., because it performs file or database I/O) and it's common for IDs to be used repeatedly, a reasonable optimization would be to write a function that does what `loadWidget` does, but also caches its results. Clogging the cache with every `Widget` that has ever been requested can lead to performance problems of its own, however, so another reasonable optimization would be to destroy cached `Widgets` when they're no longer in use.

For this caching factory function, a `std::unique_ptr` return type is not a good fit. Callers should certainly receive smart pointers to cached objects, and callers should certainly determine the lifetime of those objects, but the cache needs a pointer to the objects, too. The cache's pointers need to be able to detect when they dangle, because when factory clients are finished using an object returned by the factory, that object will be destroyed, and the corresponding cache entry will dangle. The cached pointers should therefore be `std::weak_ptrs`—pointers that can detect when they dangle. That means that the factory's return type should be a `std::shared_ptr`, because `std::weak_ptrs` can detect when they dangle only when an object's lifetime is managed by `std::shared_ptrs`.

Here's a quick-and-dirty implementation of a caching version of `loadWidget`:

```
std::shared_ptr<const Widget> fastLoadWidget(WidgetID id)
{
  static std::unordered_map<WidgetID,
                            std::weak_ptr<const Widget>> cache;

  auto objPtr = cache[id].lock();    // objPtr is std::shared_ptr
                                     // to cached object (or null
                                     // if object's not in cache)

  if (!objPtr) {                     // if not in cache,
    objPtr = loadWidget(id);         // load it
    cache[id] = objPtr;              // cache it
  }
  return objPtr;
}
```

This implementation employs one of C++11's hash table containers (std::unordered_map), though it doesn't show the WidgetID hashing and equality-comparison functions that would also have to be present.

The implementation of fastLoadWidget ignores the fact that the cache may accumulate expired std::weak_ptrs corresponding to Widgets that are no longer in use (and have therefore been destroyed). The implementation can be refined, but rather than spend time on an issue that lends no additional insight into std::weak_ptrs, let's consider a second use case: the Observer design pattern. The primary components of this pattern are subjects (objects whose state may change) and observers (objects to be notified when state changes occur). In most implementations, each subject contains a data member holding pointers to its observers. That makes it easy for subjects to issue state change notifications. Subjects have no interest in controlling the lifetime of their observers (i.e., when they're destroyed), but they have a great interest in making sure that if an observer gets destroyed, subjects don't try to subsequently access it. A reasonable design is for each subject to hold a container of std::weak_ptrs to its observers, thus making it possible for the subject to determine whether a pointer dangles before using it.

As a final example of std::weak_ptr's utility, consider a data structure with objects A, B, and C in it, where A and C share ownership of B and therefore hold std::shared_ptrs to it:

Suppose it'd be useful to also have a pointer from B back to A. What kind of pointer should this be?

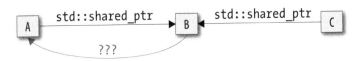

There are three choices:

- **A raw pointer.** With this approach, if A is destroyed, but C continues to point to B, B will contain a pointer to A that will dangle. B won't be able to detect that, so B may inadvertently dereference the dangling pointer. That would yield undefined behavior.

- **A std::shared_ptr.** In this design, A and B contain std::shared_ptrs to each other. The resulting std::shared_ptr cycle (A points to B and B points to A) will prevent both A and B from being destroyed. Even if A and B are unreachable from other program data structures (e.g., because C no longer points to B), each will have a reference count of one. If that happens, A and B will have been leaked, for all practical purposes: it will be impossible for the program to access them, yet their resources will never be reclaimed.

- **A `std::weak_ptr`.** This avoids both problems above. If A is destroyed, B's pointer back to it will dangle, but B will be able to detect that. Furthermore, though A and B will point to one another, B's pointer won't affect A's reference count, hence can't keep A from being destroyed when `std::shared_ptrs` no longer point to it.

Using `std::weak_ptr` is clearly the best of these choices. However, it's worth noting that the need to employ `std::weak_ptrs` to break prospective cycles of `std::shared_ptrs` is not terribly common. In strictly hierarchal data structures such as trees, child nodes are typically owned only by their parents. When a parent node is destroyed, its child nodes should be destroyed, too. Links from parents to children are thus generally best represented by `std::unique_ptrs`. Back-links from children to parents can be safely implemented as raw pointers, because a child node should never have a lifetime longer than its parent. There's thus no risk of a child node dereferencing a dangling parent pointer.

Of course, not all pointer-based data structures are strictly hierarchical, and when that's the case, as well as in situations such as caching and the implementation of lists of observers, it's nice to know that `std::weak_ptr` stands at the ready.

From an efficiency perspective, the `std::weak_ptr` story is essentially the same as that for `std::shared_ptr`. `std::weak_ptr` objects are the same size as `std::shared_ptr` objects, they make use of the same control blocks as `std::shared_ptrs` (see Item 19), and operations such as construction, destruction, and assignment involve atomic reference count manipulations. That probably surprises you, because I wrote at the beginning of this Item that `std::weak_ptrs` don't participate in reference counting. Except that's not quite what I wrote. What I wrote was that `std::weak_ptrs` don't participate in the *shared ownership* of objects and hence don't affect the *pointed-to object's reference count*. There's actually a second reference count in the control block, and it's this second reference count that `std::weak_ptrs` manipulate. For details, continue on to Item 21.

Item 21: Prefer `std::make_unique` and `std::make_shared` to direct use of new.

Let's begin by leveling the playing field for `std::make_unique` and `std::make_shared`. `std::make_shared` is part of C++11, but, sadly, `std::make_unique` isn't. It joined the Standard Library as of C++14. If you're using C++11, never fear, because a basic version of `std::make_unique` is easy to write yourself. Here, look:

```
template<typename T, typename... Ts>
std::unique_ptr<T> make_unique(Ts&&... params)
{
    return std::unique_ptr<T>(new T(std::forward<Ts>(params)...));
}
```

As you can see, `make_unique` just perfect-forwards its parameters to the constructor of the object being created, constructs a `std::unique_ptr` from the raw pointer new produces, and returns the `std::unique_ptr` so created. This form of the function doesn't support arrays (see Item 18), but it demonstrates that with only a little effort, you can create `make_unique` if you need to.[3] Just remember not to put your version in namespace `std`, because you won't want it to clash with a vendor-provided version when you upgrade to a C++14 Standard Library implementation.

`std::make_unique` and `std::make_shared` are two of the three *make functions*: functions that take an arbitrary set of arguments, perfect-forward them to the constructor for a dynamically allocated object, and return a smart pointer to that object. The third `make` function is `std::allocate_shared`. It acts just like `std::make_shared`, except its first argument is an allocator object to be used for the dynamic memory allocation.

---

[3] To create a full-featured `make_unique` with the smallest effort possible, search for the standardization document that gave rise to it, then copy the implementation you'll find there. The document you want is N3656 by Stephan T. Lavavej, dated 2013-04-18.

Even the most trivial comparison of smart pointer creation using and not using a make function reveals the first reason why using such functions is preferable. Consider:

```
auto upw1(std::make_unique<Widget>());      // with make func

std::unique_ptr<Widget> upw2(new Widget);   // without make func


auto spw1(std::make_shared<Widget>());      // with make func

std::shared_ptr<Widget> spw2(new Widget);   // without make func
```

I've highlighted the essential difference: the versions using new repeat the type being created, but the make functions don't. Repeating types runs afoul of a key tenet of software engineering: code duplication should be avoided. Duplication in source code increases compilation times, can lead to bloated object code, and generally renders a code base more difficult to work with. It often evolves into inconsistent code, and inconsistency in a code base often leads to bugs. Besides, typing something twice takes more effort than typing it once, and who's not a fan of reducing their typing burden?

The second reason to prefer make functions has to do with exception safety. Suppose we have a function to process a Widget in accord with some priority:

```
void processWidget(std::shared_ptr<Widget> spw, int priority);
```

Passing the std::shared_ptr by value may look suspicious, but Item 41 explains that if processWidget always makes a copy of the std::shared_ptr (e.g., by storing it in a data structure tracking Widgets that have been processed), this can be a reasonable design choice.

Now suppose we have a function to compute the relevant priority,

```
int computePriority();
```

and we use that in a call to processWidget that uses new instead of std::make_shared:

```
processWidget(std::shared_ptr<Widget>(new Widget),   // potential
              computePriority());                     // resource
                                                      // leak!
```

As the comment indicates, this code could leak the Widget conjured up by new. But how? Both the calling code and the called function are using std::shared_ptrs, and std::shared_ptrs are designed to prevent resource leaks. They automatically destroy what they point to when the last `std::shared_ptr` pointing there goes away. If everybody is using `std::shared_ptr`s everywhere, how can this code leak?

The answer has to do with compilers' translation of source code into object code. At runtime, the arguments for a function must be evaluated before the function can be invoked, so in the call to `processWidget`, the following things must occur before `processWidget` can begin execution:

- The expression "`new Widget`" must be evaluated, i.e., a `Widget` must be created on the heap.
- The constructor for the `std::shared_ptr<Widget>` responsible for managing the pointer produced by `new` must be executed.
- `computePriority` must run.

Compilers are not required to generate code that executes them in this order. "`new Widget`" must be executed before the `std::shared_ptr` constructor may be called, because the result of that `new` is used as an argument to that constructor, but `compute-Priority` may be executed before those calls, after them, or, crucially, *between* them. That is, compilers may emit code to execute the operations in this order:

1. Perform "`new Widget`".
2. Execute `computePriority`.
3. Run `std::shared_ptr` constructor.

If such code is generated and, at runtime, `computePriority` produces an exception, the dynamically allocated `Widget` from Step 1 will be leaked, because it will never be stored in the `std::shared_ptr` that's supposed to start managing it in Step 3.

Using `std::make_shared` avoids this problem. Calling code would look like this:

```
processWidget(std::make_shared<Widget>(),    // no potential
              computePriority());            // resource leak
```

At runtime, either `std::make_shared` or `computePriority` will be called first. If it's `std::make_shared`, the raw pointer to the dynamically allocated `Widget` is safely stored in the returned `std::shared_ptr` before `computePriority` is called. If `computePriority` then yields an exception, the `std::shared_ptr` destructor will see to it that the `Widget` it owns is destroyed. And if `computePriority` is called first and yields an exception, `std::make_shared` will not be invoked, and there will hence be no dynamically allocated `Widget` to worry about.

If we replace `std::shared_ptr` and `std::make_shared` with `std::unique_ptr` and `std::make_unique`, exactly the same reasoning applies. Using `std::make_unique` instead of `new` is thus just as important in writing exception-safe code as using `std::make_shared`.

A special feature of `std::make_shared` (compared to direct use of `new`) is improved efficiency. Using `std::make_shared` allows compilers to generate smaller, faster code that employs leaner data structures. Consider the following direct use of `new`:

```
std::shared_ptr<Widget> spw(new Widget);
```

It's obvious that this code entails a memory allocation, but it actually performs two. Item 19 explains that every `std::shared_ptr` points to a control block containing, among other things, the reference count for the pointed-to object. Memory for this control block is allocated in the `std::shared_ptr` constructor. Direct use of `new`, then, requires one memory allocation for the `Widget` and a second allocation for the control block.

If `std::make_shared` is used instead,

```
auto spw = std::make_shared<Widget>();
```

one allocation suffices. That's because `std::make_shared` allocates a single chunk of memory to hold both the `Widget` object and the control block. This optimization reduces the static size of the program, because the code contains only one memory allocation call, and it increases the speed of the executable code, because memory is allocated only once. Furthermore, using `std::make_shared` obviates the need for some of the bookkeeping information in the control block, potentially reducing the total memory footprint for the program.

The efficiency analysis for `std::make_shared` is equally applicable to `std::allocate_shared`, so the performance advantages of `std::make_shared` extend to that function, as well.

The arguments for preferring `make` functions over direct use of `new` are strong ones. Despite their software engineering, exception safety, and efficiency advantages, however, this Item's guidance is to *prefer* the `make` functions, not to rely on them exclusively. That's because there are circumstances where they can't or shouldn't be used.

For example, none of the `make` functions permit the specification of custom deleters (see Items 18 and 19), but both `std::unique_ptr` and `std::shared_ptr` have constructors that do. Given a custom deleter for a `Widget`,

```
auto widgetDeleter = [](Widget* pw) { … };
```

creating a smart pointer using it is straightforward using `new`:

```
std::unique_ptr<Widget, decltype(widgetDeleter)>
  upw(new Widget, widgetDeleter);

std::shared_ptr<Widget> spw(new Widget, widgetDeleter);
```

There's no way to do the same thing with a make function.

A second limitation of make functions stems from a syntactic detail of their implementations. Item 7 explains that when creating an object whose type overloads constructors both with and without `std::initializer_list` parameters, creating the object using braces prefers the `std::initializer_list` constructor, while creating the object using parentheses calls the non-`std::initializer_list` constructor. The make functions perfect-forward their parameters to an object's constructor, but do they do so using parentheses or using braces? For some types, the answer to this question makes a big difference. For example, in these calls,

```
auto upv = std::make_unique<std::vector<int>>(10, 20);

auto spv = std::make_shared<std::vector<int>>(10, 20);
```

do the resulting smart pointers point to `std::vectors` with 10 elements, each of value 20, or to `std::vectors` with two elements, one with value 10 and the other with value 20? Or is the result indeterminate?

The good news is that it's not indeterminate: both calls create `std::vectors` of size 10 with all values set to 20. That means that within the make functions, the perfect forwarding code uses parentheses, not braces. The bad news is that if you want to construct your pointed-to object using a braced initializer, you must use new directly. Using a make function would require the ability to perfect-forward a braced initializer, but, as Item 30 explains, braced initializers can't be perfect-forwarded. However, Item 30 also describes a workaround: use auto type deduction to create a `std::initializer_list` object from a braced initializer (see Item 2), then pass the auto-created object through the make function:

```
// create std::initializer_list
auto initList = { 10, 20 };

// create std::vector using std::initializer_list ctor
auto spv = std::make_shared<std::vector<int>>(initList);
```

For `std::unique_ptr`, these two scenarios (custom deleters and braced initializers) are the only ones where its make functions are problematic. For `std::shared_ptr` and its make functions, there are two more. Both are edge cases, but some developers live on the edge, and you may be one of them.

Some classes define their own versions of operator new and operator delete. The presence of these functions implies that the global memory allocation and deallocation routines for objects of these types are inappropriate. Often, class-specific routines are designed only to allocate and deallocate chunks of memory of precisely the size of objects of the class, e.g., operator new and operator delete for class Widget are often designed only to handle allocation and deallocation of chunks of memory of exactly size sizeof(Widget). Such routines are a poor fit for std::shared_ptr's support for custom allocation (via std::allocate_shared) and deallocation (via custom deleters), because the amount of memory that std::allocate_shared requests isn't the size of the dynamically allocated object, it's the size of that object *plus* the size of a control block. Consequently, using make functions to create objects of types with class-specific versions of operator new and operator delete is typically a poor idea.

The size and speed advantages of std::make_shared vis-à-vis direct use of new stem from std::shared_ptr's control block being placed in the same chunk of memory as the managed object. When that object's reference count goes to zero, the object is destroyed (i.e., its destructor is called). However, the memory it occupies can't be released until the control block has also been destroyed, because the same chunk of dynamically allocated memory contains both.

As I noted, the control block contains bookkeeping information beyond just the reference count itself. The reference count tracks how many std::shared_ptrs refer to the control block, but the control block contains a second reference count, one that tallies how many std::weak_ptrs refer to the control block. This second reference count is known as the *weak count*.[4] When a std::weak_ptr checks to see if it has expired (see Item 19), it does so by examining the reference count (not the weak count) in the control block that it refers to. If the reference count is zero (i.e., if the pointed-to object has no std::shared_ptrs referring to it and has thus been destroyed), the std::weak_ptr has expired. Otherwise, it hasn't.

As long as std::weak_ptrs refer to a control block (i.e., the weak count is greater than zero), that control block must continue to exist. And as long as a control block exists, the memory containing it must remain allocated. The memory allocated by a std::shared_ptr make function, then, can't be deallocated until the last std::shared_ptr *and* the last std::weak_ptr referring to it have been destroyed.

---

4 In practice, the value of the weak count isn't always equal to the number of std::weak_ptrs referring to the control block, because library implementers have found ways to slip additional information into the weak count that facilitate better code generation. For purposes of this Item, we'll ignore this and assume that the weak count's value is the number of std::weak_ptrs referring to the control block.

If the object type is quite large and the time between destruction of the last `std::shared_ptr` and the last `std::weak_ptr` is significant, a lag can occur between when an object is destroyed and when the memory it occupied is freed:

```
class ReallyBigType { … };

auto pBigObj =                              // create very large
  std::make_shared<ReallyBigType>();        // object via
                                            // std::make_shared

          …       // create std::shared_ptrs and std::weak_ptrs to
                  // large object, use them to work with it

          …       // final std::shared_ptr to object destroyed here,
                  // but std::weak_ptrs to it remain

          …       // during this period, memory formerly occupied
                  // by large object remains allocated

          …       // final std::weak_ptr to object destroyed here;
                  // memory for control block and object is released
```

With a direct use of `new`, the memory for the `ReallyBigType` object can be released as soon as the last `std::shared_ptr` to it is destroyed:

```
class ReallyBigType { … };                  // as before

std::shared_ptr<ReallyBigType> pBigObj(new ReallyBigType);
                                            // create very large
                                            // object via new

          …       // as before, create std::shared_ptrs and
                  // std::weak_ptrs to object, use them with it

          …       // final std::shared_ptr to object destroyed here,
                  // but std::weak_ptrs to it remain;
                  // memory for object is deallocated

          …       // during this period, only memory for the
                  // control block remains allocated

          …       // final std::weak_ptr to object destroyed here;
                  // memory for control block is released
```

Should you find yourself in a situation where use of `std::make_shared` is impossible or inappropriate, you'll want to guard yourself against the kind of exception-safety problems we saw earlier. The best way to do that is to make sure that when you use new directly, you immediately pass the result to a smart pointer constructor in *a statement that does nothing else*. This prevents compilers from generating code that could emit an exception between the use of new and invocation of the constructor for the smart pointer that will manage the newed object.

As an example, consider a minor revision to the exception-unsafe call to the process-Widget function we examined earlier. This time, we'll specify a custom deleter:

```
void processWidget(std::shared_ptr<Widget> spw,   // as before
                   int priority);

void cusDel(Widget *ptr);                          // custom
                                                   // deleter
```

Here's the exception-unsafe call:

```
processWidget(                                     // as before,
  std::shared_ptr<Widget>(new Widget, cusDel),     // potential
  computePriority()                                // resource
);                                                 // leak!
```

Recall: if computePriority is called after "new Widget" but before the std::shared_ptr constructor, and if computePriority yields an exception, the dynamically allocated Widget will be leaked.

Here the use of a custom deleter precludes use of std::make_shared, so the way to avoid the problem is to put the allocation of the Widget and the construction of the std::shared_ptr into their own statement, then call processWidget with the resulting std::shared_ptr. Here's the essence of the technique, though, as we'll see in a moment, we can tweak it to improve its performance:

```
std::shared_ptr<Widget> spw(new Widget, cusDel);

processWidget(spw, computePriority());             // correct, but not
                                                   // optimal; see below
```

This works, because a std::shared_ptr assumes ownership of the raw pointer passed to its constructor, even if that constructor yields an exception. In this example, if spw's constructor throws an exception (e.g., due to an inability to dynamically allocate memory for a control block), it's still guaranteed that cusDel will be invoked on the pointer resulting from "new Widget".

The minor performance hitch is that in the exception-unsafe call, we're passing an rvalue to processWidget,

```
processWidget(
    std::shared_ptr<Widget>(new Widget, cusDel),  // arg is rvalue
    computePriority()
);
```

but in the exception-safe call, we're passing an lvalue:

```
processWidget(spw, computePriority());          // arg is lvalue
```

Because processWidget's std::shared_ptr parameter is passed by value, construction from an rvalue entails only a move, while construction from an lvalue requires a copy. For std::shared_ptr, the difference can be significant, because copying a std::shared_ptr requires an atomic increment of its reference count, while moving a std::shared_ptr requires no reference count manipulation at all. For the exception-safe code to achieve the level of performance of the exception-unsafe code, we need to apply std::move to spw to turn it into an rvalue (see Item 23):

```
processWidget(std::move(spw),          // both efficient and
              computePriority());      // exception safe
```

That's interesting and worth knowing, but it's also typically irrelevant, because you'll rarely have a reason not to use a make function. And unless you have a compelling reason for doing otherwise, using a make function is what you should do.

Things to Remember

- Compared to direct use of new, make functions eliminate source code duplication, improve exception safety, and, for std::make_shared and std::allocate_shared, generate code that's smaller and faster.

- Situations where use of make functions is inappropriate include the need to specify custom deleters and a desire to pass braced initializers.

- For std::shared_ptrs, additional situations where make functions may be ill-advised include (1) classes with custom memory management and (2) systems with memory concerns, very large objects, and std::weak_ptrs that outlive the corresponding std::shared_ptrs.

Item 22: When using the Pimpl Idiom, define special member functions in the implementation file.

If you've ever had to combat excessive build times, you're familiar with the *Pimpl* ("pointer to implementation") *Idiom*. That's the technique whereby you replace the data members of a class with a pointer to an implementation class (or struct), put the data members that used to be in the primary class into the implementation class, and access those data members indirectly through the pointer. For example, suppose Widget looks like this:

```
class Widget {                    // in header "widget.h"
public:
  Widget();
  …
private:
  std::string name;
  std::vector<double> data;
  Gadget g1, g2, g3;              // Gadget is some user-
};                                // defined type
```

Because Widget's data members are of types std::string, std::vector, and Gadget, headers for those types must be present for Widget to compile, and that means that Widget clients must #include <string>, <vector>, and gadget.h. Those headers increase the compilation time for Widget clients, plus they make those clients dependent on the contents of the headers. If a header's content changes, Widget clients must recompile. The standard headers <string> and <vector> don't change very often, but it could be that gadget.h is subject to frequent revision.

Applying the Pimpl Idiom in C++98 could have Widget replace its data members with a raw pointer to a struct that has been declared, but not defined:

```
class Widget {                    // still in header "widget.h"
public:
  Widget();
  ~Widget();                      // dtor is needed—see below
  …

private:
  struct Impl;                    // declare implementation struct
  Impl *pImpl;                    // and pointer to it
};
```

Because Widget no longer mentions the types std::string, std::vector, and Gadget, Widget clients no longer need to #include the headers for these types. That speeds compilation, and it also means that if something in these headers changes, Widget clients are unaffected.

A type that has been declared, but not defined, is known as an *incomplete type*. Widget::Impl is such a type. There are very few things you can do with an incomplete type, but declaring a pointer to it is one of them. The Pimpl Idiom takes advantage of that.

Part 1 of the Pimpl Idiom is the declaration of a data member that's a pointer to an incomplete type. Part 2 is the dynamic allocation and deallocation of the object that holds the data members that used to be in the original class. The allocation and deallocation code goes in the implementation file, e.g., for Widget, in widget.cpp:

```
#include "widget.h"          // in impl. file "widget.cpp"
#include "gadget.h"
#include <string>
#include <vector>

struct Widget::Impl {        // definition of Widget::Impl
  std::string name;          // with data members formerly
  std::vector<double> data;  // in Widget
  Gadget g1, g2, g3;
};

Widget::Widget()             // allocate data members for
: pImpl(new Impl)            // this Widget object
{}

Widget::~Widget()            // destroy data members for
{ delete pImpl; }            // this object
```

Here I'm showing #include directives to make clear that the overall dependencies on the headers for std::string, std::vector, and Gadget continue to exist. However, these dependencies have been moved from widget.h (which is visible to and used by Widget clients) to widget.cpp (which is visible to and used only by the Widget implementer). I've also highlighted the code that dynamically allocates and deallocates the Impl object. The need to deallocate this object when a Widget is destroyed is what necessitates the Widget destructor.

But I've shown you C++98 code, and that reeks of a bygone millennium. It uses raw pointers and raw new and raw delete and it's all just so…raw. This chapter is built on the idea that smart pointers are preferable to raw pointers, and if what we want is to dynamically allocate a Widget::Impl object inside the Widget constructor and have it destroyed at the same time the Widget is, std::unique_ptr (see Item 18) is precisely the tool we need. Replacing the raw pImpl pointer with a std::unique_ptr yields this code for the header file,

```
class Widget {               // in "widget.h"
public:
  Widget();
  …

private:
```

```
    struct Impl;
    std::unique_ptr<Impl> pImpl;        // use smart pointer
};                                      // instead of raw pointer
```

and this for the implementation file:

```
#include "widget.h"                     // in "widget.cpp"
#include "gadget.h"
#include <string>
#include <vector>

struct Widget::Impl {                   // as before
    std::string name;
    std::vector<double> data;
    Gadget g1, g2, g3;
};

Widget::Widget()                        // per Item 21, create
: pImpl(std::make_unique<Impl>())       // std::unique_ptr
{}                                      // via std::make_unique
```

You'll note that the Widget destructor is no longer present. That's because we have no code to put into it. std::unique_ptr automatically deletes what it points to when it (the std::unique_ptr) is destroyed, so we need not delete anything ourselves. That's one of the attractions of smart pointers: they eliminate the need for us to sully our hands with manual resource release.

This code compiles, but, alas, the most trivial client use doesn't:

```
#include "widget.h"

Widget w;                               // error!
```

The error message you receive depends on the compiler you're using, but the text generally mentions something about applying sizeof or delete to an incomplete type. Those operations aren't among the things you can do with such types.

This apparent failure of the Pimpl Idiom using std::unique_ptrs is alarming, because (1) std::unique_ptr is advertised as supporting incomplete types, and (2) the Pimpl Idiom is one of std::unique_ptrs most common use cases. Fortunately, getting the code to work is easy. All that's required is a basic understanding of the cause of the problem.

The issue arises due to the code that's generated when w is destroyed (e.g., goes out of scope). At that point, its destructor is called. In the class definition using std::unique_ptr, we didn't declare a destructor, because we didn't have any code to put into it. In accord with the usual rules for compiler-generated special member functions (see Item 17), the compiler generates a destructor for us. Within that destructor, the compiler inserts code to call the destructor for Widget's data member pImpl. pImpl is a std::unique_ptr<Widget::Impl>, i.e., a std::unique_ptr using the default deleter. The default deleter is a function that uses delete on the raw pointer inside the std::unique_ptr. Prior to using delete, however, implementations typically have the default deleter employ C++11's static_assert to ensure that the raw pointer doesn't point to an incomplete type. When the compiler generates code for the destruction of the Widget w, then, it generally encounters a static_assert that fails, and that's usually what leads to the error message. This message is associated with the point where w is destroyed, because Widget's destructor, like all compiler-generated special member functions, is implicitly inline. The message itself often refers to the line where w is created, because it's the source code explicitly creating the object that leads to its later implicit destruction.

To fix the problem, you just need to make sure that at the point where the code to destroy the std::unique_ptr<Widget::Impl> is generated, Widget::Impl is a complete type. The type becomes complete when its definition has been seen, and Widget::Impl is defined inside widget.cpp. The key to successful compilation, then, is to have the compiler see the body of Widget's destructor (i.e., the place where the compiler will generate code to destroy the std::unique_ptr data member) only inside widget.cpp after Widget::Impl has been defined.

Arranging for that is simple. Declare Widget's destructor in widget.h, but don't define it there:

```
class Widget {                    // as before, in "widget.h"
public:
  Widget();
  ~Widget();                      // declaration only

  …

private:                          // as before
  struct Impl;
  std::unique_ptr<Impl> pImpl;
};
```

Define it in widget.cpp after Widget::Impl has been defined:

```
#include "widget.h"               // as before, in "widget.cpp"
#include "gadget.h"
#include <string>
#include <vector>

struct Widget::Impl {             // as before, definition of
```

```
    std::string name;                       // Widget::Impl
    std::vector<double> data;
    Gadget g1, g2, g3;
};

Widget::Widget()                            // as before
: pImpl(std::make_unique<Impl>())
{}

Widget::~Widget()                           // ~Widget definition
{}
```

This works well, and it requires the least typing, but if you want to emphasize that the compiler-generated destructor would do the right thing—that the only reason you declared it was to cause its definition to be generated in Widget's implementation file, you can define the destructor body with "= default":

```
Widget::~Widget() = default;                // same effect as above
```

Classes using the Pimpl Idiom are natural candidates for move support, because compiler-generated move operations do exactly what's desired: perform a move on the underlying std::unique_ptr. As Item 17 explains, the declaration of a destructor in Widget prevents compilers from generating the move operations, so if you want move support, you must declare the functions yourself. Given that the compiler-generated versions would behave correctly, you're likely to be tempted to implement them as follows:

```
class Widget {                                          // still in
public:                                                 // "widget.h"
  Widget();
  ~Widget();

  Widget(Widget&& rhs) noexcept = default;              // right idea,
  Widget& operator=(Widget&& rhs) noexcept = default;   // wrong code!

  ...

private:                                                // as before
  struct Impl;
  std::unique_ptr<Impl> pImpl;
};
```

This approach leads to the same kind of problem as declaring the class without a destructor, and for the same fundamental reason. The compiler-generated move assignment operator needs to destroy the object pointed to by pImpl before reassigning it, but in the Widget header file, pImpl points to an incomplete type. The situation is different for the move constructor. The problem there is that compilers must be able to generate code to destroy pImpl in the event that an exception arises inside the move constructor (even if the constructor is noexcept!), and destroying pImpl requires that Impl be complete.

Because the problem is the same as before, so is the fix—move the definition of the move operations into the implementation file:

```
class Widget {                              // still in "widget.h"
public:
  Widget();
  ~Widget();

  Widget(Widget&& rhs) noexcept;            // declarations
  Widget& operator=(Widget&& rhs) noexcept; // only

  …

private:                                    // as before
  struct Impl;
  std::unique_ptr<Impl> pImpl;
};

#include <string>                           // as before,
  …                                         // in "widget.cpp"

struct Widget::Impl { … };                  // as before

Widget::Widget()                            // as before
: pImpl(std::make_unique<Impl>())
{}

Widget::~Widget() = default;                // as before

                                            // definitions
Widget::Widget(Widget&& rhs) noexcept = default;
Widget& Widget::operator=(Widget&& rhs) noexcept = default;
```

The Pimpl Idiom is a way to reduce compilation dependencies between a class's implementation and the class's clients, but, conceptually, use of the idiom doesn't change what the class represents. The original Widget class contained std::string, std::vector, and Gadget data members, and, assuming that Gadgets, like std::strings and std::vectors, can be copied, it would make sense for Widget to support the copy operations. We have to write these functions ourselves, because (1) compilers won't generate copy operations for classes with move-only types like std::unique_ptr and (2) even if they did, the generated functions would copy only the `std::unique_ptr` (i.e., perform a *shallow copy*), and we want to copy what the pointer points to (i.e., perform a *deep copy*).

In a ritual that is by now familiar, we declare the functions in the header file and implement them in the implementation file:

```
class Widget {                              // still in "widget.h"
public:
  …                                         // other funcs, as before

  Widget(const Widget& rhs);                // declarations
  Widget& operator=(const Widget& rhs);     // only

private:                                    // as before
  struct Impl;
  std::unique_ptr<Impl> pImpl;
};


#include "widget.h"                         // as before,
…                                           // in "widget.cpp"

struct Widget::Impl { … };                  // as before

Widget::~Widget() = default;                // other funcs, as before

Widget::Widget(const Widget& rhs)                     // copy ctor
: pImpl(nullptr)
{ if (rhs.pImpl) pImpl = std::make_unique<Impl>(*rhs.pImpl); }

Widget& Widget::operator=(const Widget& rhs)    // copy operator=
{
  if (!rhs.pImpl) pImpl.reset();
  else if (!pImpl) pImpl = std::make_unique<Impl>(*rhs.pImpl);
  else *pImpl = *rhs.pImpl;

  return *this;
}
```

The implementations are straightforward, though we must handle cases where the parameter `rhs` or, in the case of the copy assignment operator, `*this` has been moved from and thus contains a null `pImpl` pointer. In general, we take advantage of the fact that compilers will create the copy operations for `Impl`, and these operations will copy each field automatically. We thus implement `Widget`'s copy operations by calling `Widget::Impl`'s compiler-generated copy operations. In both functions, note that we still follow the advice of Item 21 to prefer use of `std::make_unique` over direct use of `new`.

For purposes of implementing the Pimpl Idiom, `std::unique_ptr` is the smart pointer to use, because the `pImpl` pointer inside an object (e.g., inside a `Widget`) has exclusive ownership of the corresponding implementation object (e.g., the `Widget::Impl` object). Still, it's interesting to note that if we were to use `std::shared_ptr` instead of `std::unique_ptr` for pImpl (i.e., if the values in an Impl struct could be shared by multiple `Widget`s), we'd find that the advice of this Item no longer applied. There'd be no need to declare a destructor in `Widget`, and without a user-declared destructor, compilers would happily generate the move operations, which would do exactly what we'd want them to. That is, given this code in `widget.h`,

```
class Widget {                          // in "widget.h"
public:
  Widget();
  ...                                   // no declarations for dtor
                                        // or move operations

private:
  struct Impl;
  std::shared_ptr<Impl> pImpl;          // std::shared_ptr
};                                      // instead of std::unique_ptr
```

and this client code that `#includes widget.h`,

```
Widget w1;

auto w2(std::move(w1));                 // move-construct w2

w1 = std::move(w2);                     // move-assign w1
```

everything would compile and run as we'd hope: w1 would be default constructed, its value would be moved into w2, that value would be moved back into w1, and then both w1 and w2 would be destroyed (thus causing the pointed-to `Widget::Impl` object to be destroyed).

The difference in behavior between `std::unique_ptr` and `std::shared_ptr` for pImpl pointers stems from the differing ways these smart pointers support custom deleters. For `std::unique_ptr`, the type of the deleter is part of the type of the smart pointer, and this makes it possible for compilers to generate smaller runtime data structures and faster runtime code. A consequence of this greater efficiency is that pointed-to types must be complete when compiler-generated special functions (e.g., destructors or move operations) are used. For `std::shared_ptr`, the type of the deleter is not part of the type of the smart pointer. This necessitates larger runtime data structures and somewhat slower code, but pointed-to types need not be complete when compiler-generated special functions are employed.

For the Pimpl Idiom, there's not really a trade-off between the characteristics of `std::unique_ptr` and `std::shared_ptr`, because the relationship between classes like `Widget` and classes like `Widget::Impl` is exclusive ownership, and that makes `std::unique_ptr` the proper tool for the job. Nevertheless, it's worth knowing that in other situations—situations where shared ownership exists (and `std::shared_ptr` is hence a fitting design choice), there's no need to jump through the function-definition hoops that use of `std::unique_ptr` entails.

Things to Remember

- The Pimpl Idiom decreases build times by reducing compilation dependencies between class clients and class implementations.

- For `std::unique_ptr pImpl` pointers, declare special member functions in the class header, but implement them in the implementation file. Do this even if the default function implementations are acceptable.

- The above advice applies to `std::unique_ptr`, but not to `std::shared_ptr`.

CHAPTER 5

Rvalue References, Move Semantics, and Perfect Forwarding

When you first learn about them, move semantics and perfect forwarding seem pretty straightforward:

- **Move semantics** makes it possible for compilers to replace expensive copying operations with less expensive moves. In the same way that copy constructors and copy assignment operators give you control over what it means to copy objects, move constructors and move assignment operators offer control over the semantics of moving. Move semantics also enables the creation of move-only types, such as `std::unique_ptr`, `std::future`, and `std::thread`.

- **Perfect forwarding** makes it possible to write function templates that take arbitrary arguments and forward them to other functions such that the target functions receive exactly the same arguments as were passed to the forwarding functions.

Rvalue references are the glue that ties these two rather disparate features together. They're the underlying language mechanism that makes both move semantics and perfect forwarding possible.

The more experience you have with these features, the more you realize that your initial impression was based on only the metaphorical tip of the proverbial iceberg. The world of move semantics, perfect forwarding, and rvalue references is more nuanced than it appears. `std::move` doesn't move anything, for example, and perfect forwarding is imperfect. Move operations aren't always cheaper than copying; when they are, they're not always as cheap as you'd expect; and they're not always called in a context where moving is valid. The construct "*type*&&" doesn't always represent an rvalue reference.

No matter how far you dig into these features, it can seem that there's always more to uncover. Fortunately, there is a limit to their depths. This chapter will take you to the bedrock. Once you arrive, this part of C++11 will make a lot more sense. You'll know the usage conventions for `std::move` and `std::forward`, for example. You'll be comfortable with the ambiguous nature of "*type*&&". You'll understand the reasons for the surprisingly varied behavioral profiles of move operations. All those pieces will fall into place. At that point, you'll be back where you started, because move semantics, perfect forwarding, and rvalue references will once again seem pretty straightforward. But this time, they'll stay that way.

In the Items in this chapter, it's especially important to bear in mind that a parameter is always an lvalue, even if its type is an rvalue reference. That is, given

```
void f(Widget&& w);
```

the parameter w is an lvalue, even though its type is rvalue-reference-to-`Widget`. (If this surprises you, please review the overview of lvalues and rvalues that begins on page 2.)

Item 23: Understand `std::move` and `std::forward`.

It's useful to approach `std::move` and `std::forward` in terms of what they *don't* do. `std::move` doesn't move anything. `std::forward` doesn't forward anything. At runtime, neither does anything at all. They generate no executable code. Not a single byte.

`std::move` and `std::forward` are merely functions (actually function templates) that perform casts. `std::move` unconditionally casts its argument to an rvalue, while `std::forward` performs this cast only if a particular condition is fulfilled. That's it. The explanation leads to a new set of questions, but, fundamentally, that's the complete story.

To make the story more concrete, here's a sample implementation of `std::move` in C++11. It's not fully conforming to the details of the Standard, but it's very close.

```
template<typename T>                        // in namespace std
typename remove_reference<T>::type&&
move(T&& param)
{
  using ReturnType =                        // alias declaration;
    typename remove_reference<T>::type&&;   // see Item 9

  return static_cast<ReturnType>(param);
}
```

I've highlighted two parts of the code for you. One is the name of the function, because the return type specification is rather noisy, and I don't want you to lose your bearings in the din. The other is the cast that comprises the essence of the function. As you can see, std::move takes a reference to an object (a universal reference, to be precise—see Item 24) and it returns a reference to the same object.

The "&&" part of the function's return type implies that std::move returns an rvalue reference, but, as Item 28 explains, if the type T happens to be an lvalue reference, T&& would become an lvalue reference. To prevent this from happening, the type trait (see Item 9) std::remove_reference is applied to T, thus ensuring that "&&" is applied to a type that isn't a reference. That guarantees that std::move truly returns an rvalue reference, and that's important, because rvalue references returned from functions are rvalues. Thus, std::move casts its argument to an rvalue, and that's all it does.

As an aside, std::move can be implemented with less fuss in C++14. Thanks to function return type deduction (see Item 3) and to the Standard Library's alias template std::remove_reference_t (see Item 9), std::move can be written this way:

```
template<typename T>                    // C++14; still in
decltype(auto) move(T&& param)          // namespace std
{
    using ReturnType = remove_reference_t<T>&&;
    return static_cast<ReturnType>(param);
}
```

Easier on the eyes, no?

Because std::move does nothing but cast its argument to an rvalue, there have been suggestions that a better name for it might have been something like rvalue_cast. Be that as it may, the name we have is std::move, so it's important to remember what std::move does and doesn't do. It does cast. It doesn't move.

Of course, rvalues are candidates for moving, so applying std::move to an object tells the compiler that the object is eligible to be moved from. That's why std::move has the name it does: to make it easy to designate objects that may be moved from.

In truth, rvalues are only *usually* candidates for moving. Suppose you're writing a class representing annotations. The class's constructor takes a std::string parameter comprising the annotation, and it copies the parameter to a data member. Flush with the information in Item 41, you declare a by-value parameter:

```
class Annotation {
public:
    explicit Annotation(std::string text);  // param to be copied,
```

```
        ...                           // so per Item 41,
};                                    // pass by value
```

But `Annotation`'s constructor needs only to read `text`'s value. It doesn't need to modify it. In accord with the time-honored tradition of using `const` whenever possible, you revise your declaration such that `text` is `const`:

```
class Annotation {
public:
  explicit Annotation(const std::string text);
    ...
};
```

To avoid paying for a copy operation when copying `text` into a data member, you remain true to the advice of Item 41 and apply `std::move` to `text`, thus producing an rvalue:

```
class Annotation {
public:
  explicit Annotation(const std::string text)
  : value(std::move(text))   // "move" text into value; this code
  { ... }                    // doesn't do what it seems to!

    ...

private:
  std::string value;
};
```

This code compiles. This code links. This code runs. This code sets the data member `value` to the content of `text`. The only thing separating this code from a perfect realization of your vision is that `text` is not moved into `value`, it's *copied*. Sure, `text` is cast to an rvalue by `std::move`, but `text` is declared to be a `const std::string`, so before the cast, `text` is an lvalue `const std::string`, and the result of the cast is an rvalue `const std::string`, but throughout it all, the `const`ness remains.

Consider the effect that has when compilers have to determine which `std::string` constructor to call. There are two possibilities:

```
class string {             // std::string is actually a
public:                    // typedef for std::basic_string<char>
    ...
  string(const string& rhs);   // copy ctor
  string(string&& rhs);        // move ctor
    ...
};
```

In the Annotation constructor's member initialization list, the result of std::move(text) is an rvalue of type const std::string. That rvalue can't be passed to std::string's move constructor, because the move constructor takes an rvalue reference to a *non-const* std::string. The rvalue can, however, be passed to the copy constructor, because an lvalue-reference-to-const is permitted to bind to a const rvalue. The member initialization therefore invokes the *copy* constructor in std::string, even though text has been cast to an rvalue! Such behavior is essential to maintaining const-correctness. Moving a value out of an object generally modifies the object, so the language should not permit const objects to be passed to functions (such as move constructors) that could modify them.

There are two lessons to be drawn from this example. First, don't declare objects const if you want to be able to move from them. Move requests on const objects are silently transformed into copy operations. Second, std::move not only doesn't actually move anything, it doesn't even guarantee that the object it's casting will be eligible to be moved. The only thing you know for sure about the result of applying std::move to an object is that it's an rvalue.

The story for std::forward is similar to that for std::move, but whereas std::move *unconditionally* casts its argument to an rvalue, std::forward does it only under certain conditions. std::forward is a *conditional* cast. To understand when it casts and when it doesn't, recall how std::forward is typically used. The most common scenario is a function template taking a universal reference parameter that is to be passed to another function:

```
void process(const Widget& lvalArg);        // process lvalues
void process(Widget&& rvalArg);             // process rvalues

template<typename T>                        // template that passes
void logAndProcess(T&& param)               // param to process
{
  auto now =                                // get current time
    std::chrono::system_clock::now();

  makeLogEntry("Calling 'process'", now);
  process(std::forward<T>(param));
}
```

Consider two calls to logAndProcess, one with an lvalue, the other with an rvalue:

```
Widget w;

logAndProcess(w);                 // call with lvalue
logAndProcess(std::move(w));      // call with rvalue
```

Inside logAndProcess, the parameter param is passed to the function process. process is overloaded for lvalues and rvalues. When we call logAndProcess with an lvalue, we naturally expect that lvalue to be forwarded to process as an lvalue, and when we call logAndProcess with an rvalue, we expect the rvalue overload of process to be invoked.

But param, like all function parameters, is an lvalue. Every call to process inside logAndProcess will thus want to invoke the lvalue overload for process. To prevent this, we need a mechanism for param to be cast to an rvalue if and only if the argument with which param was initialized—the argument passed to logAndProcess—was an rvalue. This is precisely what std::forward does. That's why std::forward is a *conditional* cast: it casts to an rvalue only if its argument was initialized with an rvalue.

You may wonder how std::forward can know whether its argument was initialized with an rvalue. In the code above, for example, how can std::forward tell whether param was initialized with an lvalue or an rvalue? The brief answer is that that information is encoded in logAndProcess's template parameter T. That parameter is passed to std::forward, which recovers the encoded information. For details on exactly how that works, consult Item 28.

Given that both std::move and std::forward boil down to casts, the only difference being that std::move always casts, while std::forward only sometimes does, you might ask whether we can dispense with std::move and just use std::forward everywhere. From a purely technical perspective, the answer is yes: std::forward can do it all. std::move isn't necessary. Of course, neither function is really *necessary*, because we could write casts everywhere, but I hope we agree that that would be, well, yucky.

std::move's attractions are convenience, reduced likelihood of error, and greater clarity. Consider a class where we want to track how many times the move constructor is called. A static counter that's incremented during move construction is all we need. Assuming the only non-static data in the class is a std::string, here's the conventional way (i.e., using std::move) to implement the move constructor:

```
class Widget {
public:
  Widget(Widget&& rhs)
  : s(std::move(rhs.s))
  { ++moveCtorCalls; }

  …
```

```
private:
  static std::size_t moveCtorCalls;
  std::string s;
};
```

To implement the same behavior with `std::forward`, the code would look like this:

```
class Widget {
public:
  Widget(Widget&& rhs)                    // unconventional,
  : s(std::forward<std::string>(rhs.s))   // undesirable
  { ++moveCtorCalls; }                    // implementation

  ...

};
```

Note first that `std::move` requires only a function argument (`rhs.s`), while `std::forward` requires both a function argument (`rhs.s`) and a template type argument (`std::string`). Then note that the type we pass to `std::forward` should be a non-reference, because that's the convention for encoding that the argument being passed is an rvalue (see Item 28). Together, this means that `std::move` requires less typing than `std::forward`, and it spares us the trouble of passing a type argument that encodes that the argument we're passing is an rvalue. It also eliminates the possibility of our passing an incorrect type (e.g., `std::string&`, which would result in the data member `s` being copy constructed instead of move constructed).

More importantly, the use of `std::move` conveys an unconditional cast to an rvalue, while the use of `std::forward` indicates a cast to an rvalue only for references to which rvalues have been bound. Those are two very different actions. The first one typically sets up a move, while the second one just passes—*forwards*—an object to another function in a way that retains its original lvalueness or rvalueness. Because these actions are so different, it's good that we have two different functions (and function names) to distinguish them.

Things to Remember

- `std::move` performs an unconditional cast to an rvalue. In and of itself, it doesn't move anything.
- `std::forward` casts its argument to an rvalue only if that argument is bound to an rvalue.
- Neither `std::move` nor `std::forward` do anything at runtime.
- Move requests on `const` objects are treated as copy requests.

Item 24: Distinguish universal references from rvalue references.

It's been said that the truth shall set you free, but under the right circumstances, a well-chosen lie can be equally liberating. This Item is such a lie. Because we're dealing with software, however, let's eschew the word "lie" and instead say that this Item comprises an "abstraction."

To declare an rvalue reference to some type T, you write T&&. It thus seems reasonable to assume that if you see "T&&" in source code, you're looking at an rvalue reference. Alas, it's not quite that simple:

```
void f(Widget&& param);              // rvalue reference

Widget&& var1 = Widget();            // rvalue reference

auto&& var2 = var1;                  // not rvalue reference

template<typename T>
void f(std::vector<T>&& param);      // rvalue reference

template<typename T>
void f(T&& param);                   // not rvalue reference
```

In fact, "T&&" has two different meanings. One is rvalue reference, of course. Such references behave exactly the way you expect: they bind only to rvalues, and their primary *raison d'être* is to identify objects that may be moved from.

The other meaning for "T&&" is *either* rvalue reference *or* lvalue reference. Such references look like rvalue references in the source code (i.e., "T&&"), but they can behave as if they were lvalue references (i.e., "T&"). Their dual nature permits them to bind to rvalues (like rvalue references) as well as lvalues (like lvalue references). Furthermore, they can bind to const or non-const objects, to volatile or non-volatile objects, even to objects that are both const and volatile. They can bind to virtually *any-thing*. Such unprecedentedly flexible references deserve a name of their own. I call them *universal references*.[1]

Universal references arise in two contexts. The most common is function template parameters, such as this example from the sample code above:

---

1 Item 25 explains that universal references should almost always have std::forward applied to them, and as this book goes to press, some members of the C++ community have started referring to universal references as *forwarding references*.

```
template<typename T>
void f(T&& param);                    // param is a universal reference
```

The second context is `auto` declarations, including this one from the sample code above:

```
auto&& var2 = var1;                   // var2 is a universal reference
```

What these contexts have in common is the presence of *type deduction*. In the template `f`, the type of `param` is being deduced, and in the declaration for `var2`, `var2`'s type is being deduced. Compare that with the following examples (also from the sample code above), where type deduction is missing. If you see "T&&" without type deduction, you're looking at an rvalue reference:

```
void f(Widget&& param);               // no type deduction;
                                      // param is an rvalue reference

Widget&& var1 = Widget();             // no type deduction;
                                      // var1 is an rvalue reference
```

Because universal references are references, they must be initialized. The initializer for a universal reference determines whether it represents an rvalue reference or an lvalue reference. If the initializer is an rvalue, the universal reference corresponds to an rvalue reference. If the initializer is an lvalue, the universal reference corresponds to an lvalue reference. For universal references that are function parameters, the initializer is provided at the call site:

```
template<typename T>
void f(T&& param);        // param is a universal reference

Widget w;
f(w);                     // lvalue passed to f; param's type is
                          // Widget& (i.e., an lvalue reference)

f(std::move(w));          // rvalue passed to f; param's type is
                          // Widget&& (i.e., an rvalue reference)
```

For a reference to be universal, type deduction is necessary, but it's not sufficient. The *form* of the reference declaration must also be correct, and that form is quite constrained. It must be precisely "T&&". Look again at this example from the sample code we saw earlier:

```
template<typename T>
void f(std::vector<T>&& param);  // param is an rvalue reference
```

When f is invoked, the type T will be deduced (unless the caller explicitly specifies it, an edge case we'll not concern ourselves with). But the form of `param`'s type declaration isn't "T&&", it's "std::vector<T>&&". That rules out the possibility that `param` is a universal reference. `param` is therefore an rvalue reference, something that your compilers will be happy to confirm for you if you try to pass an lvalue to `f`:

```
std::vector<int> v;
f(v);                               // error! can't bind lvalue to
                                    // rvalue reference
```

Even the simple presence of a `const` qualifier is enough to disqualify a reference from being universal:

```
template<typename T>
void f(const T&& param);           // param is an rvalue reference
```

If you're in a template and you see a function parameter of type "T&&", you might think you can assume that it's a universal reference. You can't. That's because being in a template doesn't guarantee the presence of type deduction. Consider this `push_back` member function in `std::vector`:

```
template<class T, class Allocator = allocator<T>>   // from C++
class vector {                                       // Standards
public:
  void push_back(T&& x);
  …
};
```

`push_back`'s parameter certainly has the right form for a universal reference, but there's no type deduction in this case. That's because `push_back` can't exist without a particular `vector` instantiation for it to be part of, and the type of that instantiation fully determines the declaration for `push_back`. That is, saying

```
std::vector<Widget> v;
```

causes the `std::vector` template to be instantiated as follows:

```
class vector<Widget, allocator<Widget>> {
public:
  void push_back(Widget&& x);                // rvalue reference
  …
};
```

Now you can see clearly that `push_back` employs no type deduction. This `push_back` for `vector<T>` (there are two—the function is overloaded) always declares a parameter of type rvalue-reference-to-T.

In contrast, the conceptually similar `emplace_back` member function in `std::vector` *does* employ type deduction:

```
template<class T, class Allocator = allocator<T>>    // still from
class vector {                                        // C++
public:                                               // Standards
  template <class... Args>
  void emplace_back(Args&&... args);

  …
};
```

Here, the type parameter Args is independent of vector's type parameter T, so Args must be deduced each time emplace_back is called. (Okay, Args is really a parameter pack, not a type parameter, but for purposes of this discussion, we can treat it as if it were a type parameter.)

The fact that emplace_back's type parameter is named Args, yet it's still a universal reference, reinforces my earlier comment that it's the *form* of a universal reference that must be "T&&". There's no requirement that you use the name T. For example, the following template takes a universal reference, because the form ("*type&&*") is right, and param's type will be deduced (again, excluding the corner case where the caller explicitly specifies the type):

```
template<typename MyTemplateType>    // param is a
void someFunc(MyTemplateType&& param);    // universal reference
```

I remarked earlier that auto variables can also be universal references. To be more precise, variables declared with the type auto&& are universal references, because type deduction takes place and they have the correct form ("T&&"). auto universal references are not as common as universal references used for function template parameters, but they do crop up from time to time in C++11. They crop up a lot more in C++14, because C++14 lambda expressions may declare auto&& parameters. For example, if you wanted to write a C++14 lambda to record the time taken in an arbitrary function invocation, you could do this:

```
auto timeFuncInvocation =
  [](auto&& func, auto&&... params)                    // C++14
  {
    start timer;
    std::forward<decltype(func)>(func)(                // invoke func
      std::forward<decltype(params)>(params)...        // on params
    );
    stop timer and record elapsed time;
  };
```

If your reaction to the "std::forward<decltype(*blah blah blah*)>" code inside the lambda is, "What the...?!", that probably just means you haven't yet read Item 33. Don't worry about it. The important thing in this Item is the auto&& parameters that the lambda declares. `func` is a universal reference that can be bound to any callable object, lvalue or rvalue. `params` is zero or more universal references (i.e., a universal reference parameter pack) that can be bound to any number of objects of arbitrary types. The result, thanks to `auto` universal references, is that `timeFuncInvocation` can time pretty much any function execution. (For information on the difference between "any" and "pretty much any," turn to Item 30.)

Bear in mind that this entire Item—the foundation of universal references—is a lie… er, an "abstraction." The underlying truth is known as *reference collapsing*, a topic to which Item 28 is dedicated. But the truth doesn't make the abstraction any less useful. Distinguishing between rvalue references and universal references will help you read source code more accurately ("Does that `T&&` I'm looking at bind to rvalues only or to everything?"), and it will avoid ambiguities when you communicate with your colleagues ("I'm using a universal reference here, not an rvalue reference…"). It will also allow you to make sense of Items 25 and 26, which rely on the distinction. So embrace the abstraction. Revel in it. Just as Newton's laws of motion (which are technically incorrect) are typically just as useful as and easier to apply than Einstein's theory of relativity ("the truth"), so is the notion of universal references normally preferable to working through the details of reference collapsing.

Things to Remember

- If a function template parameter has type `T&&` for a deduced type `T`, or if an object is declared using `auto&&`, the parameter or object is a universal reference.

- If the form of the type declaration isn't precisely *type*`&&`, or if type deduction does not occur, *type*`&&` denotes an rvalue reference.

- Universal references correspond to rvalue references if they're initialized with rvalues. They correspond to lvalue references if they're initialized with lvalues.

Item 25: Use `std::move` on rvalue references, `std::forward` on universal references.

Rvalue references bind only to objects that are candidates for moving. If you have an rvalue reference parameter, you *know* that the object it's bound to may be moved:

```
class Widget {
    Widget(Widget&& rhs);        // rhs definitely refers to an
```

```
                                            // object eligible for moving
};
```

That being the case, you'll want to pass such objects to other functions in a way that permits those functions to take advantage of the object's rvalueness. The way to do that is to cast parameters bound to such objects to rvalues. As Item 23 explains, that's not only what `std::move` does, it's what it was created for:

```
class Widget {
public:
  Widget(Widget&& rhs)                  // rhs is rvalue reference
  : name(std::move(rhs.name)),
    p(std::move(rhs.p))
    { … }
  …

private:
  std::string name;
  std::shared_ptr<SomeDataStructure> p;
};
```

A universal reference, on the other hand (see Item 24), *might* be bound to an object that's eligible for moving. Universal references should be cast to rvalues only if they were initialized with rvalues. Item 23 explains that this is precisely what `std::forward` does:

```
class Widget {
public:
  template<typename T>
  void setName(T&& newName)             // newName is
  { name = std::forward<T>(newName); }  // universal reference

  …
};
```

In short, rvalue references should be *unconditionally cast* to rvalues (via `std::move`) when forwarding them to other functions, because they're *always* bound to rvalues, and universal references should be *conditionally cast* to rvalues (via `std::forward`) when forwarding them, because they're only *sometimes* bound to rvalues.

Item 23 explains that using `std::forward` on rvalue references can be made to exhibit the proper behavior, but the source code is wordy, error-prone, and unidiomatic, so you should avoid using `std::forward` with rvalue references. Even worse is the idea of using `std::move` with universal references, because that can have the effect of unexpectedly modifying lvalues (e.g., local variables):

```
class Widget {
public:
  template<typename T>
  void setName(T&& newName)           // universal reference
  { name = std::move(newName); }      // compiles, but is
  …                                   // bad, bad, bad!

private:
  std::string name;
  std::shared_ptr<SomeDataStructure> p;
};

std::string getWidgetName();          // factory function

Widget w;

auto n = getWidgetName();             // n is local variable

w.setName(n);                         // moves n into w!

…                                     // n's value now unknown
```

Here, the local variable n is passed to w.setName, which the caller can be forgiven for assuming is a read-only operation on n. But because setName internally uses std::move to unconditionally cast its reference parameter to an rvalue, n's value will be moved into w.name, and n will come back from the call to setName with an unspecified value. That's the kind of behavior that can drive callers to despair—possibly to violence.

You might argue that setName shouldn't have declared its parameter to be a universal reference. Such references can't be const (see Item 24), yet setName surely shouldn't modify its parameter. You might point out that if setName had simply been overloaded for const lvalues and for rvalues, the whole problem could have been avoided. Like this:

```
class Widget {
public:
  void setName(const std::string& newName)       // set from
  { name = newName; }                            // const lvalue

  void setName(std::string&& newName)            // set from
  { name = std::move(newName); }                 // rvalue

  …
};
```

That would certainly work in this case, but there are drawbacks. First, it's more source code to write and maintain (two functions instead of a single template). Second, it can be less efficient. For example, consider this use of setName:

```
w.setName("Adela Novak");
```

With the version of setName taking a universal reference, the string literal "Adela Novak" would be passed to setName, where it would be conveyed to the assignment operator for the std::string inside w. w's name data member would thus be assigned directly from the string literal; no temporary std::string objects would arise. With the overloaded versions of setName, however, a temporary std::string object would be created for setName's parameter to bind to, and this temporary std::string would then be moved into w's data member. A call to setName would thus entail execution of one std::string constructor (to create the temporary), one std::string move assignment operator (to move newName into w.name), and one std::string destructor (to destroy the temporary). That's almost certainly a more expensive execution sequence than invoking only the std::string assignment operator taking a const char* pointer. The additional cost is likely to vary from implementation to implementation, and whether that cost is worth worrying about will vary from application to application and library to library, but the fact is that replacing a template taking a universal reference with a pair of functions overloaded on lvalue references and rvalue references is likely to incur a runtime cost in some cases.[2]

The most serious problem with overloading on lvalues and rvalues, however, isn't the volume or idiomaticity of the source code, nor is it the code's runtime performance. It's the poor scalability of the design. Widget::setName takes only one parameter, so only two overloads are necessary, but for functions taking more parameters, each of which could be an lvalue or an rvalue, the number of overloads grows geometrically: n parameters necessitates 2^n overloads. And that's not the worst of it. Some functions —function templates, actually—take an *unlimited* number of parameters, each of which could be an lvalue or rvalue. The poster children for such functions are std::make_shared, and, as of C++14, std::make_unique (see Item 21). Check out the declarations of their most commonly used overloads:

```
template<class T, class... Args>            // from C++11
shared_ptr<T> make_shared(Args&&... args);  // Standard

template<class T, class... Args>            // from C++14
unique_ptr<T> make_unique(Args&&... args);  // Standard
```

---

2 An alternative to both universal references and overloading is pass by value. For details, see Item 41.

For functions like these, overloading on lvalues and rvalues is not an option: universal references are the only way to go. And inside such functions, I assure you, `std::forward` is applied to the universal reference parameters when they're passed to other functions. Which is exactly what you should do.

Well, usually. Eventually. But not necessarily initially. In some cases, you'll want to use the object bound to an rvalue reference or a universal reference more than once in a single function, and you'll want to make sure that it's not moved from until you're otherwise done with it. In that case, you'll want to apply `std::move` (for rvalue references) or `std::forward` (for universal references) to only the *final* use of the reference. For example:

```
template<typename T>                          // text is
void setSignText(T&& text)                    // univ. reference
{
  sign.setText(text);                         // use text, but
                                              // don't modify it

    auto now =                                // get current time
      std::chrono::system_clock::now();

    signHistory.add(now,
                    std::forward<T>(text));   // conditionally cast
}                                             // text to rvalue
```

Here, we want to make sure that `text`'s value doesn't get changed by `sign.setText`, because we want to use that value when we call `signHistory.add`. Ergo the use of `std::forward` on only the final use of the universal reference.

For `std::move`, the same thinking applies (i.e., apply `std::move` to an rvalue reference the last time it's used), but it's important to note that in rare cases, you'll want to call `std::move_if_noexcept` instead of `std::move`. To learn when and why, consult Item 14.

If you're in a function that returns *by value*, and you're returning an object bound to an rvalue reference or a universal reference, you'll want to apply `std::move` or `std::forward` when you return the reference. To see why, consider an `operator+` function to add two matrices together, where the left-hand matrix is known to be an rvalue (and can hence have its storage reused to hold the sum of the matrices):

```
Matrix                                        // by-value return
operator+(Matrix&& lhs, const Matrix& rhs)
{
  lhs += rhs;
```

```
    return std::move(lhs);                          // move lhs into
  }                                                  // return value
```

By casting `lhs` to an rvalue in the `return` statement (via `std::move`), `lhs` will be moved into the function's return value location. If the call to `std::move` were omitted,

```
  Matrix                                            // as above
  operator+(Matrix&& lhs, const Matrix& rhs)
  {
    lhs += rhs;
    return lhs;                                      // copy lhs into
  }                                                  // return value
```

the fact that `lhs` is an lvalue would force compilers to instead *copy* it into the return value location. Assuming that the `Matrix` type supports move construction, which is more efficient than copy construction, using `std::move` in the `return` statement yields more efficient code.

If `Matrix` does not support moving, casting it to an rvalue won't hurt, because the rvalue will simply be copied by `Matrix`'s copy constructor (see Item 23). If `Matrix` is later revised to support moving, `operator+` will automatically benefit the next time it is compiled. That being the case, there's nothing to be lost (and possibly much to be gained) by applying `std::move` to rvalue references being returned from functions that return by value.

The situation is similar for universal references and `std::forward`. Consider a function template `reduceAndCopy` that takes a possibly unreduced `Fraction` object, reduces it, and then returns a copy of the reduced value. If the original object is an rvalue, its value should be moved into the return value (thus avoiding the expense of making a copy), but if the original is an lvalue, an actual copy must be created. Hence:

```
  template<typename T>
  Fraction                                          // by-value return
  reduceAndCopy(T&& frac)                            // universal reference param
  {
    frac.reduce();
    return std::forward<T>(frac);                    // move rvalue into return
  }                                                  // value, copy lvalue
```

If the call to `std::forward` were omitted, `frac` would be unconditionally copied into `reduceAndCopy`'s return value.

Some programmers take the information above and try to extend it to situations where it doesn't apply. "If using `std::move` on an rvalue reference parameter being copied into a return value turns a copy construction into a move construction," they reason, "I can perform the same optimization on local variables that I'm returning." In other words, they figure that given a function returning a local variable by value, such as this,

```
Widget makeWidget()          // "Copying" version of makeWidget
{
    Widget w;                // local variable

    ...                      // configure w

    return w;                // "copy" w into return value
}
```

they can "optimize" it by turning the "copy" into a move:

```
Widget makeWidget()          // Moving version of makeWidget
{
    Widget w;
    ...
    return std::move(w);     // move w into return value
}                            // (don't do this!)
```

My liberal use of quotation marks should tip you off that this line of reasoning is flawed. But why is it flawed?

It's flawed, because the Standardization Committee is way ahead of such programmers when it comes to this kind of optimization. It was recognized long ago that the "copying" version of makeWidget can avoid the need to copy the local variable w by constructing it in the memory alloted for the function's return value. This is known as the *return value optimization* (RVO), and it's been expressly blessed by the C++ Standard for as long as there's been one.

Wording such a blessing is finicky business, because you want to permit such *copy elision* only in places where it won't affect the observable behavior of the software. Paraphrasing the legalistic (arguably toxic) prose of the Standard, this particular blessing says that compilers may elide the copying (or moving) of a local object[3] in a function that returns by value if (1) the type of the local object is the same as that returned by the function and (2) the local object is what's being returned. With that in mind, look again at the "copying" version of makeWidget:

---

3 Eligible local objects include most local variables (such as w inside makeWidget) as well as temporary objects created as part of a return statement. Function parameters don't qualify. Some people draw a distinction between application of the RVO to named and unnamed (i.e., temporary) local objects, limiting the term RVO to unnamed objects and calling its application to named objects the *named return value optimization* (NRVO).

```
Widget makeWidget()          // "Copying" version of makeWidget
{
  Widget w;
  …
  return w;                  // "copy" w into return value
}
```

Both conditions are fulfilled here, and you can trust me when I tell you that for this code, every decent C++ compiler will employ the RVO to avoid copying w. That means that the "copying" version of makeWidget doesn't, in fact, copy anything.

The moving version of makeWidget does just what its name says it does (assuming Widget offers a move constructor): it moves the contents of w into makeWidget's return value location. But why don't compilers use the RVO to eliminate the move, again constructing w in the memory alloted for the function's return value? The answer is simple: they can't. Condition (2) stipulates that the RVO may be performed only if what's being returned is a local object, but that's not what the moving version of makeWidget is doing. Look again at its return statement:

```
return std::move(w);
```

What's being returned here isn't the local object w, it's *a reference to w*—the result of std::move(w). Returning a reference to a local object doesn't satisfy the conditions required for the RVO, so compilers must move w into the function's return value location. Developers trying to help their compilers optimize by applying std::move to a local variable that's being returned are actually limiting the optimization options available to their compilers!

But the RVO is an optimization. Compilers aren't *required* to elide copy and move operations, even when they're permitted to. Maybe you're paranoid, and you worry that your compilers will punish you with copy operations, just because they can. Or perhaps you're insightful enough to recognize that there are cases where the RVO is difficult for compilers to implement, e.g., when different control paths in a function return different local variables. (Compilers would have to generate code to construct the appropriate local variable in the memory allotted for the function's return value, but how could compilers determine which local variable would be appropriate?) If so, you might be willing to pay the price of a move as insurance against the cost of a copy. That is, you might still think it's reasonable to apply std::move to a local object you're returning, simply because you'd rest easy knowing you'd never pay for a copy.

In that case, applying std::move to a local object would *still* be a bad idea. The part of the Standard blessing the RVO goes on to say that if the conditions for the RVO are met, but compilers choose not to perform copy elision, the object being returned *must be treated as an rvalue*. In effect, the Standard requires that when the RVO is permitted, either copy elision takes place or `std::move` is implicitly applied to local objects being returned. So in the "copying" version of `makeWidget`,

```
Widget makeWidget()          // as before
{
  Widget w;

  …

  return w;
}
```

compilers must either elide the copying of `w` or they must treat the function as if it were written like this:

```
Widget makeWidget()
{
  Widget w;

  …

  return std::move(w);       // treat w as rvalue, because
}                            // no copy elision was performed
```

The situation is similar for by-value function parameters. They're not eligible for copy elision with respect to their function's return value, but compilers must treat them as rvalues if they're returned. As a result, if your source code looks like this,

```
Widget makeWidget(Widget w)  // by-value parameter of same
{                            // type as function's return

  …

  return w;
}
```

compilers must treat it as if it had been written this way:

```
Widget makeWidget(Widget w)
{

  …

  return std::move(w);                // treat w as rvalue
}
```

This means that if you use `std::move` on a local object being returned from a function that's returning by value, you can't help your compilers (they have to treat the local object as an rvalue if they don't perform copy elision), but you can certainly hinder them (by precluding the RVO). There are situations where applying `std::move` to a local variable can be a reasonable thing to do (i.e., when you're passing it to a function and you know you won't be using the variable any longer), but as part of a `return` statement that would otherwise qualify for the RVO or that returns a by-value parameter isn't among them.

Item 26: Avoid overloading on universal references.

Suppose you need to write a function that takes a name as a parameter, logs the current date and time, then adds the name to a global data structure. You might come up with a function that looks something like this:

```
std::multiset<std::string> names;      // global data structure

void logAndAdd(const std::string& name)
{
  auto now =                           // get current time
    std::chrono::system_clock::now();

  log(now, "logAndAdd");               // make log entry

  names.emplace(name);                 // add name to global data
}                                      // structure; see Item 42
                                       // for info on emplace
```

This isn't unreasonable code, but it's not as efficient as it could be. Consider three potential calls:

```
std::string petName("Darla");

logAndAdd(petName);                    // pass lvalue std::string

logAndAdd(std::string("Persephone")); // pass rvalue std::string

logAndAdd("Patty Dog");                // pass string literal
```

In the first call, `logAndAdd`'s parameter `name` is bound to the variable `petName`. Within `logAndAdd`, `name` is ultimately passed to `names.emplace`. Because `name` is an lvalue, it is copied into `names`. There's no way to avoid that copy, because an lvalue (`petName`) was passed into `logAndAdd`.

In the second call, the parameter `name` is bound to an rvalue (the temporary `std::string` explicitly created from `"Persephone"`). `name` itself is an lvalue, so it's copied into `names`, but we recognize that, in principle, its value could be moved into `names`. In this call, we pay for a copy, but we should be able to get by with only a move.

In the third call, the parameter `name` is again bound to an rvalue, but this time it's to a temporary `std::string` that's implicitly created from `"Patty Dog"`. As in the second call, `name` is copied into `names`, but in this case, the argument originally passed to `logAndAdd` was a string literal. Had that string literal been passed directly to `emplace`, there would have been no need to create a temporary `std::string` at all. Instead, `emplace` would have used the string literal to create the `std::string` object directly inside the `std::multiset`. In this third call, then, we're paying to copy a `std::string`, yet there's really no reason to pay even for a move, much less a copy.

We can eliminate the inefficiencies in the second and third calls by rewriting `logAndAdd` to take a universal reference (see Item 24) and, in accord with Item 25, `std::forward`ing this reference to `emplace`. The results speak for themselves:

```cpp
template<typename T>
void logAndAdd(T&& name)
{
    auto now = std::chrono::system_clock::now();
    log(now, "logAndAdd");
    names.emplace(std::forward<T>(name));
}

std::string petName("Darla");              // as before

logAndAdd(petName);                        // as before, copy
                                           // lvalue into multiset

logAndAdd(std::string("Persephone"));      // move rvalue instead
                                           // of copying it

logAndAdd("Patty Dog");                    // create std::string
                                           // in multiset instead
                                           // of copying a temporary
                                           // std::string
```

Hurray, optimal efficiency!

Were this the end of the story, we could stop here and proudly retire, but I haven't told you that clients don't always have direct access to the names that `logAndAdd` requires. Some clients have only an index that logAndAdd uses to look up the corresponding name in a table. To support such clients, logAndAdd is overloaded:

```
std::string nameFromIdx(int idx);        // return name
                                         // corresponding to idx

void logAndAdd(int idx)                  // new overload
{
  auto now = std::chrono::system_clock::now();
  log(now, "logAndAdd");
  names.emplace(nameFromIdx(idx));
}
```

Resolution of calls to the two overloads works as expected:

```
std::string petName("Darla");            // as before

logAndAdd(petName);                      // as before, these
logAndAdd(std::string("Persephone"));    // calls all invoke
logAndAdd("Patty Dog");                  // the T&& overload

logAndAdd(22);                           // calls int overload
```

Actually, resolution works as expected only if you don't expect too much. Suppose a client has a short holding an index and passes that to logAndAdd:

```
short nameIdx;
...                                      // give nameIdx a value

logAndAdd(nameIdx);                      // error!
```

The comment on the last line isn't terribly illuminating, so let me explain what happens here.

There are two logAndAdd overloads. The one taking a universal reference can deduce T to be short&, thus yielding an exact match.[4] The overload with an int parameter can match the short argument only with a promotion. Per the normal overload resolution rules, an exact match beats a match with a promotion, so the universal reference overload is invoked.

Within that overload, the parameter name is bound to the short that's passed in. name is then std::forwarded to the emplace member function on names (a std::multiset<std::string>), which, in turn, dutifully forwards it to the std::string constructor. There is no constructor for std::string that takes a short, so the std::string constructor call inside the call to multiset::emplace

---

4 As Item 28 explains, the deduced type is short& instead of short, because nameIdx is an lvalue.

inside the call to logAndAdd fails. All because the universal reference overload was a better match for a short argument than an int.

Functions taking universal references are the greediest functions in C++. They instantiate to create exact matches for almost any type of argument. (The few kinds of arguments where this isn't the case are described in Item 30.) This is why combining overloading and universal references is almost always a bad idea: the universal reference overload vacuums up far more argument types than the developer doing the overloading generally expects.

An easy way to topple into this pit is to write a perfect forwarding constructor. A small modification to the logAndAdd example demonstrates the problem. Instead of writing a free function that can take either a std::string or an index that can be used to look up a std::string, imagine a class Person with constructors that do the same thing:

```
class Person {
public:
  template<typename T>
  explicit Person(T&& n)              // perfect forwarding ctor;
  : name(std::forward<T>(n)) {}       // initializes data member

  explicit Person(int idx)            // int ctor
  : name(nameFromIdx(idx)) {}

  …

private:
  std::string name;
};
```

As was the case with logAndAdd, passing an integral type other than int (e.g., std::size_t, short, long, etc.) will call the universal reference constructor overload instead of the int overload, and that will lead to compilation failures. The problem here is much worse, however, because there's more overloading present in Person than meets the eye. Item 17 explains that under the appropriate conditions, C++ will generate both copy and move constructors, and this is true even if the class contains a templatized constructor that could be instantiated to produce the signature of the copy or move constructor. If the copy and move constructors for Person are thus generated, Person will effectively look like this:

```
class Person {
public:
  template<typename T>                // perfect forwarding ctor
  explicit Person(T&& n)
  : name(std::forward<T>(n)) {}
```

```
    explicit Person(int idx);              // int ctor

    Person(const Person& rhs);             // copy ctor
                                           // (compiler-generated)

    Person(Person&& rhs);                  // move ctor
    ...                                    // (compiler-generated)

};
```

This leads to behavior that's intuitive only if you've spent so much time around compilers and compiler-writers, you've forgotten what it's like to be human:

```
Person p("Nancy");

auto cloneOfP(p);                          // create new Person from p;
                                           // this won't compile!
```

Here we're trying to create a Person from another Person, which seems like about as obvious a case for copy construction as one can get. (p's an lvalue, so we can banish any thoughts we might have about the "copying" being accomplished through a move operation.) But this code won't call the copy constructor. It will call the perfect-forwarding constructor. That function will then try to initialize Person's std::string data member with a Person object (p). std::string having no constructor taking a Person, your compilers will throw up their hands in exasperation, possibly punishing you with long and incomprehensible error messages as an expression of their displeasure.

"Why," you might wonder, "does the perfect-forwarding constructor get called instead of the copy constructor? We're initializing a Person with another Person!" Indeed we are, but compilers are sworn to uphold the rules of C++, and the rules of relevance here are the ones governing the resolution of calls to overloaded functions.

Compilers reason as follows. cloneOfP is being initialized with a non-const lvalue (p), and that means that the templatized constructor can be instantiated to take a non-const lvalue of type Person. After such instantiation, the Person class looks like this:

```
class Person {
public:
  explicit Person(Person& n)              // instantiated from
    : name(std::forward<Person&>(n)) {}   // perfect-forwarding
                                          // template

  explicit Person(int idx);               // as before
```

```
    Person(const Person& rhs);            // copy ctor
    …                                      // (compiler-generated)
};
```

In the statement,

```
auto cloneOfP(p);
```

p could be passed to either the copy constructor or the instantiated template. Calling the copy constructor would require adding const to p to match the copy constructor's parameter's type, but calling the instantiated template requires no such addition. The overload generated from the template is thus a better match, so compilers do what they're designed to do: generate a call to the better-matching function. "Copying" non-const lvalues of type Person is thus handled by the perfect-forwarding constructor, not the copy constructor.

If we change the example slightly so that the object to be copied is const, we hear an entirely different tune:

```
const Person cp("Nancy");      // object is now const

auto cloneOfP(cp);             // calls copy constructor!
```

Because the object to be copied is now const, it's an exact match for the parameter taken by the copy constructor. The templatized constructor can be instantiated to have the same signature,

```
class Person {
public:
    explicit Person(const Person& n);      // instantiated from
                                           // template

    Person(const Person& rhs);             // copy ctor
                                           // (compiler-generated)
    …
};
```

but this doesn't matter, because one of the overload-resolution rules in C++ is that in situations where a template instantiation and a non-template function (i.e., a "normal" function) are equally good matches for a function call, the normal function is preferred. The copy constructor (a normal function) thereby trumps an instantiated template with the same signature.

(If you're wondering why compilers generate a copy constructor when they could instantiate a templatized constructor to get the signature that the copy constructor would have, review Item 17.)

The interaction among perfect-forwarding constructors and compiler-generated copy and move operations develops even more wrinkles when inheritance enters the picture. In particular, the conventional implementations of derived class copy and move operations behave quite surprisingly. Here, take a look:

```
class SpecialPerson: public Person {
public:
  SpecialPerson(const SpecialPerson& rhs)   // copy ctor; calls
  : Person(rhs)                             // base class
  { … }                                     // forwarding ctor!

  SpecialPerson(SpecialPerson&& rhs)        // move ctor; calls
  : Person(std::move(rhs))                  // base class
  { … }                                     // forwarding ctor!
};
```

As the comments indicate, the derived class copy and move constructors don't call their base class's copy and move constructors, they call the base class's perfect-forwarding constructor! To understand why, note that the derived class functions are using arguments of type SpecialPerson to pass to their base class, then work through the template instantiation and overload-resolution consequences for the constructors in class Person. Ultimately, the code won't compile, because there's no std::string constructor taking a SpecialPerson.

I hope that by now I've convinced you that overloading on universal reference parameters is something you should avoid if at all possible. But if overloading on universal references is a bad idea, what do you do if you need a function that forwards most argument types, yet needs to treat some argument types in a special fashion? That egg can be unscrambled in a number of ways. So many, in fact, that I've devoted an entire Item to them. It's Item 27. The next Item. Keep reading, you'll bump right into it.

Things to Remember

- Overloading on universal references almost always leads to the universal reference overload being called more frequently than expected.
- Perfect-forwarding constructors are especially problematic, because they're typically better matches than copy constructors for non-const lvalues, and they can hijack derived class calls to base class copy and move constructors.

Item 27: Familiarize yourself with alternatives to overloading on universal references.

Item 26 explains that overloading on universal references can lead to a variety of problems, both for freestanding and for member functions (especially constructors). Yet it also gives examples where such overloading could be useful. If only it would behave the way we'd like! This Item explores ways to achieve the desired behavior, either through designs that avoid overloading on universal references or by employing them in ways that constrain the types of arguments they can match.

The discussion that follows builds on the examples introduced in Item 26. If you haven't read that Item recently, you'll want to review it before continuing.

Abandon overloading

The first example in Item 26, `logAndAdd`, is representative of the many functions that can avoid the drawbacks of overloading on universal references by simply using different names for the would-be overloads. The two `logAndAdd` overloads, for example, could be broken into `logAndAddName` and `logAndAddNameIdx`. Alas, this approach won't work for the second example we considered, the `Person` constructor, because constructor names are fixed by the language. Besides, who wants to give up overloading?

Pass by const T&

An alternative is to revert to C++98 and replace pass-by-universal-reference with pass-by-lvalue-reference-to-`const`. In fact, that's the first approach Item 26 considers (shown on page 177). The drawback is that the design isn't as efficient as we'd prefer. Knowing what we now know about the interaction of universal references and overloading, giving up some efficiency to keep things simple might be a more attractive trade-off than it initially appeared.

Pass by value

An approach that often allows you to dial up performance without any increase in complexity is to replace pass-by-reference parameters with, counterintuitively, pass by value. The design adheres to the advice in Item 41 to consider passing objects by value when you know you'll copy them, so I'll defer to that Item for a detailed discussion of how things work and how efficient they are. Here, I'll just show how the technique could be used in the `Person` example:

```
class Person {
public:
    explicit Person(std::string n) // replaces T&& ctor; see
```

```
  : name(std::move(n)) {}          // Item 41 for use of std::move

  explicit Person(int idx)         // as before
  : name(nameFromIdx(idx)) {}
  …

private:
  std::string name;
};
```

Because there's no `std::string` constructor taking only an integer, all `int` and `int`-like arguments to a `Person` constructor (e.g., `std::size_t`, `short`, `long`) get funneled to the `int` overload. Similarly, all arguments of type `std::string` (and things from which `std::string`s can be created, e.g., literals such as `"Ruth"`) get passed to the constructor taking a `std::string`. There are thus no surprises for callers. You could argue, I suppose, that some people might be surprised that using `0` or `NULL` to indicate a null pointer would invoke the `int` overload, but such people should be referred to Item 8 and required to read it repeatedly until the thought of using `0` or `NULL` as a null pointer makes them recoil.

Use Tag dispatch

Neither pass by lvalue-reference-to-`const` nor pass by value offers support for perfect forwarding. If the motivation for the use of a universal reference is perfect forwarding, we have to use a universal reference; there's no other choice. Yet we don't want to abandon overloading. So if we don't give up overloading and we don't give up universal references, how can we avoid overloading on universal references?

It's actually not that hard. Calls to overloaded functions are resolved by looking at all the parameters of all the overloads as well as all the arguments at the call site, then choosing the function with the best overall match—taking into account all parameter/argument combinations. A universal reference parameter generally provides an exact match for whatever's passed in, but if the universal reference is part of a parameter list containing other parameters that are *not* universal references, sufficiently poor matches on the non-universal reference parameters can knock an overload with a universal reference out of the running. That's the basis behind the *tag dispatch* approach, and an example will make the foregoing description easier to understand.

We'll apply tag dispatch to the `logAndAdd` example on page 178. Here's the code for that example, lest you get sidetracked looking it up:

```
std::multiset<std::string> names;     // global data structure

template<typename T>                   // make log entry and add
```

```
void logAndAdd(T&& name)                  // name to data structure
{
  auto now = std::chrono::system_clock::now();
  log(now, "logAndAdd");
  names.emplace(std::forward<T>(name));
}
```

By itself, this function works fine, but were we to introduce the overload taking an int that's used to look up objects by index, we'd be back in the troubled land of Item 26. The goal of this Item is to avoid that. Rather than adding the overload, we'll reimplement logAndAdd to delegate to two other functions, one for integral values and one for everything else. logAndAdd itself will accept all argument types, both integral and non-integral.

The two functions doing the real work will be named logAndAddImpl, i.e., we'll use overloading. One of the functions will take a universal reference. So we'll have both overloading and universal references. But each function will also take a second parameter, one that indicates whether the argument being passed is integral. This second parameter is what will prevent us from tumbling into the morass described in Item 26, because we'll arrange it so that the second parameter will be the factor that determines which overload is selected.

Yes, I know, "Blah, blah, blah. Stop talking and show me the code!" No problem. Here's an almost-correct version of the updated logAndAdd:

```
template<typename T>
void logAndAdd(T&& name)
{
  logAndAddImpl(std::forward<T>(name),
                std::is_integral<T>());      // not quite correct
}
```

This function forwards its parameter to logAndAddImpl, but it also passes an argument indicating whether that parameter's type (T) is integral. At least, that's what it's supposed to do. For integral arguments that are rvalues, it's also what it does. But, as Item 28 explains, if an lvalue argument is passed to the universal reference name, the type deduced for T will be an lvalue reference. So if an lvalue of type int is passed to logAndAdd, T will be deduced to be int&. That's not an integral type, because references aren't integral types. That means that std::is_integral<T> will be false for any lvalue argument, even if the argument really does represent an integral value.

Recognizing the problem is tantamount to solving it, because the ever-handy Standard C++ Library has a type trait (see Item 9), std::remove_reference, that does both what its name suggests and what we need: remove any reference qualifiers from a type. The proper way to write logAndAdd is therefore:

```
template<typename T>
void logAndAdd(T&& name)
{
  logAndAddImpl(
    std::forward<T>(name),
    std::is_integral<typename std::remove_reference<T>::type>()
  );
}
```

This does the trick. (In C++14, you can save a few keystrokes by using `std::remove_reference_t<T>` in place of the highlighted text. For details, see Item 9.)

With that taken care of, we can shift our attention to the function being called, `logAndAddImpl`. There are two overloads, and the first is applicable only to non-integral types (i.e., to types where `std::is_integral<typename std::remove_reference<T>::type>` is false):

```
template<typename T>                            // non-integral
void logAndAddImpl(T&& name, std::false_type)   // argument:
{                                               // add it to
  auto now = std::chrono::system_clock::now();  // global data
  log(now, "logAndAdd");                        // structure
  names.emplace(std::forward<T>(name));
}
```

This is straightforward code, once you understand the mechanics behind the highlighted parameter. Conceptually, `logAndAdd` passes a boolean to `logAndAddImpl` indicating whether an integral type was passed to `logAndAdd`, but `true` and `false` are *runtime* values, and we need to use overload resolution—a *compile-time* phenomenon—to choose the correct `logAndAddImpl` overload. That means we need a *type* that corresponds to `true` and a different type that corresponds to `false`. This need is common enough that the Standard Library provides what is required under the names `std::true_type` and `std::false_type`. The argument passed to `logAndAddImpl` by `logAndAdd` is an object of a type that inherits from `std::true_type` if T is integral and from `std::false_type` if T is not integral. The net result is that this `logAndAddImpl` overload is a viable candidate for the call in `logAndAdd` only if T is not an integral type.

The second overload covers the opposite case: when T is an integral type. In that event, `logAndAddImpl` simply finds the name corresponding to the passed-in index and passes that name back to `logAndAdd`:

```
std::string nameFromIdx(int idx);               // as in Item 26
```

```
void logAndAddImpl(int idx, std::true_type)    // integral
{                                              // argument: look
  logAndAdd(nameFromIdx(idx));                 // up name and
}                                              // call logAndAdd
                                               // with it
```

By having `logAndAddImpl` for an index look up the corresponding name and pass it to `logAndAdd` (from where it will be `std::forwarded` to the other `logAndAddImpl` overload), we avoid the need to put the logging code in both `logAndAddImpl` overloads.

In this design, the types `std::true_type` and `std::false_type` are "tags" whose only purpose is to force overload resolution to go the way we want. Notice that we don't even name those parameters. They serve no purpose at runtime, and in fact we hope that compilers will recognize that the tag parameters are unused and will optimize them out of the program's execution image. (Some compilers do, at least some of the time.) The call to the overloaded implementation functions inside `logAndAdd` "dispatches" the work to the correct overload by causing the proper tag object to be created. Hence the name for this design: *tag dispatch*. It's a standard building block of template metaprogramming, and the more you look at code inside contemporary C++ libraries, the more often you'll encounter it.

For our purposes, what's important about tag dispatch is less how it works and more how it permits us to combine universal references and overloading without the problems described in Item 26. The dispatching function—`logAndAdd`—takes an unconstrained universal reference parameter, but this function is not overloaded. The implementation functions—`logAndAddImpl`—are overloaded, and one takes a universal reference parameter, but resolution of calls to these functions depends not just on the universal reference parameter, but also on the tag parameter, and the tag values are designed so that no more than one overload will be a viable match. As a result, it's the tag that determines which overload gets called. The fact that the universal reference parameter will always generate an exact match for its argument is immaterial.

Constraining templates that take universal references

A keystone of tag dispatch is the existence of a single (unoverloaded) function as the client API. This single function dispatches the work to be done to the implementation functions. Creating an unoverloaded dispatch function is usually easy, but the second problem case Item 26 considers, that of a perfect-forwarding constructor for the `Person` class (shown on page 180), is an exception. Compilers may generate copy and move constructors themselves, so even if you write only one constructor and use tag dispatch within it, some constructor calls may be handled by compiler-generated functions that bypass the tag dispatch system.

In truth, the real problem is not that the compiler-generated functions sometimes bypass the tag dispatch design, it's that they don't *always* pass it by. You virtually always want the copy constructor for a class to handle requests to copy lvalues of that type, but, as Item 26 demonstrates, providing a constructor taking a universal reference causes the universal reference constructor (rather than the copy constructor) to be called when copying non-`const` lvalues. That Item also explains that when a base class declares a perfect-forwarding constructor, that constructor will typically be called when derived classes implement their copy and move constructors in the conventional fashion, even though the correct behavior is for the base class's copy and move constructors to be invoked.

For situations like these, where an overloaded function taking a universal reference is greedier than you want, yet not greedy enough to act as a single dispatch function, tag dispatch is not the droid you're looking for. You need a different technique, one that lets you rachet down the conditions under which the function template that the universal reference is part of is permitted to be employed. What you need, my friend, is `std::enable_if`.

`std::enable_if` gives you a way to force compilers to behave as if a particular template didn't exist. Such templates are said to be *disabled*. By default, all templates are *enabled*, but a template using `std::enable_if` is enabled only if the condition specified by `std::enable_if` is satisfied. In our case, we'd like to enable the `Person` perfect-forwarding constructor only if the type being passed isn't `Person`. If the type being passed is `Person`, we want to disable the perfect-forwarding constructor (i.e., cause compilers to ignore it), because that will cause the class's copy or move constructor to handle the call, which is what we want when a `Person` object is initialized with another `Person`.

The way to express that idea isn't particularly difficult, but the syntax is off-putting, especially if you've never seen it before, so I'll ease you into it. There's some boilerplate that goes around the condition part of `std::enable_if`, so we'll start with that. Here's the declaration for the perfect-forwarding constructor in `Person`, showing only as much of the `std::enable_if` as is required simply to use it. I'm showing only the declaration for this constructor, because the use of `std::enable_if` has no effect on the function's implementation. The implementation remains the same as in Item 26.

```
class Person {
public:
  template<typename T,
           typename = typename std::enable_if<condition>::type>
  explicit Person(T&& n);

  …
```

```
};
```

To understand exactly what's going on in the highlighted text, I must regretfully suggest that you consult other sources, because the details take a while to explain, and there's just not enough space for it in this book. (During your research, look into "SFINAE" as well as `std::enable_if`, because SFINAE is the technology that makes `std::enable_if` work.) Here, I want to focus on expression of the condition that will control whether this constructor is enabled.

The condition we want to specify is that T isn't `Person`, i.e., that the templatized constructor should be enabled only if T is a type other than `Person`. Thanks to a type trait that determines whether two types are the same (`std::is_same`), it would seem that the condition we want is `!std::is_same<Person, T>::value`. (Notice the "!" at the beginning of the expression. We want for `Person` and T to *not* be the same.) This is close to what we need, but it's not quite correct, because, as Item 28 explains, the type deduced for a universal reference initialized with an lvalue is always an lvalue reference. That means that for code like this,

```
Person p("Nancy");

auto cloneOfP(p);              // initialize from lvalue
```

the type T in the universal constructor will be deduced to be `Person&`. The types `Person` and `Person&` are not the same, and the result of `std::is_same` will reflect that: `std::is_same<Person, Person&>::value` is false.

If we think more precisely about what we mean when we say that the templatized constructor in `Person` should be enabled only if T isn't `Person`, we'll realize that when we're looking at T, we want to ignore

- **Whether it's a reference.** For the purpose of determining whether the universal reference constructor should be enabled, the types `Person`, `Person&`, and `Person&&` are all the same as `Person`.

- **Whether it's const or volatile.** As far as we're concerned, a `const Person` and a `volatile Person` and a `const volatile Person` are all the same as a `Person`.

This means we need a way to strip any references, `const`s, and `volatile`s from T before checking to see if that type is the same as `Person`. Once again, the Standard Library gives us what we need in the form of a type trait. That trait is `std::decay`. `std::decay<T>::type` is the same as T, except that references and *cv-qualifiers* (i.e., `const` or `volatile` qualifiers) are removed. (I'm fudging the truth here, because `std::decay`, as its name suggests, also turns array and function types into pointers (see Item 1), but for purposes of this discussion, `std::decay` behaves as I've described.) The condition we want to control whether our constructor is enabled, then, is

```
!std::is_same<Person, typename std::decay<T>::type>::value
```

i.e., `Person` is not the same type as T, ignoring any references or cv-qualifiers. (As Item 9 explains, the "`typename`" in front of `std::decay` is required, because the type `std::decay<T>::type` depends on the template parameter T.)

Inserting this condition into the `std::enable_if` boilerplate above, plus formatting the result to make it easier to see how the pieces fit together, yields this declaration for `Person`'s perfect-forwarding constructor:

```
class Person {
public:
  template<
    typename T,
    typename = typename std::enable_if<
                 !std::is_same<Person,
                                typename std::decay<T>::type
                 >::value
               >::type
  >
  explicit Person(T&& n);

  ...

};
```

If you've never seen anything like this before, count your blessings. There's a reason I saved this design for last. When you can use one of the other mechanisms to avoid mixing universal references and overloading (and you almost always can), you should. Still, once you get used to the functional syntax and the proliferation of angle brackets, it's not that bad. Furthermore, this gives you the behavior you've been striving for. Given the declaration above, constructing a `Person` from another `Person`—lvalue or rvalue, `const` or non-`const`, `volatile` or non-`volatile`—will never invoke the constructor taking a universal reference.

Success, right? We're done!

Um, no. Belay that celebration. There's still one loose end from Item 26 that continues to flap about. We need to tie it down.

Suppose a class derived from `Person` implements the copy and move operations in the conventional manner:

```
class SpecialPerson: public Person {
public:
  SpecialPerson(const SpecialPerson& rhs)   // copy ctor; calls
  : Person(rhs)                             // base class
  { … }                                     // forwarding ctor!

  SpecialPerson(SpecialPerson&& rhs)        // move ctor; calls
  : Person(std::move(rhs))                  // base class
  { … }                                     // forwarding ctor!

  …
};
```

This is the same code I showed on page 183, including the comments, which, alas, remain accurate. When we copy or move a SpecialPerson object, we expect to copy or move its base class parts using the base class's copy and move constructors, but in these functions, we're passing SpecialPerson objects to the base class's constructors, and because SpecialPerson isn't the same as Person (not even after application of std::decay), the universal reference constructor in the base class is enabled, and it happily instantiates to perform an exact match for a SpecialPerson argument. This exact match is better than the derived-to-base conversions that would be necessary to bind the SpecialPerson objects to the Person parameters in Person's copy and move constructors, so with the code we have now, copying and moving Special-Person objects would use the Person perfect-forwarding constructor to copy or move their base class parts! It's déjà Item 26 all over again.

The derived class is just following the normal rules for implementing derived class copy and move constructors, so the fix for this problem is in the base class and, in particular, in the condition that controls whether Person's universal reference constructor is enabled. We now realize that we don't want to enable the templatized constructor for any argument type other than Person, we want to enable it for any argument type other than Person *or a type derived from Person*. Pesky inheritance!

You should not be surprised to hear that among the standard type traits is one that determines whether one type is derived from another. It's called std::is_base_of. std::is_base_of<T1, T2>::value is true if T2 is derived from T1. User-defined types are considered to be derived from themselves, so std::is_base_of<T, T>::value is true if T is a user-defined type. (When T is a built-in type, std::is_base_of<T, T>::value is false.) This is handy, because we want to revise our condition controlling Person's perfect-forwarding constructor such that the constructor is enabled only if the type T, after stripping it of references and cv-qualifiers, is neither Person nor a class derived from Person. Using std::is_base_of instead of std::is_same gives us what we need:

```
class Person {
public:
  template<
    typename T,
    typename = typename std::enable_if<
                 !std::is_base_of<Person,
                                  typename std::decay<T>::type
                 >::value
             >::type
  >
  explicit Person(T&& n);

  …

};
```

Now we're finally done. Provided we're writing the code in C++11, that is. If we're using C++14, this code will still work, but we can employ alias templates for `std::enable_if` and `std::decay` to get rid of the "`typename`" and "`::type`" cruft, thus yielding this somewhat more palatable code:

```
class Person {                                           // C++14
public:
  template<
    typename T,
    typename = std::enable_if_t<                // less code here
                 !std::is_base_of<Person,
                                  std::decay_t<T>   // and here
                 >::value
             >                                       // and here
  >
  explicit Person(T&& n);

  …

};
```

Okay, I admit it: I lied. We're still not done. But we're close. Tantalizingly close. Honest.

We've seen how to use `std::enable_if` to selectively disable `Person`'s universal reference constructor for argument types we want to have handled by the class's copy and move constructors, but we haven't yet seen how to apply it to distinguish integral and non-integral arguments. That was, after all, our original goal; the constructor ambiguity problem was just something we got dragged into along the way.

All we need to do—and I really do mean that this is everything—is (1) add a `Person` constructor overload to handle integral arguments and (2) further constrain the templatized constructor so that it's disabled for such arguments. Pour these ingredients into the pot with everything else we've discussed, simmer over a low flame, and savor the aroma of success:

```cpp
class Person {
public:
  template<
    typename T,
    typename = std::enable_if_t<
      !std::is_base_of<Person, std::decay_t<T>>::value
      &&
      !std::is_integral<std::remove_reference_t<T>>::value
    >
  >
  explicit Person(T&& n)          // ctor for std::strings and
  : name(std::forward<T>(n))      // args convertible to
  { ... }                         // std::strings

  explicit Person(int idx)        // ctor for integral args
  : name(nameFromIdx(idx))
  { ... }

  ...                             // copy and move ctors, etc.

private:
  std::string name;
};
```

Voilà! A thing of beauty! Well, okay, the beauty is perhaps most pronounced for those with something of a template metaprogramming fetish, but the fact remains that this approach not only gets the job done, it does it with unique aplomb. Because it uses perfect forwarding, it offers maximal efficiency, and because it controls the combination of universal references and overloading rather than forbidding it, this technique can be applied in circumstances (such as constructors) where overloading is unavoidable.

Trade-offs

The first three techniques considered in this Item—abandoning overloading, passing by `const T&`, and passing by value—specify a type for each parameter in the function(s) to be called. The last two techniques—tag dispatch and constraining template eligibility—use perfect forwarding, hence don't specify types for the parameters. This fundamental decision—to specify a type or not—has consequences.

As a rule, perfect forwarding is more efficient, because it avoids the creation of temporary objects solely for the purpose of conforming to the type of a parameter declaration. In the case of the `Person` constructor, perfect forwarding permits a string literal such as `"Nancy"` to be forwarded to the constructor for the `std::string` inside `Person`, whereas techniques not using perfect forwarding must create a temporary `std::string` object from the string literal to satisfy the parameter specification for the `Person` constructor.

But perfect forwarding has drawbacks. One is that some kinds of arguments can't be perfect-forwarded, even though they can be passed to functions taking specific types. Item 30 explores these perfect forwarding failure cases.

A second issue is the comprehensibility of error messages when clients pass invalid arguments. Suppose, for example, a client creating a `Person` object passes a string literal made up of `char16_t`s (a type introduced in C++11 to represent 16-bit characters) instead of `char`s (which is what a `std::string` consists of):

```
Person p(u"Konrad Zuse");    // "Konrad Zuse" consists of
                             // characters of type const char16_t
```

With the first three approaches examined in this Item, compilers will see that the available constructors take either `int` or `std::string`, and they'll produce a more or less straightforward error message explaining that there's no conversion from `const char16_t[12]` to `int` or `std::string`.

With an approach based on perfect forwarding, however, the array of `const char16_t`s gets bound to the constructor's parameter without complaint. From there it's forwarded to the constructor of `Person`'s `std::string` data member, and it's only at that point that the mismatch between what the caller passed in (a `const char16_t` array) and what's required (any type acceptable to the `std::string` constructor) is discovered. The resulting error message is likely to be, er, impressive. With one of the compilers I use, it's more than 160 lines long.

In this example, the universal reference is forwarded only once (from the `Person` constructor to the `std::string` constructor), but the more complex the system, the more likely that a universal reference is forwarded through several layers of function calls before finally arriving at a site that determines whether the argument type(s) are acceptable. The more times the universal reference is forwarded, the more baffling the error message may be when something goes wrong. Many developers find that this issue alone is grounds to reserve universal reference parameters for interfaces where performance is a foremost concern.

In the case of `Person`, we know that the forwarding function's universal reference parameter is supposed to be an initializer for a `std::string`, so we can use a

static_assert to verify that it can play that role. The std::is_constructible
type trait performs a compile-time test to determine whether an object of one type
can be constructed from an object (or set of objects) of a different type (or set of
types), so the assertion is easy to write:

```
class Person {
public:
  template<                                        // as before
    typename T,
    typename = std::enable_if_t<
      !std::is_base_of<Person, std::decay_t<T>>::value
      &&
      !std::is_integral<std::remove_reference_t<T>>::value
    >
  >
  explicit Person(T&& n)
  : name(std::forward<T>(n))
  {
    // assert that a std::string can be created from a T object
    static_assert(
      std::is_constructible<std::string, T>::value,
      "Parameter n can't be used to construct a std::string"
    );

    …                                        // the usual ctor work goes here

  }

  …                                        // remainder of Person class (as before)

};
```

This causes the specified error message to be produced if client code tries to create a
Person from a type that can't be used to construct a std::string. Unfortunately, in
this example the static_assert is in the body of the constructor, but the forwarding code, being part of the member initialization list, precedes it. With the compilers
I use, the result is that the nice, readable message arising from the static_assert
appears only *after* the usual error messages (up to 160-plus lines of them) have been
emitted.

- Alternatives to the combination of universal references and overloading include the use of distinct function names, passing parameters by lvalue-reference-to-`const`, passing parameters by value, and using tag dispatch.

- Constraining templates via `std::enable_if` permits the use of universal references and overloading together, but it controls the conditions under which compilers may use the universal reference overloads.

- Universal reference parameters often have efficiency advantages, but they typically have usability disadvantages.

Item 28: Understand reference collapsing.

Item 23 remarks that when an argument is passed to a template function, the type deduced for the template parameter encodes whether the argument is an lvalue or an rvalue. The Item fails to mention that this happens only when the argument is used to initialize a parameter that's a universal reference, but there's a good reason for the omission: universal references aren't introduced until Item 24. Together, these observations about universal references and lvalue/rvalue encoding mean that for this template,

```
template<typename T>
void func(T&& param);
```

the deduced template parameter T will encode whether the argument passed to `param` was an lvalue or an rvalue.

The encoding mechanism is simple. When an lvalue is passed as an argument, T is deduced to be an lvalue reference. When an rvalue is passed, T is deduced to be a non-reference. (Note the asymmetry: lvalues are encoded as lvalue references, but rvalues are encoded as *non-references*.) Hence:

```
Widget widgetFactory();      // function returning rvalue

Widget w;                    // a variable (an lvalue)

func(w);                     // call func with lvalue; T deduced
                             // to be Widget&

func(widgetFactory());       // call func with rvalue; T deduced
                             // to be Widget
```

In both calls to `func`, a `Widget` is passed, yet because one `Widget` is an lvalue and one is an rvalue, different types are deduced for the template parameter T. This, as we shall soon see, is what determines whether universal references become rvalue references or lvalue references, and it's also the underlying mechanism through which `std::forward` does its work.

Before we can look more closely at `std::forward` and universal references, we must note that references to references are illegal in C++. Should you try to declare one, your compilers will reprimand you:

```
int x;
…
auto& & rx = x;    // error! can't declare reference to reference
```

But consider what happens when an lvalue is passed to a function template taking a universal reference:

```
template<typename T>
void func(T&& param);    // as before

func(w);                         // invoke func with lvalue;
                                 // T deduced as Widget&
```

If we take the type deduced for T (i.e., `Widget&`) and use it to instantiate the template, we get this:

```
void func(Widget& && param);
```

A reference to a reference! And yet compilers issue no protest. We know from Item 24 that because the universal reference `param` is being initialized with an lvalue, `param`'s type is supposed to be an lvalue reference, but how does the compiler get from the result of taking the deduced type for T and substituting it into the template to the following, which is the ultimate function signature?

```
void func(Widget& param);
```

The answer is *reference collapsing*. Yes, *you* are forbidden from declaring references to references, but *compilers* may produce them in particular contexts, template instantiation being among them. When compilers generate references to references, reference collapsing dictates what happens next.

There are two kinds of references (lvalue and rvalue), so there are four possible reference-reference combinations (lvalue to lvalue, lvalue to rvalue, rvalue to lvalue, and rvalue to rvalue). If a reference to a reference arises in a context where this is permitted (e.g., during template instantiation), the references *collapse* to a single reference according to this rule:

> If either reference is an lvalue reference, the result is an lvalue reference. Otherwise (i.e., if both are rvalue references) the result is an rvalue reference.

In our example above, substitution of the deduced type `Widget&` into the template `func` yields an rvalue reference to an lvalue reference, and the reference-collapsing rule tells us that the result is an lvalue reference.

Reference collapsing is a key part of what makes `std::forward` work. As explained in Item 25, `std::forward` is applied to universal reference parameters, so a common use case looks like this:

```
template<typename T>
void f(T&& fParam)
{
    ...                                      // do some work

    someFunc(std::forward<T>(fParam));   // forward fParam to
}                                        // someFunc
```

Because `fParam` is a universal reference, we know that the type parameter `T` will encode whether the argument passed to `f` (i.e., the expression used to initialize `fParam`) was an lvalue or an rvalue. `std::forward`'s job is to cast `fParam` (an lvalue) to an rvalue if and only if `T` encodes that the argument passed to `f` was an rvalue, i.e., if `T` is a non-reference type.

Here's how `std::forward` can be implemented to do that:

```
template<typename T>                          // in
T&& forward(typename                          // namespace
            remove_reference<T>::type& param)  // std
{
    return static_cast<T&&>(param);
}
```

This isn't quite Standards-conformant (I've omitted a few interface details), but the differences are irrelevant for the purpose of understanding how `std::forward` behaves.

Suppose that the argument passed to `f` is an lvalue of type `Widget`. `T` will be deduced as `Widget&`, and the call to `std::forward` will instantiate as `std::forward<Widget&>`. Plugging `Widget&` into the `std::forward` implementation yields this:

```
Widget& && forward(typename
                   remove_reference<Widget&>::type& param)
{ return static_cast<Widget& &&>(param); }
```

The type trait `std::remove_reference<Widget&>::type` yields `Widget` (see Item 9), so `std::forward` becomes:

```
Widget& && forward(Widget& param)
{ return static_cast<Widget& &&>(param); }
```

Reference collapsing is also applied to the return type and the cast, and the result is the final version of `std::forward` for the call:

```
Widget& forward(Widget& param)                    // still in
{ return static_cast<Widget&>(param); }           // namespace std
```

As you can see, when an lvalue argument is passed to the function template f, `std::forward` is instantiated to take and return an lvalue reference. The cast inside `std::forward` does nothing, because `param`'s type is already `Widget&`, so casting it to `Widget&` has no effect. An lvalue argument passed to `std::forward` will thus return an lvalue reference. By definition, lvalue references are lvalues, so passing an lvalue to `std::forward` causes an lvalue to be returned, just like it's supposed to.

Now suppose that the argument passed to f is an rvalue of type `Widget`. In this case, the deduced type for f's type parameter T will simply be `Widget`. The call inside f to `std::forward` will thus be to `std::forward<Widget>`. Substituting `Widget` for T in the `std::forward` implementation gives this:

```
Widget&& forward(typename
                 remove_reference<Widget>::type& param)
{ return static_cast<Widget&&>(param); }
```

Applying `std::remove_reference` to the non-reference type `Widget` yields the same type it started with (`Widget`), so `std::forward` becomes this:

```
Widget&& forward(Widget& param)
{ return static_cast<Widget&&>(param); }
```

There are no references to references here, so there's no reference collapsing, and this is the final instantiated version of `std::forward` for the call.

Rvalue references returned from functions are defined to be rvalues, so in this case, `std::forward` will turn f's parameter `fParam` (an lvalue) into an rvalue. The end result is that an rvalue argument passed to f will be forwarded to `someFunc` as an rvalue, which is precisely what is supposed to happen.

In C++14, the existence of `std::remove_reference_t` makes it possible to implement `std::forward` a bit more concisely:

```
template<typename T>                        // C++14; still in
T&& forward(remove_reference_t<T>& param)   // namespace std
{
    return static_cast<T&&>(param);
}
```

Reference collapsing occurs in four contexts. The first and most common is template instantiation. The second is type generation for `auto` variables. The details are essentially the same as for templates, because type deduction for `auto` variables is essentially the same as type deduction for templates (see Item 2). Consider again this example from earlier in the Item:

```
template<typename T>
void func(T&& param);

Widget widgetFactory();     // function returning rvalue

Widget w;                   // a variable (an lvalue)

func(w);                    // call func with lvalue; T deduced
                            // to be Widget&

func(widgetFactory());      // call func with rvalue; T deduced
                            // to be Widget
```

This can be mimicked in `auto` form. The declaration

```
auto&& w1 = w;
```

initializes `w1` with an lvalue, thus deducing the type `Widget&` for `auto`. Plugging `Widget&` in for `auto` in the declaration for `w1` yields this reference-to-reference code,

```
Widget& && w1 = w;
```

which, after reference collapsing, becomes

```
Widget& w1 = w;
```

As a result, `w1` is an lvalue reference.

On the other hand, this declaration,

```
auto&& w2 = widgetFactory();
```

initializes `w2` with an rvalue, causing the non-reference type `Widget` to be deduced for `auto`. Substituting `Widget` for `auto` gives us this:

```
Widget&& w2 = widgetFactory();
```

There are no references to references here, so we're done; w2 is an rvalue reference.

We're now in a position to truly understand the universal references introduced in Item 24. A universal reference isn't a new kind of reference, it's actually an rvalue reference in a context where two conditions are satisfied:

- **Type deduction distinguishes lvalues from rvalues.** Lvalues of type T are deduced to have type T&, while rvalues of type T yield T as their deduced type.
- **Reference collapsing occurs.**

The concept of universal references is useful, because it frees you from having to recognize the existence of reference collapsing contexts, to mentally deduce different types for lvalues and rvalues, and to apply the reference collapsing rule after mentally substituting the deduced types into the contexts in which they occur.

I said there were four such contexts, but we've discussed only two: template instantiation and auto type generation. The third is the generation and use of typedefs and alias declarations (see Item 9). If, during creation or evaluation of a typedef, references to references arise, reference collapsing intervenes to eliminate them. For example, suppose we have a Widget class template with an embedded typedef for an rvalue reference type,

```
template<typename T>
class Widget {
public:
  typedef T&& RvalueRefToT;
  …
};
```

and suppose we instantiate Widget with an lvalue reference type:

```
Widget<int&> w;
```

Substituting int& for T in the Widget template gives us the following typedef:

```
typedef int& && RvalueRefToT;
```

Reference collapsing reduces it to this,

```
typedef int& RvalueRefToT;
```

which makes clear that the name we chose for the typedef is perhaps not as descriptive as we'd hoped: *RvalueRefToT* is a typedef for an *lvalue reference* when Widget is instantiated with an lvalue reference type.

The final context in which reference collapsing takes place is uses of `decltype`. If, during analysis of a type involving `decltype`, a reference to a reference arises, reference collapsing will kick in to eliminate it. (For information about `decltype`, see Item 3.)

> ### Things to Remember
>
> - Reference collapsing occurs in four contexts: template instantiation, `auto` type generation, creation and use of `typedefs` and alias declarations, and `decltype`.
> - When compilers generate a reference to a reference in a reference collapsing context, the result becomes a single reference. If either of the original references is an lvalue reference, the result is an lvalue reference. Otherwise it's an rvalue reference.
> - Universal references are rvalue references in contexts where type deduction distinguishes lvalues from rvalues and where reference collapsing occurs.

Item 29: Assume that move operations are not present, not cheap, and not used.

Move semantics is arguably *the* premier feature of C++11. "Moving containers is now as cheap as copying pointers!" you're likely to hear, and "Copying temporary objects is now so efficient, coding to avoid it is tantamount to premature optimization!" Such sentiments are easy to understand. Move semantics is truly an important feature. It doesn't just allow compilers to replace expensive copy operations with comparatively cheap moves, it actually *requires* that they do so (when the proper conditions are fulfilled). Take your C++98 code base, recompile with a C++11-conformant compiler and Standard Library, and—*shazam!*—your software runs faster.

Move semantics can really pull that off, and that grants the feature an aura worthy of legend. Legends, however, are generally the result of exaggeration. The purpose of this Item is to keep your expectations grounded.

Let's begin with the observation that many types fail to support move semantics. The entire C++98 Standard Library was overhauled for C++11 to add move operations for types where moving could be implemented faster than copying, and the implementation of the library components was revised to take advantage of these operations, but chances are that you're working with a code base that has not been completely revised to take advantage of C++11. For types in your applications (or in the libraries you use) where no modifications for C++11 have been made, the existence of move support in your compilers is likely to do you little good. True, C++11 is willing to generate move operations for classes that lack them, but that happens only for classes declaring no copy operations, move operations, or destructors (see Item 17). Data members or base classes of types that have disabled moving (e.g., by deleting the move operations—see Item 11) will also suppress compiler-generated move operations. For types without explicit support for moving and that don't qualify for compiler-generated move operations, there is no reason to expect C++11 to deliver any kind of performance improvement over C++98.

Even types with explicit move support may not benefit as much as you'd hope. All containers in the standard C++11 library support moving, for example, but it would be a mistake to assume that moving all containers is cheap. For some containers, this is because there's no truly cheap way to move their contents. For others, it's because the truly cheap move operations the containers offer come with caveats the container elements can't satisfy.

Consider `std::array`, a new container in C++11. `std::array` is essentially a built-in array with an STL interface. This is fundamentally different from the other standard containers, each of which stores its contents on the heap. Objects of such container types hold (as data members), conceptually, only a pointer to the heap memory storing the contents of the container. (The reality is more complex, but for purposes of this analysis, the differences are not important.) The existence of this pointer makes it possible to move the contents of an entire container in constant time: just copy the pointer to the container's contents from the source container to the target, and set the source's pointer to null:

```
std::vector<Widget> vw1;

// put data into vw1
```

```
...
```

```
// move vw1 into vw2. Runs in
// constant time. Only ptrs
// in vw1 and vw2 are modified
auto vw2 = std::move(vw1);
```

`std::array` objects lack such a pointer, because the data for a `std::array`'s contents are stored directly in the `std::array` object:

```
std::array<Widget, 10000> aw1;

// put data into aw1
```

aw1

Widgets

```
...
```

```
// move aw1 into aw2. Runs in
// linear time. All elements in
// aw1 are moved into aw2
auto aw2 = std::move(aw1);
```

aw1

Widgets (moved from)

aw2

Widgets (moved to)

Note that the elements in aw1 are *moved* into aw2. Assuming that Widget is a type where moving is faster than copying, moving a std::array of Widget will be faster than copying the same std::array. So std::array certainly offers move support. Yet both moving and copying a std::array have linear-time computational complexity, because each element in the container must be copied or moved. This is far from the "moving a container is now as cheap as assigning a couple of pointers" claim that one sometimes hears.

On the other hand, std::string offers constant-time moves and linear-time copies. That makes it sound like moving is faster than copying, but that may not be the case. Many string implementations employ the *small string optimization* (SSO). With the SSO, "small" strings (e.g., those with a capacity of no more than 15 characters) are stored in a buffer within the std::string object; no heap-allocated storage is used. Moving small strings using an SSO-based implementation is no faster than copying them, because the copy-only-a-pointer trick that generally underlies the performance advantage of moves over copies isn't applicable.

The motivation for the SSO is extensive evidence that short strings are the norm for many applications. Using an internal buffer to store the contents of such strings eliminates the need to dynamically allocate memory for them, and that's typically an efficiency win. An implication of the win, however, is that moves are no faster than copies, though one could just as well take a glass-half-full approach and say that for such strings, copying is no slower than moving.

Even for types supporting speedy move operations, some seemingly sure-fire move situations can end up making copies. Item 14 explains that some container operations in the Standard Library offer the strong exception safety guarantee and that to ensure that legacy C++98 code dependent on that guarantee isn't broken when upgrading to C++11, the underlying copy operations may be replaced with move operations only if the move operations are known to not throw. A consequence is that even if a type offers move operations that are more efficient than the corresponding copy operations, and even if, at a particular point in the code, a move operation would generally be appropriate (e.g., if the source object is an rvalue), compilers might still be forced to invoke a copy operation because the corresponding move operation isn't declared noexcept.

There are thus several scenarios in which C++11's move semantics do you no good:

- **No move operations:** The object to be moved from fails to offer move operations. The move request therefore becomes a copy request.

- **Move not faster:** The object to be moved from has move operations that are no faster than its copy operations.

- **Move not usable:** The context in which the moving would take place requires a move operation that emits no exceptions, but that operation isn't declared noexcept.

It's worth mentioning, too, another scenario where move semantics offers no efficiency gain:

- **Source object is lvalue:** With very few exceptions (see e.g., Item 25) only rvalues may be used as the source of a move operation.

But the title of this Item is to *assume* that move operations are not present, not cheap, and not used. This is typically the case in generic code, e.g., when writing templates, because you don't know all the types you're working with. In such circumstances, you must be as conservative about copying objects as you were in C++98—before move semantics existed. This is also the case for "unstable" code, i.e., code where the characteristics of the types being used are subject to relatively frequent modification.

Often, however, you know the types your code uses, and you can rely on their characteristics not changing (e.g., whether they support inexpensive move operations). When that's the case, you don't need to make assumptions. You can simply look up the move support details for the types you're using. If those types offer cheap move operations, and if you're using objects in contexts where those move operations will be invoked, you can safely rely on move semantics to replace copy operations with their less expensive move counterparts.

Things to Remember
- Assume that move operations are not present, not cheap, and not used.
- In code with known types or support for move semantics, there is no need for assumptions.

Item 30: Familiarize yourself with perfect forwarding failure cases.

One of the features most prominently emblazoned on the C++11 box is perfect forwarding. *Perfect* forwarding. It's *perfect*! Alas, tear the box open, and you'll find that there's "perfect" (the ideal), and then there's "perfect" (the reality). C++11's perfect forwarding is very good, but it achieves true perfection only if you're willing to overlook an epsilon or two. This Item is devoted to familiarizing you with the epsilons.

Before embarking on our epsilon exploration, it's worthwhile to review what's meant by "perfect forwarding." "Forwarding" just means that one function passes—*forwards* —its parameters to another function. The goal is for the second function (the one being forwarded to) to receive the same objects that the first function (the one doing the forwarding) received. That rules out by-value parameters, because they're *copies* of what the original caller passed in. We want the forwarded-to function to be able to work with the originally-passed-in objects. Pointer parameters are also ruled out, because we don't want to force callers to pass pointers. When it comes to general-purpose forwarding, we'll be dealing with parameters that are references.

Perfect forwarding means we don't just forward objects, we also forward their salient characteristics: their types, whether they're lvalues or rvalues, and whether they're const or volatile. In conjunction with the observation that we'll be dealing with reference parameters, this implies that we'll be using universal references (see Item 24), because only universal reference parameters encode information about the lvalueness and rvalueness of the arguments that are passed to them.

Let's assume we have some function f, and we'd like to write a function (in truth, a function template) that forwards to it. The core of what we need looks like this:

```
template<typename T>
void fwd(T&& param)              // accept any argument
{
    f(std::forward<T>(param));   // forward it to f
}
```

Forwarding functions are, by their nature, generic. The fwd template, for example, accepts any type of argument, and it forwards whatever it gets. A logical extension of this genericity is for forwarding functions to be not just templates, but *variadic* templates, thus accepting any number of arguments. The variadic form for fwd looks like this:

```
template<typename... Ts>
void fwd(Ts&&... params)         // accept any arguments
{
```

```
    f(std::forward<Ts>(params)...);      // forward them to f
}
```

This is the form you'll see in, among other places, the standard containers' emplacement functions (see Item 42) and the smart pointer factory functions, `std::make_shared` and `std::make_unique` (see Item 21).

Given our target function f and our forwarding function fwd, perfect forwarding *fails* if calling f with a particular argument does one thing, but calling fwd with the same argument does something different:

```
    f( expression );       // if this does one thing,
    fwd( expression );     // but this does something else, fwd fails
                           // to perfectly forward expression to f
```

Several kinds of arguments lead to this kind of failure. Knowing what they are and how to work around them is important, so let's tour the kinds of arguments that can't be perfect-forwarded.

Braced initializers

Suppose f is declared like this:

```
    void f(const std::vector<int>& v);
```

In that case, calling f with a braced initializer compiles,

```
    f({ 1, 2, 3 });        // fine, "{1, 2, 3}" implicitly
                           // converted to std::vector<int>
```

but passing the same braced initializer to fwd doesn't compile:

```
    fwd({ 1, 2, 3 });      // error! doesn't compile
```

That's because the use of a braced initializer is a perfect forwarding failure case.

All such failure cases have the same cause. In a direct call to f (such as f({ 1, 2, 3 })), compilers see the arguments passed at the call site, and they see the types of the parameters declared by f. They compare the arguments at the call site to the parameter declarations to see if they're compatible, and, if necessary, they perform implicit conversions to make the call succeed. In the example above, they generate a temporary `std::vector<int>` object from { 1, 2, 3 } so that f's parameter v has a `std::vector<int>` object to bind to.

When calling f indirectly through the forwarding function template fwd, compilers no longer compare the arguments passed at fwd's call site to the parameter declarations in f. Instead, they *deduce* the types of the arguments being passed to fwd, and they compare the deduced types to f's parameter declarations. Perfect forwarding fails when either of the following occurs:

- **Compilers are unable to deduce a type** for one or more of fwd's parameters. In this case, the code fails to compile.

- **Compilers deduce the "wrong" type** for one or more of fwd's parameters. Here, "wrong" could mean that fwd's instantiation won't compile with the types that were deduced, but it could also mean that the call to f using fwd's deduced types behaves differently from a direct call to f with the arguments that were passed to fwd. One source of such divergent behavior would be if f were an overloaded function name, and, due to "incorrect" type deduction, the overload of f called inside fwd were different from the overload that would be invoked if f were called directly.

In the "fwd({ 1, 2, 3 })" call above, the problem is that passing a braced initializer to a function template parameter that's not declared to be a std::initializer_list is decreed to be, as the Standard puts it, a "non-deduced context." In plain English, that means that compilers are forbidden from deducing a type for the expression { 1, 2, 3 } in the call to fwd, because fwd's parameter isn't declared to be a std::initializer_list. Being prevented from deducing a type for fwd's parameter, compilers must understandably reject the call.

Interestingly, Item 2 explains that type deduction succeeds for auto variables initialized with a braced initializer. Such variables are deemed to be std::initializer_list objects, and this affords a simple workaround for cases where the type the forwarding function should deduce is a std::initializer_list—declare a local variable using auto, then pass the local variable to the forwarding function:

```
auto il = { 1, 2, 3 };      // il's type deduced to be
                            // std::initializer_list<int>

fwd(il);                    // fine, perfect-forwards il to f
```

0 or NULL as null pointers

Item 8 explains that when you try to pass 0 or NULL as a null pointer to a template, type deduction goes awry, deducing an integral type (typically int) instead of a pointer type for the argument you pass. The result is that neither 0 nor NULL can be perfect-forwarded as a null pointer. The fix is easy, however: pass nullptr instead of 0 or NULL. For details, consult Item 8.

Declaration-only integral `static const` and `constexpr` data members

As a general rule, there's no need to define integral `static const` and `constexpr` data members in classes; declarations alone suffice. That's because compilers perform *const propagation* on such members' values, thus eliminating the need to set aside memory for them. For example, consider this code:

```
class Widget {
public:
  static constexpr std::size_t MinVals = 28; // MinVals' declaration
  …
};
…                                             // no defn. for MinVals

std::vector<int> widgetData;
widgetData.reserve(Widget::MinVals);          // use of MinVals
```

Here, we're using `Widget::MinVals` (henceforth simply `MinVals`) to specify `widget-Data`'s initial capacity, even though `MinVals` lacks a definition. Compilers work around the missing definition (as they are required to do) by plopping the value 28 into all places where `MinVals` is mentioned. The fact that no storage has been set aside for `MinVals`' value is unproblematic. If `MinVals`' address were to be taken (e.g., if somebody created a pointer to `MinVals`), then `MinVals` would require storage (so that the pointer had something to point to), and the code above, though it would compile, would fail at link-time until a definition for `MinVals` was provided.

With that in mind, imagine that `f` (the function `fwd` forwards its argument to) is declared like this:

```
void f(std::size_t val);
```

Calling `f` with `MinVals` is fine, because compilers will just replace `MinVals` with its value:

```
f(Widget::MinVals);          // fine, treated as "f(28)"
```

Alas, things may not go so smoothly if we try to call `f` through `fwd`:

```
fwd(Widget::MinVals);        // error! shouldn't link
```

This code will compile, but it shouldn't link. If that reminds you of what happens if we write code that takes `MinVals`' address, that's good, because the underlying problem is the same.

Although nothing in the source code takes `MinVals`' address, `fwd`'s parameter is a universal reference, and references, in the code generated by compilers, are usually treated like pointers. In the program's underlying binary code (and on the hardware), pointers and references are essentially the same thing. At this level, there's truth to the adage that references are simply pointers that are automatically dereferenced. That being the case, passing MinVals by reference is effectively the same as passing it by pointer, and as such, there has to be some memory for the pointer to point to. Passing integral static const and constexpr data members by reference, then, generally requires that they be defined, and that requirement can cause code using perfect forwarding to fail where the equivalent code without perfect forwarding succeeds.

But perhaps you noticed the weasel words I sprinkled through the preceding discussion. The code "shouldn't" link. References are "usually" treated like pointers. Passing integral static const and constexpr data members by reference "generally" requires that they be defined. It's almost like I know something I don't really want to tell you…

That's because I do. According to the Standard, passing MinVals by reference requires that it be defined. But not all implementations enforce this requirement. So, depending on your compilers and linkers, you may find that you can perfect-forward integral static const and constexpr data members that haven't been defined. If you do, congratulations, but there is no reason to expect such code to port. To make it portable, simply provide a definition for the integral static const or constexpr data member in question. For MinVals, that'd look like this:

```
constexpr std::size_t Widget::MinVals;    // in Widget's .cpp file
```

Note that the definition doesn't repeat the initializer (28, in the case of MinVals). Don't stress over this detail, however. If you forget and provide the initializer in both places, your compilers will complain, thus reminding you to specify it only once.

Overloaded function names and template names

Suppose our function f (the one we keep wanting to forward arguments to via fwd) can have its behavior customized by passing it a function that does some of its work. Assuming this function takes and returns ints, f could be declared like this:

```
void f(int (*pf)(int));        // pf = "processing function"
```

It's worth noting that f could also be declared using a simpler non-pointer syntax. Such a declaration would look like this, though it'd have the same meaning as the declaration above:

```
void f(int pf(int));            // declares same f as above
```

Either way, now suppose we have an overloaded function, processVal:

```
int processVal(int value);
int processVal(int value, int priority);
```

We can pass `processVal` to `f`,

```
f(processVal);                          // fine
```

but it's something of a surprise that we can. `f` demands a pointer to a function as its argument, but `processVal` isn't a function pointer or even a function, it's the name of two different functions. However, compilers know which `processVal` they need: the one matching `f`'s parameter type. They thus choose the `processVal` taking one `int`, and they pass that function's address to `f`.

What makes this work is that `f`'s declaration lets compilers figure out which version of `processVal` is required. `fwd`, however, being a function template, doesn't have any information about what type it needs, and that makes it impossible for compilers to determine which overload should be passed:

```
fwd(processVal);                        // error! which processVal?
```

`processVal` alone has no type. Without a type, there can be no type deduction, and without type deduction, we're left with another perfect forwarding failure case.

The same problem arises if we try to use a function template instead of (or in addition to) an overloaded function name. A function template doesn't represent one function, it represents *many* functions:

```
template<typename T>
T workOnVal(T param)            // template for processing values
{ … }

fwd(workOnVal);                 // error! which workOnVal
                                // instantiation?
```

The way to get a perfect-forwarding function like `fwd` to accept an overloaded function name or a template name is to manually specify the overload or instantiation you want to have forwarded. For example, you can create a function pointer of the same type as `f`'s parameter, initialize that pointer with `processVal` or `workOnVal` (thus causing the proper version of `processVal` to be selected or the proper instantiation of `workOnVal` to be generated), and pass the pointer to `fwd`:

```
using ProcessFuncType =                 // make typedef;
  int (*)(int);                         // see Item 9

ProcessFuncType processValPtr = processVal;   // specify needed
                                              // signature for
                                              // processVal

fwd(processValPtr);                     // fine

fwd(static_cast<ProcessFuncType>(workOnVal)); // also fine
```

Of course, this requires that you know the type of function pointer that `fwd` is forwarding to. It's not unreasonable to assume that a perfect-forwarding function will document that. After all, perfect-forwarding functions are designed to accept *anything*, so if there's no documentation telling you what to pass, how would you know?

Bitfields

The final failure case for perfect forwarding is when a bitfield is used as a function argument. To see what this means in practice, observe that an IPv4 header can be modeled as follows:[5]

```
struct IPv4Header {
  std::uint32_t version:4,
                IHL:4,
                DSCP:6,
                ECN:2,
                totalLength:16;
  ...
};
```

If our long-suffering function `f` (the perennial target of our forwarding function `fwd`) is declared to take a `std::size_t` parameter, calling it with, say, the `totalLength` field of an `IPv4Header` object compiles without fuss:

```
void f(std::size_t sz);       // function to call

IPv4Header h;
...
f(h.totalLength);             // fine
```

Trying to forward `h.totalLength` to `f` via `fwd`, however, is a different story:

```
fwd(h.totalLength);           // error!
```

The problem is that `fwd`'s parameter is a reference, and `h.totalLength` is a non-`const` bitfield. That may not sound so bad, but the C++ Standard condemns the combination in unusually clear prose: "A non-`const` reference shall not be bound to a bit-field." There's an excellent reason for the prohibition. Bitfields may consist of arbitrary parts of machine words (e.g., bits 3-5 of a 32-bit `int`), but there's no way to directly address such things. I mentioned earlier that references and pointers are the same thing at the hardware level, and just as there's no way to create a pointer to

---

5 This assumes that bitfields are laid out lsb (least significant bit) to msb (most significant bit). C++ doesn't guarantee that, but compilers often provide a mechanism that allows programmers to control bitfield layout.

arbitrary bits (C++ dictates that the smallest thing you can point to is a char), there's no way to bind a reference to arbitrary bits, either.

Working around the impossibility of perfect-forwarding a bitfield is easy, once you realize that any function that accepts a bitfield as an argument will receive a *copy* of the bitfield's value. After all, no function can bind a reference to a bitfield, nor can any function accept pointers to bitfields, because pointers to bitfields don't exist. The only kinds of parameters to which a bitfield can be passed are by-value parameters and, interestingly, references-to-const. In the case of by-value parameters, the called function obviously receives a copy of the value in the bitfield, and it turns out that in the case of a reference-to-const parameter, the Standard requires that the reference actually bind to a *copy* of the bitfield's value that's stored in an object of some standard integral type (e.g., int). References-to-const don't bind to bitfields, they bind to "normal" objects into which the values of the bitfields have been copied.

The key to passing a bitfield into a perfect-forwarding function, then, is to take advantage of the fact that the forwarded-to function will always receive a copy of the bitfield's value. You can thus make a copy yourself and call the forwarding function with the copy. In the case of our example with IPv4Header, this code would do the trick:

```
// copy bitfield value; see Item 6 for info on init. form
auto length = static_cast<std::uint16_t>(h.totalLength);

fwd(length);                            // forward the copy
```

Upshot

In most cases, perfect forwarding works exactly as advertised. You rarely have to think about it. But when it doesn't work—when reasonable-looking code fails to compile or, worse, compiles, but doesn't behave the way you anticipate—it's important to know about perfect forwarding's imperfections. Equally important is knowing how to work around them. In most cases, this is straightforward.

Things to Remember
- Perfect forwarding fails when template type deduction fails or when it deduces the wrong type.
- The kinds of arguments that lead to perfect forwarding failure are braced initializers, null pointers expressed as 0 or NULL, declaration-only integral const static data members, template and overloaded function names, and bitfields.

CHAPTER 6

Lambda Expressions

Lambda expressions—*lambdas*—are a game changer in C++ programming. That's somewhat surprising, because they bring no new expressive power to the language. Everything a lambda can do is something you can do by hand with a bit more typing. But lambdas are such a convenient way to create function objects, the impact on day-to-day C++ software development is enormous. Without lambdas, the STL "_if" algorithms (e.g., `std::find_if`, `std::remove_if`, `std::count_if`, etc.) tend to be employed with only the most trivial predicates, but when lambdas are available, use of these algorithms with nontrivial conditions blossoms. The same is true of algorithms that can be customized with comparison functions (e.g., `std::sort`, `std::nth_element`, `std::lower_bound`, etc.). Outside the STL, lambdas make it possible to quickly create custom deleters for `std::unique_ptr` and `std::shared_ptr` (see Items 18 and 19), and they make the specification of predicates for condition variables in the threading API equally straightforward (see Item 39). Beyond the Standard Library, lambdas facilitate the on-the-fly specification of callback functions, interface adaption functions, and context-specific functions for one-off calls. Lambdas really make C++ a more pleasant programming language.

The vocabulary associated with lambdas can be confusing. Here's a brief refresher:

- A *lambda expression* is just that: an expression. It's part of the source code. In

```
std::find_if(container.begin(), container.end(),
             [](int val) { return 0 < val && val < 10; });
```

the highlighted expression is the lambda.

- A *closure* is the runtime object created by a lambda. Depending on the capture mode, closures hold copies of or references to the captured data. In the call to `std::find_if` above, the closure is the object that's passed at runtime as the third argument to `std::find_if`.

- A *closure class* is a class from which a closure is instantiated. Each lambda causes compilers to generate a unique closure class. The statements inside a lambda become executable instructions in the member functions of its closure class.

A lambda is often used to create a closure that's used only as an argument to a function. That's the case in the call to `std::find_if` above. However, closures may generally be copied, so it's usually possible to have multiple closures of a closure type corresponding to a single lambda. For example, in the following code,

```
{
    int x;                              // x is local variable
    …

    auto c1 =                           // c1 is copy of the
      [x](int y) { return x * y > 55; }; // closure produced
                                        // by the lambda

    auto c2 = c1;                       // c2 is copy of c1

    auto c3 = c2;                       // c3 is copy of c2

    …

}
```

`c1`, `c2`, and `c3` are all copies of the closure produced by the lambda.

Informally, it's perfectly acceptable to blur the lines between lambdas, closures, and closure classes. But in the Items that follow, it's often important to distinguish what exists during compilation (lambdas and closure classes), what exists at runtime (closures), and how they relate to one another.

Item 31: Avoid default capture modes.

There are two default capture modes in C++11: by-reference and by-value. Default by-reference capture can lead to dangling references. Default by-value capture lures you into thinking you're immune to that problem (you're not), and it lulls you into thinking your closures are self-contained (they may not be).

That's the executive summary for this Item. If you're more engineer than executive, you'll want some meat on those bones, so let's start with the danger of default by-reference capture.

A by-reference capture causes a closure to contain a reference to a local variable or to a parameter that's available in the scope where the lambda is defined. If the lifetime of a closure created from that lambda exceeds the lifetime of the local variable or parameter, the reference in the closure will dangle. For example, suppose we have a container of filtering functions, each of which takes an `int` and returns a `bool` indicating whether a passed-in value satisfies the filter:

```cpp
using FilterContainer =                         // see Item 9 for
    std::vector<std::function<bool(int)>>;      // "using", Item 5
                                                // for std::function

FilterContainer filters;                        // filtering funcs
```

We could add a filter for multiples of 5 like this:

```cpp
filters.emplace_back(                           // see Item 42 for
    [](int value) { return value % 5 == 0; }    // info on
);                                              // emplace_back
```

However, it may be that we need to compute the divisor at runtime, i.e., we can't just hard-code 5 into the lambda. So adding the filter might look more like this:

```cpp
void addDivisorFilter()
{
  auto calc1 = computeSomeValue1();
  auto calc2 = computeSomeValue2();

  auto divisor = computeDivisor(calc1, calc2);

  filters.emplace_back(                            // danger!
    [&](int value) { return value % divisor == 0; } // ref to
  );                                               // divisor
}                                                  // will
                                                   // dangle!
```

This code is a problem waiting to happen. The lambda refers to the local variable `divisor`, but that variable ceases to exist when `addDivisorFilter` returns. That's immediately after `filters.emplace_back` returns, so the function that's added to `filters` is essentially dead on arrival. Using that filter yields undefined behavior from virtually the moment it's created.

Now, the same problem would exist if `divisor`'s by-reference capture were explicit,

```cpp
filters.emplace_back(
  [&divisor](int value)                  // danger! ref to
  { return value % divisor == 0; }       // divisor will
);                                       // still dangle!
```

but with an explicit capture, it's easier to see that the viability of the lambda is dependent on `divisor`'s lifetime. Also, writing out the name, "divisor," reminds us to ensure that `divisor` lives at least as long as the lambda's closures. That's a more specific memory jog than the general "make sure nothing dangles" admonition that "[&]" conveys.

If you know that a closure will be used immediately (e.g., by being passed to an STL algorithm) and won't be copied, there is no risk that references it holds will outlive the local variables and parameters in the environment where its lambda is created. In that case, you might argue, there's no risk of dangling references, hence no reason to avoid a default by-reference capture mode. For example, our filtering lambda might be used only as an argument to C++11's `std::all_of`, which returns whether all elements in a range satisfy a condition:

```
template<typename C>
void workWithContainer(const C& container)
{
    auto calc1 = computeSomeValue1();            // as above
    auto calc2 = computeSomeValue2();            // as above

    auto divisor = computeDivisor(calc1, calc2); // as above

    using ContElemT = typename C::value_type;    // type of
                                                 // elements in
                                                 // container

    using std::begin;                            // for
    using std::end;                              // genericity;
                                                 // see Item 13

    if (std::all_of(                             // if all values
          begin(container), end(container),      // in container
          [&](const ContElemT& value)            // are multiples
          { return value % divisor == 0; })      // of divisor...
       ) {
        …                                        // they are...
    } else {
        …                                        // at least one
    }                                            // isn't...
}
```

It's true, this is safe, but its safety is somewhat precarious. If the lambda were found to be useful in other contexts (e.g., as a function to be added to the `filters` container) and was copy-and-pasted into a context where its closure could outlive `divi-`

sor, you'd be back in dangle-city, and there'd be nothing in the capture clause to specifically remind you to perform lifetime analysis on divisor.

Long-term, it's simply better software engineering to explicitly list the local variables and parameters that a lambda depends on.

By the way, the ability to use auto in C++14 lambda parameter specifications means that the code above can be simplified in C++14. The ContElemT typedef can be eliminated, and the if condition can be revised as follows:

```
if (std::all_of(begin(container), end(container),
                [&](const auto& value)              // C++14
                { return value % divisor == 0; }))
```

One way to solve our problem with divisor would be a default by-value capture mode. That is, we could add the lambda to filters as follows:

```
filters.emplace_back(                                 // now
  [=](int value) { return value % divisor == 0; }    // divisor
);                                                     // can't
                                                       // dangle
```

This suffices for this example, but, in general, default by-value capture isn't the anti-dangling elixir you might imagine. The problem is that if you capture a pointer by value, you copy the pointer into the closures arising from the lambda, but you don't prevent code outside the lambda from deleteing the pointer and causing your copies to dangle.

"That could never happen!" you protest. "Having read Chapter 4, I worship at the house of smart pointers. Only loser C++98 programmers use raw pointers and delete." That may be true, but it's irrelevant because you do, in fact, use raw pointers, and they can, in fact, be deleted out from under you. It's just that in your modern C++ programming style, there's often little sign of it in the source code.

Suppose one of the things Widgets can do is add entries to the container of filters:

```
class Widget {
public:
  …                                   // ctors, etc.
  void addFilter() const;             // add an entry to filters

private:
  int divisor;                        // used in Widget's filter
};
```

Widget::addFilter could be defined like this:

```
void Widget::addFilter() const
{
  filters.emplace_back(
    [=](int value) { return value % divisor == 0; }
  );
}
```

To the blissfully uninitiated, this looks like safe code. The lambda is dependent on divisor, but the default by-value capture mode ensures that divisor is copied into any closures arising from the lambda, right?

Wrong. Completely wrong. Horribly wrong. Fatally wrong.

Captures apply only to non-static local variables (including parameters) visible in the scope where the lambda is created. In the body of Widget::addFilter, divisor is not a local variable, it's a data member of the Widget class. It can't be captured. Yet if the default capture mode is eliminated, the code won't compile:

```
void Widget::addFilter() const
{
  filters.emplace_back(                             // error!
    [](int value) { return value % divisor == 0; }  // divisor
  );                                                // not
}                                                   // available
```

Furthermore, if an attempt is made to explicitly capture divisor (either by value or by reference—it doesn't matter), the capture won't compile, because divisor isn't a local variable or a parameter:

```
void Widget::addFilter() const
{
  filters.emplace_back(
    [divisor](int value)                  // error! no local
    { return value % divisor == 0; }       // divisor to capture
  );
}
```

So if the default by-value capture clause isn't capturing divisor, yet without the default by-value capture clause, the code won't compile, what's going on?

The explanation hinges on the implicit use of a raw pointer: this. Every non-static member function has a this pointer, and you use that pointer every time you mention a data member of the class. Inside any Widget member function, for example, compilers internally replace uses of divisor with this->divisor. In the version of Widget::addFilter with a default by-value capture,

```
void Widget::addFilter() const
{
  filters.emplace_back(
    [=](int value) { return value % divisor == 0; }
  );
}
```

what's being captured is the Widget's this pointer, not divisor. Compilers treat the code as if it had been written as follows:

```
void Widget::addFilter() const
{
  auto currentObjectPtr = this;

  filters.emplace_back(
    [currentObjectPtr](int value)
    { return value % currentObjectPtr->divisor == 0; }
  );
}
```

Understanding this is tantamount to understanding that the viability of the closures arising from this lambda is tied to the lifetime of the Widget whose this pointer they contain a copy of. In particular, consider this code, which, in accord with Chapter 4, uses pointers of only the smart variety:

```
using FilterContainer =                  // as before
  std::vector<std::function<bool(int)>>;

FilterContainer filters;                 // as before

void doSomeWork()
{
  auto pw =                              // create Widget; see
    std::make_unique<Widget>();          // Item 21 for
                                         // std::make_unique

  pw->addFilter();                       // add filter that uses
                                         // Widget::divisor

  ...
}                                        // destroy Widget; filters
                                         // now holds dangling pointer!
```

When a call is made to doSomeWork, a filter is created that depends on the Widget object produced by std::make_unique, i.e., a filter that contains a copy of a pointer to that Widget—the Widget's this pointer. This filter is added to filters, but when doSomeWork finishes, the Widget is destroyed by the std::unique_ptr managing its lifetime (see Item 18). From that point on, `filters` contains an entry with a dangling pointer.

This particular problem can be solved by making a local copy of the data member you want to capture and then capturing the copy:

```
void Widget::addFilter() const
{
  auto divisorCopy = divisor;                 // copy data member

  filters.emplace_back(
    [divisorCopy](int value)                  // capture the copy
    { return value % divisorCopy == 0; }      // use the copy
  );
}
```

To be honest, if you take this approach, default by-value capture will work, too,

```
void Widget::addFilter() const
{
  auto divisorCopy = divisor;                 // copy data member

  filters.emplace_back(
    [=](int value)                            // capture the copy
    { return value % divisorCopy == 0; }      // use the copy
  );
}
```

but why tempt fate? A default capture mode is what made it possible to accidentally capture `this` when you thought you were capturing `divisor` in the first place.

In C++14, a better way to capture a data member is to use generalized lambda capture (see Item 32):

```
void Widget::addFilter() const
{
  filters.emplace_back(                       // C++14:
    [divisor = divisor](int value)            // copy divisor to closure
    { return value % divisor == 0; }          // use the copy
  );
}
```

There's no such thing as a default capture mode for a generalized lambda capture, however, so even in C++14, the advice of this Item—to avoid default capture modes—stands.

An additional drawback to default by-value captures is that they can suggest that the corresponding closures are self-contained and insulated from changes to data outside the closures. In general, that's not true, because lambdas may be dependent not just on local variables and parameters (which may be captured), but also on objects with *static storage duration*. Such objects are defined at global or namespace scope or are declared `static` inside classes, functions, or files. These objects can be used inside lambdas, but they can't be captured. Yet specification of a default by-value capture mode can lend the impression that they are. Consider this revised version of the `addDivisorFilter` function we saw earlier:

```
void addDivisorFilter()
{
  static auto calc1 = computeSomeValue1();    // now static
  static auto calc2 = computeSomeValue2();    // now static

  static auto divisor =                       // now static
    computeDivisor(calc1, calc2);

  filters.emplace_back(
    [=](int value)                            // captures nothing!
    { return value % divisor == 0; }          // refers to above static
  );

  ++divisor;                                  // modify divisor
}
```

A casual reader of this code could be forgiven for seeing "[=]" and thinking, "Okay, the lambda makes a copy of all the objects it uses and is therefore self-contained." But it's not self-contained. This lambda doesn't use any non-static local variables, so nothing is captured. Rather, the code for the lambda refers to the `static` variable `divisor`. When, at the end of each invocation of `addDivisorFilter`, `divisor` is incremented, any lambdas that have been added to `filters` via this function will exhibit new behavior (corresponding to the new value of `divisor`). Practically speaking, this lambda captures `divisor` by reference, a direct contradiction to what the default by-value capture clause seems to imply. If you stay away from default by-value capture clauses, you eliminate the risk of your code being misread in this way.

Things to Remember

- Default by-reference capture can lead to dangling references.
- Default by-value capture is susceptible to dangling pointers (especially `this`), and it misleadingly suggests that lambdas are self-contained.

Item 32: Use init capture to move objects into closures.

Sometimes neither by-value capture nor by-reference capture is what you want. If you have a move-only object (e.g., a `std::unique_ptr` or a `std::future`) that you want to get into a closure, C++11 offers no way to do it. If you have an object that's expensive to copy but cheap to move (e.g., most containers in the Standard Library), and you'd like to get that object into a closure, you'd much rather move it than copy it. Again, however, C++11 gives you no way to accomplish that.

But that's C++11. C++14 is a different story. It offers direct support for moving objects into closures. If your compilers are C++14-compliant, rejoice and read on. If you're still working with C++11 compilers, you should rejoice and read on, too, because there are ways to approximate move capture in C++11.

The absence of move capture was recognized as a shortcoming even as C++11 was adopted. The straightforward remedy would have been to add it in C++14, but the Standardization Committee chose a different path. They introduced a new capture mechanism that's so flexible, capture-by-move is only one of the tricks it can perform. The new capability is called *init capture*. It can do virtually everything the C++11 capture forms can do, plus more. The one thing you can't express with an init capture is a default capture mode, but Item 31 explains that you should stay away from those, anyway. (For situations covered by C++11 captures, init capture's syntax is a bit wordier, so in cases where a C++11 capture gets the job done, it's perfectly reasonable to use it.)

Using an init capture makes it possible for you to specify

1. **the name of a data member** in the closure class generated from the lambda and

2. **an expression** initializing that data member.

Here's how you can use init capture to move a `std::unique_ptr` into a closure:

```
class Widget {                              // some useful type
public:
  …

  bool isValidated() const;
  bool isProcessed() const;
  bool isArchived() const;

private:
  …
};
```

```
auto pw = std::make_unique<Widget>();   // create Widget; see
                                         // Item 21 for info on
                                         // std::make_unique


...                                      // configure *pw

auto func = [pw = std::move(pw)]              // init data mbr
            { return pw->isValidated()        // in closure w/
                   && pw->isArchived(); };    // std::move(pw)
```

The highlighted text comprises the init capture. To the left of the "=" is the name of the data member in the closure class you're specifying, and to the right is the initializing expression. Interestingly, the scope on the left of the "=" is different from the scope on the right. The scope on the left is that of the closure class. The scope on the right is the same as where the lambda is being defined. In the example above, the name pw on the left of the "=" refers to a data member in the closure class, while the name pw on the right refers to the object declared above the lambda, i.e., the variable initialized by the call to std::make_unique. So "pw = std::move(pw)" means "create a data member pw in the closure, and initialize that data member with the result of applying std::move to the local variable pw."

As usual, code in the body of the lambda is in the scope of the closure class, so uses of pw there refer to the closure class data member.

The comment "configure *pw" in this example indicates that after the Widget is created by std::make_unique and before the std::unique_ptr to that Widget is captured by the lambda, the Widget is modified in some way. If no such configuration is necessary, i.e., if the Widget created by std::make_unique is in a state suitable to be captured by the lambda, the local variable pw is unnecessary, because the closure class's data member can be directly initialized by std::make_unique:

```
auto func = [pw = std::make_unique<Widget>()]   // init data mbr
            { return pw->isValidated()           // in closure w/
                   && pw->isArchived(); };       // result of call
                                                 // to make_unique
```

This should make clear that the C++14 notion of "capture" is considerably generalized from C++11, because in C++11, it's not possible to capture the result of an expression. As a result, another name for init capture is *generalized lambda capture*.

But what if one or more of the compilers you use lacks support for C++14's init capture? How can you accomplish move capture in a language lacking support for move capture?

Recall that a lambda expression is just a way to cause a class and a class instance to be generated. Anything you can do with a lambda, you can do by hand. The example C++14 code we just saw, for example, can be written in C++11 like this:[1]

```
class IsValAndArch {              // "is validated
public:                           // and archived"
  using DataType = std::unique_ptr<Widget>;

  explicit IsValAndArch(DataType&& ptr)    // Item 25 explains
  : pw(std::move(ptr)) {}                  // use of std::move

  bool operator()() const
  { return pw->isValidated() && pw->isArchived(); }

private:
  DataType pw;
};

auto func = IsValAndArch(std::make_unique<Widget>());
```

That's more work than writing the lambda, but it doesn't change the fact that if you want a class in C++11 that supports move-initialization of its data members, the only thing between you and your desire is a bit of time with your keyboard.

If you want to stick with lambdas (and given their convenience, you probably do), move capture can be emulated in C++11 by

1. **moving the object to be captured into a function object produced by `std::bind`** and

2. **giving the lambda a reference to the "captured" object.**

If you're familiar with `std::bind`, the code is pretty straightforward. If you're not familiar with `std::bind`, the code takes a little getting used to, but it's worth the trouble.

Suppose you'd like to create a local `std::vector`, put an appropriate set of values into it, then move it into a closure. In C++14, this is easy:

```
std::vector<double> data;              // object to be moved
                                       // into closure

...                                    // populate data

auto func = [data = std::move(data)]   // C++14 init capture
              { /* uses of data */ };
```

_____

1 I use `make_unique` in this code, even though it's not part of C++11, because Item 21 demonstrates that `make_unique` is easy to implement in C++11.

I've highlighted key parts of this code: the type of object you want to move (std::vector<double>), the name of that object (data), and the initializing expression for the init capture (std::move(data)). The C++11 equivalent is as follows, where I've highlighted the same key things:

```
std::vector<double> data;                    // as above

...                                          // as above

auto func =
  std::bind(                                 // C++11 emulation
    [](const std::vector<double>& data)      // of init capture
    { /* uses of data */ },
    std::move(data)
  );
```

Like lambda expressions, std::bind produces function objects. I call function objects returned by std::bind *bind objects*. The first argument to std::bind is a callable object. Subsequent arguments represent values to be passed to that object.

A bind object contains copies of all the arguments passed to std::bind. For each lvalue argument, the corresponding object in the bind object is copy constructed. For each rvalue, it's move constructed. In this example, the second argument is an rvalue (the result of std::move—see Item 23), so data is move constructed into the bind object. This move construction is the crux of move capture emulation, because moving an rvalue into a bind object is how we work around the inability to move an rvalue into a C++11 closure.

When a bind object is "called" (i.e., its function call operator is invoked) the arguments it stores are passed to the callable object originally passed to std::bind. In this example, that means that when func (the bind object) is called, the move-constructed copy of data inside func is passed as an argument to the lambda that was passed to std::bind.

This lambda is the same as the lambda we'd use in C++14, except a parameter, data, has been added to correspond to our pseudo-move-captured object. This parameter is an lvalue reference to the copy of data in the bind object. (It's not an rvalue reference, because although the expression used to initialize the copy of data ("std::move(data)") is an rvalue, the copy of data itself is an lvalue.) Uses of data inside the lambda will thus operate on the move-constructed copy of data inside the bind object.

By default, the operator() member function inside the closure class generated from a lambda is const. That has the effect of rendering all data members in the closure const within the body of the lambda. The move-constructed copy of data inside the bind object is not const, however, so to prevent that copy of data from being modified inside the lambda, the lambda's parameter is declared reference-to-const. If the lambda were declared mutable, operator() in its closure class would not be declared const, and it would be appropriate to omit const in the lambda's parameter declaration:

```
auto func =
  std::bind(                                    // C++11 emulation
    [](std::vector<double>& data) mutable  // of init capture
    { /* uses of data */ },                     // for mutable lambda
    std::move(data)
  );
```

Because a bind object stores copies of all the arguments passed to std::bind, the bind object in our example contains a copy of the closure produced by the lambda that is its first argument. The lifetime of the closure is therefore the same as the lifetime of the bind object. That's important, because it means that as long as the closure exists, the bind object containing the pseudo-move-captured object exists, too.

If this is your first exposure to std::bind, you may need to consult your favorite C++11 reference before all the details of the foregoing discussion fall into place. Even if that's the case, these fundamental points should be clear:

- It's not possible to move-construct an object into a C++11 closure, but it is possible to move-construct an object into a C++11 bind object.

- Emulating move-capture in C++11 consists of move-constructing an object into a bind object, then passing the move-constructed object to the lambda by reference.

- Because the lifetime of the bind object is the same as that of the closure, it's possible to treat objects in the bind object as if they were in the closure.

As a second example of using std::bind to emulate move capture, here's the C++14 code we saw earlier to create a std::unique_ptr in a closure:

```
auto func = [pw = std::make_unique<Widget>()]    // as before,
              { return pw->isValidated()          // create pw
                && pw->isArchived(); };           // in closure
```

And here's the C++11 emulation:

```
auto func = std::bind(
              [](const std::unique_ptr<Widget>& pw)
              { return pw->isValidated()
                && pw->isArchived(); },
```

```
            std::make_unique<Widget>()
        );
```

It's ironic that I'm showing how to use `std::bind` to work around limitations in C++11 lambdas, because in Item 34, I advocate the use of lambdas over `std::bind`. However, that Item explains that there are some cases in C++11 where `std::bind` can be useful, and this is one of them. (In C++14, features such as init capture and `auto` parameters eliminate those cases.)

Things to Remember

- Use C++14's init capture to move objects into closures.
- In C++11, emulate init capture via hand-written classes or `std::bind`.

Item 33: Use decltype on auto&& parameters to std::forward them.

One of the most exciting features of C++14 is *generic lambdas*—lambdas that use `auto` in their parameter specifications. The implementation of this feature is straight-forward: `operator()` in the lambda's closure class is a template. Given this lambda, for example,

```
auto f = [](auto x){ return normalize(x); };
```

the closure class's function call operator looks like this:

```
class SomeCompilerGeneratedClassName {
public:
  template<typename T>              // see Item 3 for
  auto operator()(T x) const        // auto return type
  { return normalize(x); }

  ...                               // other closure class
};                                  // functionality
```

In this example, the only thing the lambda does with its parameter x is forward it to `normalize`. If `normalize` treats lvalues differently from rvalues, this lambda isn't written properly, because it always passes an lvalue (the parameter x) to `normalize`, even if the argument that was passed to the lambda was an rvalue.

The correct way to write the lambda is to have it perfect-forward x to `normalize`. Doing that requires two changes to the code. First, x has to become a universal reference (see Item 24), and second, it has to be passed to `normalize` via `std::forward` (see Item 25). In concept, these are trivial modifications:

```
auto f = [](auto&& x)
              { return normalize(std::forward<???>(x)); };
```

Between concept and realization, however, is the question of what type to pass to `std::forward`, i.e., to determine what should go where I've written ??? above.

Normally, when you employ perfect forwarding, you're in a template function taking a type parameter T, so you just write `std::forward<T>`. In the generic lambda, though, there's no type parameter T available to you. There is a T in the templatized `operator()` inside the closure class generated by the lambda, but it's not possible to refer to it from the lambda, so it does you no good.

Item 28 explains that if an lvalue argument is passed to a universal reference parameter, the type of that parameter becomes an lvalue reference. If an rvalue is passed, the parameter becomes an rvalue reference. This means that in our lambda, we can determine whether the argument passed was an lvalue or an rvalue by inspecting the type of the parameter x. `decltype` gives us a way to do that (see Item 3). If an lvalue was passed in, `decltype(x)` will produce a type that's an lvalue reference. If an rvalue was passed, `decltype(x)` will produce an rvalue reference type.

Item 28 also explains that when calling `std::forward`, convention dictates that the type argument be an lvalue reference to indicate an lvalue and a non-reference to indicate an rvalue. In our lambda, if x is bound to an lvalue, `decltype(x)` will yield an lvalue reference. That conforms to convention. However, if x is bound to an rvalue, `decltype(x)` will yield an rvalue reference instead of the customary non-reference.

But look at the sample C++14 implementation for `std::forward` from Item 28:

```
template<typename T>                          // in namespace
T&& forward(remove_reference_t<T>& param)     // std
{
  return static_cast<T&&>(param);
}
```

If client code wants to perfect-forward an rvalue of type `Widget`, it normally instantiates `std::forward` with the type `Widget` (i.e., a non-reference type), and the `std::forward` template yields this function:

```
Widget&& forward(Widget& param)               // instantiation of
{                                             // std::forward when
  return static_cast<Widget&&>(param);        // T is Widget
}
```

But consider what would happen if the client code wanted to perfect-forward the same rvalue of type Widget, but instead of following the convention of specifying T to be a non-reference type, it specified it to be an rvalue reference. That is, consider what would happen if T were specified to be Widget&&. After initial instantiation of std::forward and application of std::remove_reference_t, but before reference collapsing (once again, see Item 28), std::forward would look like this:

```
Widget&& && forward(Widget& param)         // instantiation of
{                                          // std::forward when
  return static_cast<Widget&& &&>(param);  // T is Widget&&
}                                          // (before reference-
                                           // collapsing)
```

Applying the reference-collapsing rule that an rvalue reference to an rvalue reference becomes a single rvalue reference, this instantiation emerges:

```
Widget&& forward(Widget& param)            // instantiation of
{                                          // std::forward when
  return static_cast<Widget&&>(param);     // T is Widget&&
}                                          // (after reference-
                                           // collapsing)
```

If you compare this instantiation with the one that results when std::forward is called with T set to Widget, you'll see that they're identical. That means that instantiating std::forward with an rvalue reference type yields the same result as instantiating it with a non-reference type.

That's wonderful news, because decltype(x) yields an rvalue reference type when an rvalue is passed as an argument to our lambda's parameter x. We established above that when an lvalue is passed to our lambda, decltype(x) yields the customary type to pass to std::forward, and now we realize that for rvalues, decltype(x) yields a type to pass to std::forward that's not conventional, but that nevertheless yields the same outcome as the conventional type. So for both lvalues and rvalues, passing decltype(x) to std::forward gives us the result we want. Our perfect-forwarding lambda can therefore be written like this:

```
auto f = [](auto&& x)
         { return normalize(std::forward<decltype(x)>(x)); };
```

From there, it's just a hop, skip, and six dots to a perfect-forwarding lambda that accepts not just a single parameter, but any number of parameters, because C++14 lambdas can also be variadic:

```
auto f = [](auto&&... xs)
         { return normalize(std::forward<decltype(xs)>(xs)...); };
```

Item 34: Prefer lambdas to `std::bind`.

`std::bind` is the C++11 successor to C++98's `std::bind1st` and `std::bind2nd`, but, informally, it's been part of the Standard Library since 2005. That's when the Standardization Committee adopted a document known as TR1, which included `bind`'s specification. (In TR1, `bind` was in a different namespace, so it was `std::tr1::bind`, not `std::bind`, and a few interface details were different.) This history means that some programmers have a decade or more of experience using `std::bind`. If you're one of them, you may be reluctant to abandon a tool that's served you well. That's understandable, but in this case, change is good, because in C++11, lambdas are almost always a better choice than `std::bind`. As of C++14, the case for lambdas isn't just stronger, it's downright ironclad.

This Item assumes that you're familiar with `std::bind`. If you're not, you'll want to acquire a basic understanding before continuing. Such an understanding is worthwhile in any case, because you never know when you might encounter uses of `std::bind` in a code base you have to read or maintain.

As in Item 32, I refer to the function objects returned from `std::bind` as *bind objects*.

The most important reason to prefer lambdas over `std::bind` is that lambdas are more readable. Suppose, for example, we have a function to set up an audible alarm:

```
// typedef for a point in time (see Item 9 for syntax)
using Time = std::chrono::steady_clock::time_point;

// see Item 10 for "enum class"
enum class Sound { Beep, Siren, Whistle };

// typedef for a length of time
using Duration = std::chrono::steady_clock::duration;

// at time t, make sound s for duration d
void setAlarm(Time t, Sound s, Duration d);
```

Further suppose that at some point in the program, we've determined we'll want an alarm that will go off an hour after it's set and that will stay on for 30 seconds. The alarm sound, however, remains undecided. We can write a lambda that revises setAlarm's interface so that only a sound needs to be specified:

```
// setSoundL ("L" for "lambda") is a function object allowing a
// sound to be specified for a 30-sec alarm to go off an hour
// after it's set
auto setSoundL =
  [](Sound s)
  {
    // make std::chrono components available w/o qualification
    using namespace std::chrono;

    setAlarm(steady_clock::now() + hours(1),  // alarm to go off
             s,                                // in an hour for
             seconds(30));                     // 30 seconds
  };
```

I've highlighted the call to setAlarm inside the lambda. This is a normal-looking function call, and even a reader with little lambda experience can see that the parameter s passed to the lambda is passed as an argument to setAlarm.

We can streamline this code in C++14 by availing ourselves of the standard suffixes for seconds (s), milliseconds (ms), hours (h), etc., that build on C++11's support for user-defined literals. These suffixes are implemented in the std::literals namespace, so the above code can be rewritten as follows:

```
auto setSoundL =
  [](Sound s)
  {
    using namespace std::chrono;
    using namespace std::literals;       // for C++14 suffixes

    setAlarm(steady_clock::now() + 1h,   // C++14, but
             s,                          // same meaning
             30s);                       // as above
  };
```

Our first attempt at writing the corresponding `std::bind` call is below. It has an error that we'll fix in a moment, but the correct code is more complicated, and even this simplified version brings out some important issues:

```
using namespace std::chrono;            // as above
using namespace std::literals;

using namespace std::placeholders;      // needed for use of "_1"

auto setSoundB =                        // "B" for "bind"
  std::bind(setAlarm,
            steady_clock::now() + 1h,   // incorrect! see below
            _1,
            30s);
```

I'd like to highlight the call to `setAlarm` here as I did in the lambda, but there's no call to highlight. Readers of this code simply have to know that calling `setSoundB` invokes `setAlarm` with the time and duration specified in the call to `std::bind`. To the uninitiated, the placeholder "_1" is essentially magic, but even readers in the know have to mentally map from the number in that placeholder to its position in the `std::bind` parameter list in order to understand that the first argument in a call to `setSoundB` is passed as the second argument to `setAlarm`. The type of this argument is not identified in the call to `std::bind`, so readers have to consult the `setAlarm` declaration to determine what kind of argument to pass to `setSoundB`.

But, as I said, the code isn't quite right. In the lambda, it's clear that the expression "`steady_clock::now() + 1h`" is an argument to `setAlarm`. It will be evaluated when `setAlarm` is called. That makes sense: we want the alarm to go off an hour after invoking `setAlarm`. In the `std::bind` call, however, "`steady_clock::now() + 1h`" is passed as an argument to `std::bind`, not to `setAlarm`. That means that the expression will be evaluated when `std::bind` is called, and the time resulting from that expression will be stored inside the generated bind object. As a consequence, the alarm will be set to go off an hour *after the call to `std::bind`*, not an hour after the call to `setAlarm`!

Fixing the problem requires telling `std::bind` to defer evaluation of the expression until `setAlarm` is called, and the way to do that is to nest two more calls to `std::bind` inside the first one:

```
auto setSoundB =
  std::bind(setAlarm,
            std::bind(std::plus<>(),
                      std::bind(steady_clock::now),
                      1h),
            _1,
            30s);
```

If you're familiar with the `std::plus` template in C++98, you may be surprised to see that this code contains "`std::plus<>`", not "`std::plus<type>`". In C++14, the template type argument for the standard operator templates can generally be omitted, so there's no need to provide it here. C++11 offers no such feature, so the C++11 `std::bind` equivalent to the lambda is:

```
struct genericAdder {
  template<typename T1, typename T2>
  auto operator()(T1&& param1, T2&& param2)
    -> decltype(std::forward<T1>(param1) + std::forward<T2>(param2))
  {
    return std::forward<T1>(param1) + std::forward<T2>(param2);
  }
};

auto setSoundB =
  std::bind(setAlarm,
            std::bind(genericAdder(),
                      std::bind(steady_clock::now),
                      hours(1)),
            _1,
            seconds(30));
```

If, at this point, the lambda's not looking a lot more attractive, you should probably have your eyesight checked.

When `setAlarm` is overloaded, a new issue arises. Suppose there's an overload taking a fourth parameter specifying the alarm volume:

```
enum class Volume { Normal, Loud, LoudPlusPlus };

void setAlarm(Time t, Sound s, Duration d, Volume v);
```

The lambda continues to work as before, because overload resolution chooses the three-argument version of `setAlarm`:

```
auto setSoundL =                              // same as before
  [](Sound s)
  {
    using namespace std::chrono;
    using namespace std::literals;

    setAlarm(steady_clock::now() + 1h,        // fine, calls
             s,                               // 3-arg version
             30s);                            // of setAlarm
  };
```

The `std::bind` call, on the other hand, now fails to compile:

```
auto setSoundB =                              // error! which
  std::bind(setAlarm,                         // setAlarm?
```

```
std::bind(std::plus<>(),
          std::bind(steady_clock::now),
          1h),
_1,
30s);
```

The problem is that compilers have no way to determine which of the two setAlarm functions they should pass to std::bind. All they have is a function name, and the name alone is ambiguous.

To get the std::bind call to compile, setAlarm must be cast to the proper function pointer type:

```
using SetAlarm3ParamType = void(*)(Time t, Sound s, Duration d);
```

```
auto setSoundB =                                     // now
  std::bind(static_cast<SetAlarm3ParamType>(setAlarm),  // okay
            std::bind(std::plus<>(),
                      std::bind(steady_clock::now),
                      1h),
            _1,
            30s);
```

But this brings up another difference between lambdas and std::bind. Inside the function call operator for setSoundL (i.e., the function call operator of the lambda's closure class), the call to setAlarm is a normal function invocation that can be inlined by compilers in the usual fashion:

```
setSoundL(Sound::Siren);      // body of setAlarm may
                              // well be inlined here
```

The call to std::bind, however, passes a function pointer to setAlarm, and that means that inside the function call operator for setSoundB (i.e., the function call operator for the bind object), the call to setAlarm takes place through a function pointer. Compilers are less likely to inline function calls through function pointers, and that means that calls to setAlarm through setSoundB are less likely to be fully inlined than those through setSoundL:

```
setSoundB(Sound::Siren);      // body of setAlarm is less
                              // likely to be inlined here
```

It's thus possible that using lambdas generates faster code than using std::bind.

The setAlarm example involves only a simple function call. If you want to do anything more complicated, the scales tip even further in favor of lambdas. For example, consider this C++14 lambda, which returns whether its argument is between a minimum value (lowVal) and a maximum value (highVal), where lowVal and highVal are local variables:

```
auto betweenL =
  [lowVal, highVal]
  (const auto& val)                          // C++14
  { return lowVal <= val && val <= highVal; };
```

`std::bind` can express the same thing, but the construct is an example of job security through code obscurity:

```
using namespace std::placeholders;          // as above

auto betweenB =
  std::bind(std::logical_and<>(),            // C++14
            std::bind(std::less_equal<>(), lowVal, _1),
            std::bind(std::less_equal<>(), _1, highVal));
```

In C++11, we'd have to specify the types we wanted to compare, and the `std::bind` call would then look like this:

```
auto betweenB =                              // C++11 version
  std::bind(std::logical_and<bool>(),
            std::bind(std::less_equal<int>(), lowVal, _1),
            std::bind(std::less_equal<int>(), _1, highVal));
```

Of course, in C++11, the lambda couldn't take an `auto` parameter, so it'd have to commit to a type, too:

```
auto betweenL =                              // C++11 version
  [lowVal, highVal]
  (int val)
  { return lowVal <= val && val <= highVal; };
```

Either way, I hope we can agree that the lambda version is not just shorter, but also more comprehensible and maintainable.

Earlier, I remarked that for those with little `std::bind` experience, its placeholders (e.g., _1, _2, etc.) are essentially magic. But it's not just the behavior of the placeholders that's opaque. Suppose we have a function to create compressed copies of Widgets,

```
enum class CompLevel { Low, Normal, High };  // compression
                                             // level

Widget compress(const Widget& w,             // make compressed
                CompLevel lev);              // copy of w
```

and we want to create a function object that allows us to specify how much a particular Widget w should be compressed. This use of `std::bind` will create such an object:

```
Widget w;

using namespace std::placeholders;

auto compressRateB = std::bind(compress, w, _1);
```

Now, when we pass w to std::bind, it has to be stored for the later call to compress. It's stored inside the object compressRateB, but how is it stored—by value or by reference? It makes a difference, because if w is modified between the call to std::bind and a call to compressRateB, storing w by reference will reflect the changes, while storing it by value won't.

The answer is that it's stored by value,[2] but the only way to know that is to memorize how std::bind works; there's no sign of it in the call to std::bind. Contrast that with a lambda approach, where whether w is captured by value or by reference is explicit:

```
auto compressRateL =                    // w is captured by
  [w](CompLevel lev)                    // value; lev is
  { return compress(w, lev); };         // passed by value
```

Equally explicit is how parameters are passed to the lambda. Here, it's clear that the parameter lev is passed by value. Hence:

```
compressRateL(CompLevel::High);         // arg is passed
                                        // by value
```

But in the call to the object resulting from std::bind, how is the argument passed?

```
compressRateB(CompLevel::High);         // how is arg
                                        // passed?
```

Again, the only way to know is to memorize how std::bind works. (The answer is that all arguments passed to bind objects are passed by reference, because the function call operator for such objects uses perfect forwarding.)

Compared to lambdas, then, code using std::bind is less readable, less expressive, and possibly less efficient. In C++14, there are no reasonable use cases for std::bind. In C++11, however, std::bind can be justified in two constrained situations:

---

2 std::bind always copies its arguments, but callers can achieve the effect of having an argument stored by reference by applying std::ref to it. The result of
```
    auto compressRateB = std::bind(compress, std::ref(w), _1);
```
is that compressRateB acts as if it holds a reference to w, rather than a copy.

- **Move capture**. C++11 lambdas don't offer move capture, but it can be emulated through a combination of a lambda and `std::bind`. For details, consult Item 32, which also explains that in C++14, lambdas' support for init capture eliminates the need for the emulation.

- **Polymorphic function objects**. Because the function call operator on a bind object uses perfect forwarding, it can accept arguments of any type (modulo the restrictions on perfect forwarding described in Item 30). This can be useful when you want to bind an object with a templatized function call operator. For example, given this class,

```
class PolyWidget {
public:
    template<typename T>
    void operator()(const T& param) const;
    ...
};
```

`std::bind` can bind a `PolyWidget` as follows:

```
PolyWidget pw;

auto boundPW = std::bind(pw, _1);
```

`boundPW` can then be called with different types of arguments:

```
boundPW(1930);              // pass int to
                            // PolyWidget::operator()

boundPW(nullptr);           // pass nullptr to
                            // PolyWidget::operator()

boundPW("Rosebud");         // pass string literal to
                            // PolyWidget::operator()
```

There is no way to do this with a C++11 lambda. In C++14, however, it's easily achieved via a lambda with an `auto` parameter:

```
auto boundPW = [pw](const auto& param)    // C++14
               { pw(param); };
```

These are edge cases, of course, and they're transient edge cases at that, because compilers supporting C++14 lambdas are increasingly common.

When `bind` was unofficially added to C++ in 2005, it was a big improvement over its 1998 predecessors. The addition of lambda support to C++11 rendered `std::bind` all but obsolete, however, and as of C++14, there are just no good use cases for it.

Things to Remember

- Lambdas are more readable, more expressive, and may be more efficient than using `std::bind`.

- In C++11 only, `std::bind` may be useful for implementing move capture or for binding objects with templatized function call operators.

CHAPTER 7

The Concurrency API

One of C++11's great triumphs is the incorporation of concurrency into the language and library. Programmers familiar with other threading APIs (e.g., pthreads or Windows threads) are sometimes surprised at the comparatively Spartan feature set that C++ offers, but that's because a great deal of C++'s support for concurrency is in the form of constraints on compiler writers. The resulting language assurances mean that for the first time in C++'s history, programmers can write multithreaded programs with standard behavior across all platforms. This establishes a solid foundation on which expressive libraries can be built, and the concurrency elements of the Standard Library (tasks, futures, threads, mutexes, condition variables, atomic objects, and more) are merely the beginning of what is sure to become an increasingly rich set of tools for the development of concurrent C++ software.

In the Items that follow, bear in mind that the Standard Library has two templates for futures: `std::future` and `std::shared_future`. In many cases, the distinction is not important, so I often simply talk about *futures*, by which I mean both kinds.

Item 35: Prefer task-based programming to thread-based.

If you want to run a function doAsyncWork asynchronously, you have two basic choices. You can create a `std::thread` and run doAsyncWork on it, thus employing a *thread-based* approach:

```
int doAsyncWork();
```

```
std::thread t(doAsyncWork);
```

Or you can pass doAsyncWork to `std::async`, an example of a strategy known as *task-based*:

```
auto fut = std::async(doAsyncWork);        // "fut" for "future"
```

In such calls, the function object passed to `std::async` (e.g., `doAsyncWork`) is considered a *task*.

The task-based approach is typically superior to its thread-based counterpart, and the tiny amount of code we've seen already demonstrates some reasons why. Here, `doAsyncWork` produces a return value, which we can reasonably assume the code invoking `doAsyncWork` is interested in. With the thread-based invocation, there's no straightforward way to get access to it. With the task-based approach, it's easy, because the future returned from `std::async` offers the `get` function. The `get` function is even more important if `doAsyncWork` emits an exception, because `get` provides access to that, too. With the thread-based approach, if `doAsyncWork` throws, the program dies (via a call to `std::terminate`).

A more fundamental difference between thread-based and task-based programming is the higher level of abstraction that task-based embodies. It frees you from the details of thread management, an observation that reminds me that I need to summarize the three meanings of "thread" in concurrent C++ software:

- *Hardware threads* are the threads that actually perform computation. Contemporary machine architectures offer one or more hardware threads per CPU core.

- *Software threads* (also known as *OS threads* or *system threads*) are the threads that the operating system[1] manages across all processes and schedules for execution on hardware threads. It's typically possible to create more software threads than hardware threads, because when a software thread is blocked (e.g., on I/O or waiting for a mutex or condition variable), throughput can be improved by executing other, unblocked, threads.

- `std::threads` are objects in a C++ process that act as handles to underlying software threads. Some `std::thread` objects represent "null" handles, i.e., correspond to no software thread, because they're in a default-constructed state (hence have no function to execute), have been moved from (the moved-to `std::thread` then acts as the handle to the underlying software thread), have been `joined` (the function they were to run has finished), or have been `detached` (the connection between them and their underlying software thread has been severed).

Software threads are a limited resource. If you try to create more than the system can provide, a `std::system_error` exception is thrown. This is true even if the function you want to run can't throw. For example, even if `doAsyncWork` is `noexcept`,

---

1 Assuming you have one. Some embedded systems don't.

```
int doAsyncWork() noexcept;          // see Item 14 for noexcept
```

this statement could result in an exception:

```
std::thread t(doAsyncWork);          // throws if no more
                                     // threads are available
```

Well-written software must somehow deal with this possibility, but how? One approach is to run doAsyncWork on the current thread, but that could lead to unbalanced loads and, if the current thread is a GUI thread, responsiveness issues. Another option is to wait for some existing software threads to complete and then try to create a new std::thread again, but it's possible that the existing threads are waiting for an action that doAsyncWork is supposed to perform (e.g., produce a result or notify a condition variable).

Even if you don't run out of threads, you can have trouble with *oversubscription*. That's when there are more ready-to-run (i.e., unblocked) software threads than hardware threads. When that happens, the thread scheduler (typically part of the OS) time-slices the software threads on the hardware. When one thread's time-slice is finished and another's begins, a context switch is performed. Such context switches increase the overall thread management overhead of the system, and they can be particularly costly when the hardware thread on which a software thread is scheduled is on a different core than was the case for the software thread during its last time-slice. In that case, (1) the CPU caches are typically cold for that software thread (i.e., they contain little data and few instructions useful to it) and (2) the running of the "new" software thread on that core "pollutes" the CPU caches for "old" threads that had been running on that core and are likely to be scheduled to run there again.

Avoiding oversubscription is difficult, because the optimal ratio of software to hardware threads depends on how often the software threads are runnable, and that can change dynamically, e.g., when a program goes from an I/O-heavy region to a computation-heavy region. The best ratio of software to hardware threads is also dependent on the cost of context switches and how effectively the software threads use the CPU caches. Furthermore, the number of hardware threads and the details of the CPU caches (e.g., how large they are and their relative speeds) depend on the machine architecture, so even if you tune your application to avoid oversubscription (while still keeping the hardware busy) on one platform, there's no guarantee that your solution will work well on other kinds of machines.

Your life will be easier if you dump these problems on somebody else, and using std::async does exactly that:

```
auto fut = std::async(doAsyncWork);   // onus of thread mgmt is
                                      // on implementer of
                                      // the Standard Library
```

This call shifts the thread management responsibility to the implementer of the C++ Standard Library. For example, the likelihood of receiving an out-of-threads exception is significantly reduced, because this call will probably never yield one. "How can that be?" you might wonder. "If I ask for more software threads than the system can provide, why does it matter whether I do it by creating `std::thread`s or by calling `std::async`?" It matters, because `std::async`, when called in this form (i.e., with the default launch policy—see Item 36), doesn't guarantee that it will create a new software thread. Rather, it permits the scheduler to arrange for the specified function (in this example, `doAsyncWork`) to be run on the thread requesting `doAsyncWork`'s result (i.e., on the thread calling `get` or `wait` on `fut`), and reasonable schedulers take advantage of that freedom if the system is oversubscribed or is out of threads.

If you pulled this "run it on the thread needing the result" trick yourself, I remarked that it could lead to load-balancing issues, and those issues don't go away simply because it's `std::async` and the runtime scheduler that confront them instead of you. When it comes to load balancing, however, the runtime scheduler is likely to have a more comprehensive picture of what's happening on the machine than you do, because it manages the threads from all processes, not just the one your code is running in.

With `std::async`, responsiveness on a GUI thread can still be problematic, because the scheduler has no way of knowing which of your threads has tight responsiveness requirements. In that case, you'll want to pass the `std::launch::async` launch policy to `std::async`. That will ensure that the function you want to run really executes on a different thread (see Item 36).

State-of-the-art thread schedulers employ system-wide thread pools to avoid oversubscription, and they improve load balancing across hardware cores through work-stealing algorithms. The C++ Standard does not require the use of thread pools or work-stealing, and, to be honest, there are some technical aspects of the C++11 concurrency specification that make it more difficult to employ them than we'd like. Nevertheless, some vendors take advantage of this technology in their Standard Library implementations, and it's reasonable to expect that progress will continue in this area. If you take a task-based approach to your concurrent programming, you automatically reap the benefits of such technology as it becomes more widespread. If, on the other hand, you program directly with `std::thread`s, you assume the burden of dealing with thread exhaustion, oversubscription, and load balancing yourself, not to mention how your solutions to these problems mesh with the solutions implemented in programs running in other processes on the same machine.

Compared to thread-based programming, a task-based design spares you the travails of manual thread management, and it provides a natural way to examine the results of asynchronously executed functions (i.e., return values or exceptions). Nevertheless, there are some situations where using threads directly may be appropriate. They include:

- **You need access to the API of the underlying threading implementation.** The C++ concurrency API is typically implemented using a lower-level platform-specific API, usually pthreads or Windows' Threads. Those APIs are currently richer than what C++ offers. (For example, C++ has no notion of thread priorities or affinities.) To provide access to the API of the underlying threading implementation, `std::thread` objects typically offer the `native_handle` member function. There is no counterpart to this functionality for `std::futures` (i.e., for what `std::async` returns).

- **You need to and are able to optimize thread usage for your application.** This could be the case, for example, if you're developing server software with a known execution profile that will be deployed as the only significant process on a machine with fixed hardware characteristics.

- **You need to implement threading technology beyond the C++ concurrency API**, e.g., thread pools on platforms where your C++ implementations don't offer them.

These are uncommon cases, however. Most of the time, you should choose task-based designs instead of programming with threads.

Things to Remember

- The `std::thread` API offers no direct way to get return values from asynchronously run functions, and if those functions throw, the program is terminated.

- Thread-based programming calls for manual management of thread exhaustion, oversubscription, load balancing, and adaptation to new platforms.

- Task-based programming via `std::async` with the default launch policy handles most of these issues for you.

Item 36: Specify `std::launch::async` if asynchronicity is essential.

When you call `std::async` to execute a function (or other callable object), you're generally intending to run the function asynchronously. But that's not necessarily what you're asking `std::async` to do. You're really requesting that the function be run in accord with a `std::async` *launch policy*. There are two standard policies, each represented by an enumerator in the std::launch scoped enum. (See Item 10 for information on scoped enums.) Assuming a function f is passed to std::async for execution,

- **The std::launch::async launch policy** means that f must be run asynchronously, i.e., on a different thread.

- **The std::launch::deferred launch policy** means that f may run only when get or wait is called on the future returned by std::async.[2] That is, f's execution is *deferred* until such a call is made. When get or wait is invoked, f will execute synchronously, i.e., the caller will block until f finishes running. If neither get nor wait is called, f will never run.

Perhaps surprisingly, std::async's default launch policy—the one it uses if you don't expressly specify one—is neither of these. Rather, it's these or-ed together. The following two calls have exactly the same meaning:

```
auto fut1 = std::async(f);                  // run f using
                                            // default launch
                                            // policy

auto fut2 = std::async(std::launch::async | // run f either
                       std::launch::deferred, // async or
                       f);                  // deferred
```

The default policy thus permits f to be run either asynchronously or synchronously. As Item 35 points out, this flexibility permits std::async and the thread-management components of the Standard Library to assume responsibility for thread creation and destruction, avoidance of oversubscription, and load balancing. That's among the things that make concurrent programming with std::async so convenient.

But using std::async with the default launch policy has some interesting implications. Given a thread t executing this statement,

```
auto fut = std::async(f);    // run f using default launch policy
```

---

2 This is a simplification. What matters isn't the future on which get or wait is invoked, it's the shared state to which the future refers. (Item 38 discusses the relationship between futures and shared states.) Because std::futures support moving and can also be used to construct std::shared_futures, and because std::shared_futures can be copied, the future object referring to the shared state arising from the call to std::async to which f was passed is likely to be different from the one returned by std::async. That's a mouthful, however, so it's common to fudge the truth and simply talk about invoking get or wait on the future returned from std::async.

- **It's not possible to predict whether f will run concurrently with t**, because f might be scheduled to run deferred.

- **It's not possible to predict whether f runs on a thread different from the thread invoking get or wait on fut.** If that thread is t, the implication is that it's not possible to predict whether f runs on a thread different from t.

- **It may not be possible to predict whether f runs at all**, because it may not be possible to guarantee that get or wait will be called on fut along every path through the program.

The default launch policy's scheduling flexibility often mixes poorly with the use of thread_local variables, because it means that if f reads or writes such *thread-local storage* (TLS), it's not possible to predict which thread's variables will be accessed:

```
auto fut = std::async(f);        // TLS for f possibly for
                                 // independent thread, but
                                 // possibly for thread
                                 // invoking get or wait on fut
```

It also affects wait-based loops using timeouts, because calling wait_for or wait_until on a task (see Item 35) that's deferred yields the value std::future_status::deferred. This means that the following loop, which looks like it should eventually terminate, may, in reality, run forever:

```
using namespace std::literals;       // for C++14 duration
                                     // suffixes; see Item 34

void f()                             // f sleeps for 1 second,
{                                    // then returns
  std::this_thread::sleep_for(1s);
}

auto fut = std::async(f);            // run f asynchronously
                                     // (conceptually)

while (fut.wait_for(100ms) !=        // loop until f has
       std::future_status::ready)    // finished running...
{                                    // which may never happen!
  …
}
```

If f runs concurrently with the thread calling std::async (i.e., if the launch policy chosen for f is std::launch::async), there's no problem here (assuming f eventually finishes), but if f is deferred, fut.wait_for will always return std::future_status::deferred. That will never be equal to std::future_status::ready, so the loop will never terminate.

This kind of bug is easy to overlook during development and unit testing, because it may manifest itself only under heavy loads. Those are the conditions that push the machine towards oversubscription or thread exhaustion, and that's when a task may be most likely to be deferred. After all, if the hardware isn't threatened by oversubscription or thread exhaustion, there's no reason for the runtime system not to schedule the task for concurrent execution.

The fix is simple: just check the future corresponding to the std::async call to see whether the task is deferred, and, if so, avoid entering the timeout-based loop. Unfortunately, there's no direct way to ask a future whether its task is deferred. Instead, you have to call a timeout-based function—a function such as wait_for. In this case, you don't really want to wait for anything, you just want to see if the return value is std::future_status::deferred, so stifle your mild disbelief at the necessary circumlocution and call wait_for with a zero timeout:

```
auto fut = std::async(f);                        // as above

if (fut.wait_for(0s) ==                          // if task is
    std::future_status::deferred)                // deferred...
{
                          // ...use wait or get on fut
    …                     // to call f synchronously


} else {                 // task isn't deferred
    while (fut.wait_for(100ms) !=                // infinite loop not
        std::future_status::ready) {             // possible (assuming
                                                 // f finishes)

        …                 // task is neither deferred nor ready,
                          // so do concurrent work until it's ready
    }

    …                     // fut is ready

}
```

The upshot of these various considerations is that using `std::async` with the default launch policy for a task is fine as long as the following conditions are fulfilled:

- The task need not run concurrently with the thread calling `get` or `wait`.
- It doesn't matter which thread's `thread_local` variables are read or written.
- Either there's a guarantee that `get` or `wait` will be called on the future returned by `std::async` or it's acceptable that the task may never execute.
- Code using `wait_for` or `wait_until` takes the possibility of deferred status into account.

If any of these conditions fails to hold, you probably want to guarantee that `std::async` will schedule the task for truly asynchronous execution. The way to do that is to pass `std::launch::async` as the first argument when you make the call:

```
auto fut = std::async(std::launch::async, f);   // launch f
                                                 // asynchronously
```

In fact, having a function that acts like `std::async`, but that automatically uses `std::launch::async` as the launch policy, is a convenient tool to have around, so it's nice that it's easy to write. Here's the C++11 version:

```
template<typename F, typename... Ts>
inline
std::future<typename std::result_of<F(Ts...)>::type>
reallyAsync(F&& f, Ts&&... params)       // return future
{                                        // for asynchronous
  return std::async(std::launch::async,  // call to f(params...)
                    std::forward<F>(f),
                    std::forward<Ts>(params)...);
}
```

This function receives a callable object `f` and zero or more parameters `params` and perfect-forwards them (see Item 25) to `std::async`, passing `std::launch::async` as the launch policy. Like `std::async`, it returns a `std::future` for the result of invoking `f` on `params`. Determining the type of that result is easy, because the type trait `std::result_of` gives it to you. (See Item 9 for general information on type traits.)

`reallyAsync` is used just like `std::async`:

```
auto fut = reallyAsync(f);       // run f asynchronously;
                                 // throw if std::async
                                 // would throw
```

In C++14, the ability to deduce `reallyAsync`'s return type streamlines the function declaration:

```
template<typename F, typename... Ts>
inline
auto                                      // C++14
reallyAsync(F&& f, Ts&&... params)
{
  return std::async(std::launch::async,
                    std::forward<F>(f),
                    std::forward<Ts>(params)...);
}
```

This version makes it crystal clear that `reallyAsync` does nothing but invoke `std::async` with the `std::launch::async` launch policy.

Things to Remember

- The default launch policy for `std::async` permits both asynchronous and synchronous task execution.

- This flexibility leads to uncertainty when accessing `thread_locals`, implies that the task may never execute, and affects program logic for timeout-based `wait` calls.

- Specify `std::launch::async` if asynchronous task execution is essential.

Item 37: Make `std::threads` unjoinable on all paths.

Every `std::thread` object is in one of two states: *joinable* or *unjoinable*. A joinable `std::thread` corresponds to an underlying asynchronous thread of execution that is or could be running. A `std::thread` corresponding to an underlying thread that's blocked or waiting to be scheduled is joinable, for example. `std::thread` objects corresponding to underlying threads that have run to completion are also considered joinable.

An unjoinable `std::thread` is what you'd expect: a `std::thread` that's not joinable. Unjoinable `std::thread` objects include:

- **Default-constructed `std::threads`.** Such `std::threads` have no function to execute, hence don't correspond to an underlying thread of execution.

- **std::thread objects that have been moved from**. The result of a move is that the underlying thread of execution a std::thread used to correspond to (if any) now corresponds to a different std::thread.

- **std::threads that have been joined**. After a join, the std::thread object no longer corresponds to the underlying thread of execution that has finished running.

- **std::threads that have been detached**. A detach severs the connection between a std::thread object and the underlying thread of execution it corresponds to.

One reason a std::thread's joinability is important is that if the destructor for a joinable thread is invoked, execution of the program (i.e., all threads) is terminated. For example, suppose we have a function doWork that takes a filtering function, filter, and a maximum value, maxVal, as parameters. doWork makes sure that all conditions necessary for its computation are satisfied, then performs the computation with all the values between 0 and maxVal that pass the filter. If it's time-consuming to do the filtering and it's also time-consuming to determine whether doWork's conditions are satisfied, it would be reasonable to do those two things concurrently.

Our preference would be to employ a task-based design for this (see Item 35), but let's assume we'd like to set the priority of the thread doing the filtering. Item 35 explains that that requires use of the thread's native handle, and that's accessible only through the std::thread API; the task-based API (i.e., futures) doesn't provide it. Our approach will therefore be based on threads, not tasks.

We could come up with code like this:

```
constexpr auto tenMillion = 10000000;          // see Item 15
                                               // for constexpr

bool doWork(std::function<bool(int)> filter,   // returns whether
            int maxVal = tenMillion)           // computation was
{                                              // performed; see
                                               // Item 5 for
                                               // std::function

    std::vector<int> goodVals;                 // values that
                                               // satisfy filter

    std::thread t([&filter, maxVal, &goodVals] // populate
                  {                            // goodVals
                      for (auto i = 0; i <= maxVal; ++i)
                          { if (filter(i)) goodVals.push_back(i); }
```

```
                      });

    auto nh = t.native_handle();              // use t's native
    …                                          // handle to set
                                               // t's priority
    if (conditionsAreSatisfied()) {
      t.join();                                // let t finish
      performComputation(goodVals);
      return true;                             // computation was
    }                                          // performed

    return false;                              // computation was
  }                                            // not performed
```

Before I explain why this code is problematic, I'll remark that tenMillion's initializing value can be made more readable in C++14 by taking advantage of C++14's ability to use an apostrophe as a digit separator:

```
    constexpr auto tenMillion = 10'000'000;    // C++14
```

I'll also remark that setting t's priority after it has started running is a bit like closing the proverbial barn door after the equally proverbial horse has bolted. A better design would be to start t in a suspended state (thus making it possible to adjust its priority before it does any computation), but I don't want to distract you with that code. If you're more distracted by the code's absence, turn to Item 39, because it shows how to start threads suspended.

But back to doWork. If conditionsAreSatisfied() returns true, all is well, but if it returns false or throws an exception, the std::thread object t will be joinable when its destructor is called at the end of doWork. That would cause program execution to be terminated.

You might wonder why the std::thread destructor behaves this way. It's because the two other obvious options are arguably worse. They are:

- **An implicit join**. In this case, a std::thread's destructor would wait for its underlying asynchronous thread of execution to complete. That sounds reasonable, but it could lead to performance anomalies that would be difficult to track down. For example, it would be counterintuitive that doWork would wait for its filter to be applied to all values if conditionsAreSatisfied() had already returned false.

- **An implicit detach**. In this case, a std::thread's destructor would sever the connection between the std::thread object and its underlying thread of execution. The underlying thread would continue to run. This sounds no less reasonable than the join approach, but the debugging problems it can lead to are worse. In doWork, for example, goodVals is a local variable that is captured by reference. It's also modified inside the lambda (via the call to push_back). Suppose, then, that while the lambda is running asynchronously, *conditionsAre-Satisfied()* returns false. In that case, doWork would return, and its local variables (including goodVals) would be destroyed. Its stack frame would be popped, and execution of its thread would continue at doWork's call site.

Statements following that call site would, at some point, make additional function calls, and at least one such call would probably end up using some or all of the memory that had once been occupied by the doWork stack frame. Let's call such a function f. While f was running, the lambda that doWork initiated would still be running asynchronously. That lambda could call push_back on the stack memory that used to be goodVals but that is now somewhere inside f's stack frame. Such a call would modify the memory that used to be goodVals, and that means that from f's perspective, the content of memory in its stack frame could spontaneously change! Imagine the fun you'd have debugging *that*.

The Standardization Committee decided that the consequences of destroying a joinable thread were sufficiently dire that they essentially banned it (by specifying that destruction of a joinable thread causes program termination).

This puts the onus on you to ensure that if you use a std::thread object, it's made unjoinable on every path out of the scope in which it's defined. But covering every path can be complicated. It includes flowing off the end of the scope as well as jumping out via a return, continue, break, goto or exception. That can be a lot of paths.

Any time you want to perform some action along every path out of a block, the normal approach is to put that action in the destructor of a local object. Such objects are known as *RAII objects*, and the classes they come from are known as *RAII classes*. (*RAII* itself stands for "Resource Acquisition Is Initialization," although the crux of the technique is destruction, not initialization). RAII classes are common in the Standard Library. Examples include the STL containers (each container's destructor destroys the container's contents and releases its memory), the standard smart pointers (Items 18–20 explain that std::unique_ptr's destructor invokes its deleter on the object it points to, and the destructors in std::shared_ptr and std::weak_ptr decrement reference counts), std::fstream objects (their destructors close the files they correspond to), and many more. And yet there is no standard RAII class for std::thread objects, perhaps because the Standardization Committee, having rejected both join and detach as default options, simply didn't know what such a class should do.

Fortunately, it's not difficult to write one yourself. For example, the following class allows callers to specify whether `join` or `detach` should be called when a Thread-RAII object (an RAII object for a `std::thread`) is destroyed:

```
class ThreadRAII {
public:
  enum class DtorAction { join, detach };     // see Item 10 for
                                              // enum class info

  ThreadRAII(std::thread&& t, DtorAction a)   // in dtor, take
  : action(a), t(std::move(t)) {}             // action a on t

  ~ThreadRAII()
  {                                           // see below for
    if (t.joinable()) {                       // joinability test

      if (action == DtorAction::join) {
        t.join();
      } else {
        t.detach();
      }

    }
  }

  std::thread& get() { return t; }            // see below

private:
  DtorAction action;
  std::thread t;
};
```

I hope this code is largely self-explanatory, but the following points may be helpful:

- The constructor accepts only `std::thread` rvalues, because we want to move the passed-in `std::thread` into the ThreadRAII object. (Recall that `std::thread` objects aren't copyable.)

- The parameter order in the constructor is designed to be intuitive to callers (specifying the `std::thread` first and the destructor action second makes more sense than vice versa), but the member initialization list is designed to match the order of the data members' declarations. That order puts the `std::thread` object last. In this class, the order makes no difference, but in general, it's possible for the initialization of one data member to depend on another, and because `std::thread` objects may start running a function immediately after they are initialized, it's a good habit to declare them last in a class. That guarantees that at the time they are constructed, all the data members that precede them have already been initialized and can therefore be safely accessed by the asynchronously running thread that corresponds to the std::thread data member.

- ThreadRAII offers a get function to provide access to the underlying std::thread object. This is analogous to the get functions offered by the standard smart pointer classes that give access to their underlying raw pointers. Providing get avoids the need for ThreadRAII to replicate the full std::thread interface, and it also means that ThreadRAII objects can be used in contexts where std::thread objects are required.

- Before the ThreadRAII destructor invokes a member function on the std::thread object t, it checks to make sure that t is joinable. This is necessary, because invoking join or detach on an unjoinable thread yields undefined behavior. It's possible that a client constructed a std::thread, created a ThreadRAII object from it, used get to acquire access to t, and then did a move from t or called join or detach on it. Each of those actions would render t unjoinable.

If you're worried that in this code,

```
if (t.joinable()) {

  if (action == DtorAction::join) {
    t.join();
  } else {
    t.detach();
  }
}
```

a race exists, because between execution of t.joinable() and invocation of join or detach, another thread could render t unjoinable, your intuition is commendable, but your fears are unfounded. A std::thread object can change state from joinable to unjoinable only through a member function call, e.g., join, detach, or a move operation. At the time a ThreadRAII object's destructor is invoked, no other thread should be making member function calls on that object. If there are simultaneous calls, there is certainly a race, but it isn't inside the destructor, it's in the client code that is trying to invoke two member functions (the destructor and something else) on one object at the same time. In general, simultaneous member function calls on a single object are safe only if all are to const member functions (see Item 16).

Employing ThreadRAII in our doWork example would look like this:

```
bool doWork(std::function<bool(int)> filter,   // as before
            int maxVal = tenMillion)
{
  std::vector<int> goodVals;                    // as before

  ThreadRAII t(                                 // use RAII object
    std::thread([&filter, maxVal, &goodVals]
                {
                  for (auto i = 0; i <= maxVal; ++i)
                    { if (filter(i)) goodVals.push_back(i); }
                }),
                ThreadRAII::DtorAction::join   // RAII action
  );

  auto nh = t.get().native_handle();
  …

  if (conditionsAreSatisfied()) {
    t.get().join();
    performComputation(goodVals);
    return true;
  }

  return false;
}
```

In this case, we've chosen to do a join on the asynchronously running thread in the ThreadRAII destructor, because, as we saw earlier, doing a detach could lead to some truly nightmarish debugging. We also saw earlier that doing a join could lead to performance anomalies (that, to be frank, could also be unpleasant to debug), but given a choice between undefined behavior (which detach would get us), program termination (which use of a raw std::thread would yield), or performance anomalies, performance anomalies seems like the best of a bad lot.

Alas, Item 39 demonstrates that using ThreadRAII to perform a join on std::thread destruction can sometimes lead not just to a performance anomaly, but to a hung program. The "proper" solution to these kinds of problems would be to communicate to the asynchronously running lambda that we no longer need its work and that it should return early, but there's no support in C++11 for *interruptible threads.* They can be implemented by hand, but that's a topic beyond the scope of this book.[3]

Item 17 explains that because ThreadRAII declares a destructor, there will be no compiler-generated move operations, but there is no reason ThreadRAII objects shouldn't be movable. If compilers were to generate these functions, the functions would do the right thing, so explicitly requesting their creation is appropriate:

```
class ThreadRAII {
public:
  enum class DtorAction { join, detach };      // as before

  ThreadRAII(std::thread&& t, DtorAction a)     // as before
  : action(a), t(std::move(t)) {}

  ~ThreadRAII()
  {
    ...                                          // as before
  }

  ThreadRAII(ThreadRAII&&) = default;            // support
  ThreadRAII& operator=(ThreadRAII&&) = default; // moving

  std::thread& get() { return t; }               // as before

private:                                         // as before
  DtorAction action;
  std::thread t;
};
```

Things to Remember

- Make std::threads unjoinable on all paths.
- join-on-destruction can lead to difficult-to-debug performance anomalies.
- detach-on-destruction can lead to difficult-to-debug undefined behavior.
- Declare std::thread objects last in lists of data members.

---

3 You'll find a nice treatment in Anthony Williams' *C++ Concurrency in Action* (Manning Publications, 2012), section 9.2.

Item 38: Be aware of varying thread handle destructor behavior.

Item 37 explains that a joinable `std::thread` corresponds to an underlying system thread of execution. A future for a non-deferred task (see Item 36) has a similar relationship to a system thread. As such, both `std::thread` objects and future objects can be thought of as *handles* to system threads.

From this perspective, it's interesting that `std::thread`s and futures have such different behaviors in their destructors. As noted in Item 37, destruction of a joinable `std::thread` terminates your program, because the two obvious alternatives—an implicit `join` and an implicit `detach`—were considered worse choices. Yet the destructor for a future sometimes behaves as if it did an implicit `join`, sometimes as if it did an implicit `detach`, and sometimes neither. It never causes program termination. This thread handle behavioral bouillabaisse deserves closer examination.

We'll begin with the observation that a future is one end of a communications channel through which a callee transmits a result to a caller.[4] The callee (usually running asynchronously) writes the result of its computation into the communications channel (typically via a `std::promise` object), and the caller reads that result using a future. You can think of it as follows, where the dashed arrow shows the flow of information from callee to caller:

But where is the callee's result stored? The callee could finish before the caller invokes `get` on a corresponding future, so the result can't be stored in the callee's `std::promise`. That object, being local to the callee, would be destroyed when the callee finished.

The result can't be stored in the caller's future, either, because (among other reasons) a `std::future` may be used to create a `std::shared_future` (thus transferring ownership of the callee's result from the `std::future` to the `std::shared_future`), which may then be copied many times after the original `std::future` is destroyed. Given that not all result types can be copied (i.e., move-only types) and that the result

---

4 Item 39 explains that the kind of communications channel associated with a future can be employed for other purposes. For this Item, however, we'll consider only its use as a mechanism for a callee to convey its result to a caller.

must live at least as long as the last future referring to it, which of the potentially many futures corresponding to the callee should be the one to contain its result?

Because neither objects associated with the callee nor objects associated with the caller are suitable places to store the callee's result, it's stored in a location outside both. This location is known as the *shared state*. The shared state is typically represented by a heap-based object, but its type, interface, and implementation are not specified by the Standard. Standard Library authors are free to implement shared states in any way they like.

We can envision the relationship among the callee, the caller, and the shared state as follows, where dashed arrows once again represent the flow of information:

The existence of the shared state is important, because the behavior of a future's destructor—the topic of this Item—is determined by the shared state associated with the future. In particular,

- **The destructor for the last future referring to a shared state for a non-deferred task launched via std::async blocks** until the task completes. In essence, the destructor for such a future does an implicit join on the thread on which the asynchronously executing task is running.

- **The destructor for all other futures simply destroys the future object**. For asynchronously running tasks, this is akin to an implicit detach on the underlying thread. For deferred tasks for which this is the final future, it means that the deferred task will never run.

These rules sound more complicated than they are. What we're really dealing with is a simple "normal" behavior and one lone exception to it. The normal behavior is that a future's destructor destroys the future object. That's it. It doesn't join with anything, it doesn't detach from anything, it doesn't run anything. It just destroys the future's data members. (Well, actually, it does one more thing. It decrements the reference count inside the shared state that's manipulated by both the futures referring to it and the callee's std::promise. This reference count makes it possible for the library to know when the shared state can be destroyed. For general information about reference counting, see Item 19.)

The exception to this normal behavior arises only for a future for which all of the following apply:

- **It refers to a shared state that was created due to a call to std::async.**

- **The task's launch policy is std::launch::async** (see Item 36), either because that was chosen by the runtime system or because it was specified in the call to std::async.

- **The future is the last future referring to the shared state**. For std::futures, this will always be the case. For std::shared_futures, if other std::shared_futures refer to the same shared state as the future being destroyed, the future being destroyed follows the normal behavior (i.e., it simply destroys its data members).

Only when all of these conditions are fulfilled does a future's destructor exhibit special behavior, and that behavior is to block until the asynchronously running task completes. Practically speaking, this amounts to an implicit join with the thread running the std::async-created task.

It's common to hear this exception to normal future destructor behavior summarized as "Futures from std::async block in their destructors." To a first approximation, that's correct, but sometimes you need more than a first approximation. Now you know the truth in all its glory and wonder.

Your wonder may take a different form. It may be of the "I wonder why there's a special rule for shared states for non-deferred tasks that are launched by std::async" variety. It's a reasonable question. From what I can tell, the Standardization Committee wanted to avoid the problems associated with an implicit detach (see Item 37), but they didn't want to adopt as radical a policy as mandatory program termination (as they did for joinable std::threads—again, see Item 37), so they compromised on an implicit join. The decision was not without controversy, and there was serious talk about abandoning this behavior for C++14. In the end, no change was made, so the behavior of destructors for futures is consistent in C++11 and C++14.

The API for futures offers no way to determine whether a future refers to a shared state arising from a call to std::async, so given an arbitrary future object, it's not possible to know whether it will block in its destructor waiting for an asynchronously running task to finish. This has some interesting implications:

```
// this container might block in its dtor, because one or more
// contained futures could refer to a shared state for a non-
// deferred task launched via std::async
std::vector<std::future<void>> futs;    // see Item 39 for info
                                        // on std::future<void>

class Widget {                          // Widget objects might
public:                                 // block in their dtors
```

...

```
private:
  std::shared_future<double> fut;
};
```

Of course, if you have a way of knowing that a given future *does not* satisfy the conditions that trigger the special destructor behavior (e.g., due to program logic), you're assured that that future won't block in its destructor. For example, only shared states arising from calls to std::async qualify for the special behavior, but there are other ways that shared states get created. One is the use of std::packaged_task. A std::packaged_task object prepares a function (or other callable object) for asynchronous execution by wrapping it such that its result is put into a shared state. A future referring to that shared state can then be obtained via std::packaged_task's get_future function:

```
int calcValue();                    // func to run

std::packaged_task<int()>           // wrap calcValue so it
  pt(calcValue);                    // can run asynchronously

auto fut = pt.get_future();         // get future for pt
```

At this point, we know that the future fut doesn't refer to a shared state created by a call to std::async, so its destructor will behave normally.

Once created, the std::packaged_task pt can be run on a thread. (It could be run via a call to std::async, too, but if you want to run a task using std::async, there's little reason to create a std::packaged_task, because std::async does everything std::packaged_task does before it schedules the task for execution.)

std::packaged_tasks aren't copyable, so when pt is passed to the std::thread constructor, it must be cast to an rvalue (via std::move—see Item 23):

```
std::thread t(std::move(pt));       // run pt on t
```

This example lends some insight into the normal behavior for future destructors, but it's easier to see if the statements are put together inside a block:

```
{                                   // begin block

  std::packaged_task<int()>
    pt(calcValue);

  auto fut = pt.get_future();
```

```
std::thread t(std::move(pt));

...                                          // see below

}                                            // end block
```

The most interesting code here is the "..." that follows creation of the `std::thread` object t and precedes the end of the block. What makes it interesting is what can happen to t inside the "..." region. There are three basic possibilities:

- **Nothing happens to t**. In this case, t will be joinable at the end of the scope. That will cause the program to be terminated (see Item 37).

- **A join is done on t**. In this case, there would be no need for `fut` to block in its destructor, because the `join` is already present in the calling code.

- **A detach is done on t**. In this case, there would be no need for `fut` to detach in its destructor, because the calling code already does that.

In other words, when you have a future corresponding to a shared state that arose due to a `std::packaged_task`, there's usually no need to adopt a special destruction policy, because the decision among termination, joining, or detaching will be made in the code that manipulates the `std::thread` on which the `std::packaged_task` is typically run.

Things to Remember
- Future destructors normally just destroy the future's data members.
- The final future referring to a shared state for a non-deferred task launched via `std::async` blocks until the task completes.

Item 39: Consider `void` futures for one-shot event communication.

Sometimes it's useful for a task to tell a second, asynchronously running task that a particular event has occurred, because the second task can't proceed until the event has taken place. Perhaps a data structure has been initialized, a stage of computation has been completed, or a significant sensor value has been detected. When that's the case, what's the best way for this kind of inter-thread communication to take place?

An obvious approach is to use a condition variable (*condvar*). If we call the task that detects the condition the *detecting task* and the task reacting to the condition the *reacting task*, the strategy is simple: the reacting task waits on a condition variable, and the detecting thread notifies that condvar when the event occurs. Given

```
std::condition_variable cv;              // condvar for event

std::mutex m;                            // mutex for use with cv
```

the code in the detecting task is as simple as simple can be:

```
...                                      // detect event

cv.notify_one();                         // tell reacting task
```

If there were multiple reacting tasks to be notified, it would be appropriate to replace notify_one with notify_all, but for now, we'll assume there's only one reacting task.

The code for the reacting task is a bit more complicated, because before calling wait on the condvar, it must lock a mutex through a std::unique_lock object. (Locking a mutex before waiting on a condition variable is typical for threading libraries. The need to lock the mutex through a std::unique_lock object is simply part of the C++11 API.) Here's the conceptual approach:

```
...                                      // prepare to react

{                                        // open critical section

  std::unique_lock<std::mutex> lk(m);    // lock mutex

  cv.wait(lk);                           // wait for notify;
                                         // this isn't correct!

  ...                                    // react to event
                                         // (m is locked)

}                                        // close crit. section;
                                         // unlock m via lk's dtor

...                                      // continue reacting
                                         // (m now unlocked)
```

The first issue with this approach is what's sometimes termed a *code smell*: even if the code works, something doesn't seem quite right. In this case, the odor emanates from the need to use a mutex. Mutexes are used to control access to shared data, but it's entirely possible that the detecting and reacting tasks have no need for such mediation. For example, the detecting task might be responsible for initializing a global data structure, then turning it over to the reacting task for use. If the detecting task never accesses the data structure after initializing it, and if the reacting task never accesses it before the detecting task indicates that it's ready, the two tasks will stay out of each other's way through program logic. There will be no need for a mutex. The fact that the condvar approach requires one leaves behind the unsettling aroma of suspect design.

Even if you look past that, there are two other problems you should definitely pay attention to:

- **If the detecting task notifies the condvar before the reacting task waits, the reacting task will hang.** In order for notification of a condvar to wake another task, the other task must be waiting on that condvar. If the detecting task happens to execute the notification before the reacting task executes the wait, the reacting task will miss the notification, and it will wait forever.

- **The wait statement fails to account for spurious wakeups.** A fact of life in threading APIs (in many languages—not just C++) is that code waiting on a condition variable may be awakened even if the condvar wasn't notified. Such awakenings are known as *spurious wakeups*. Proper code deals with them by confirming that the condition being waited for has truly occurred, and it does this as its first action after waking. The C++ condvar API makes this exceptionally easy, because it permits a lambda (or other function object) that tests for the waited-for condition to be passed to wait. That is, the wait call in the reacting task could be written like this:

```
cv.wait(lk,
        []{ return whether the event has occurred; });
```

Taking advantage of this capability requires that the reacting task be able to determine whether the condition it's waiting for is true. But in the scenario we've been considering, the condition it's waiting for is the occurrence of an event that the detecting thread is responsible for recognizing. The reacting thread may have no way of determining whether the event it's waiting for has taken place. That's why it's waiting on a condition variable!

There are many situations where having tasks communicate using a condvar is a good fit for the problem at hand, but this doesn't seem to be one of them.

For many developers, the next trick in their bag is a shared boolean flag. The flag is initially false. When the detecting thread recognizes the event it's looking for, it sets the flag:

```
std::atomic<bool> flag(false);      // shared flag; see
                                    // Item 40 for std::atomic

...                                 // detect event
```

```
flag = true;                          // tell reacting task
```

For its part, the reacting thread simply polls the flag. When it sees that the flag is set, it knows that the event it's been waiting for has occurred:

```
...                                   // prepare to react

while (!flag);                        // wait for event

...                                   // react to event
```

This approach suffers from none of the drawbacks of the condvar-based design. There's no need for a mutex, no problem if the detecting task sets the flag before the reacting task starts polling, and nothing akin to a spurious wakeup. Good, good, good.

Less good is the cost of polling in the reacting task. During the time the task is waiting for the flag to be set, the task is essentially blocked, yet it's still running. As such, it occupies a hardware thread that another task might be able to make use of, it incurs the cost of a context switch each time it starts or completes its time-slice, and it could keep a core running that might otherwise be shut down to save power. A truly blocked task would do none of these things. That's an advantage of the condvar-based approach, because a task in a `wait` call is truly blocked.

It's common to combine the condvar and flag-based designs. A flag indicates whether the event of interest has occurred, but access to the flag is synchronized by a mutex. Because the mutex prevents concurrent access to the flag, there is, as Item 40 explains, no need for the flag to be `std::atomic`; a simple `bool` will do. The detecting task would then look like this:

```
std::condition_variable cv;           // as before
std::mutex m;

bool flag(false);                     // not std::atomic

...                                   // detect event

{
  std::lock_guard<std::mutex> g(m);   // lock m via g's ctor

  flag = true;                        // tell reacting task
                                      // (part 1)

}                                     // unlock m via g's dtor
```

```
    cv.notify_one();                        // tell reacting task
                                            // (part 2)
```

And here's the reacting task:

```
    ...                                     // prepare to react

    {                                       // as before
      std::unique_lock<std::mutex> lk(m);   // as before

      cv.wait(lk, [] { return flag; });     // use lambda to avoid
                                            // spurious wakeups

      ...                                   // react to event
                                            // (m is locked)
    }

    ...                                     // continue reacting
                                            // (m now unlocked)
```

This approach avoids the problems we've discussed. It works regardless of whether the reacting task waits before the detecting task notifies, it works in the presence of spurious wakeups, and it doesn't require polling. Yet an odor remains, because the detecting task communicates with the reacting task in a very curious fashion. Notifying the condition variable tells the reacting task that the event it's been waiting for has probably occurred, but the reacting task must check the flag to be sure. Setting the flag tells the reacting task that the event has definitely occurred, but the detecting task still has to notify the condition variable so that the reacting task will awaken and check the flag. The approach works, but it doesn't seem terribly clean.

An alternative is to avoid condition variables, mutexes, and flags by having the reacting task wait on a future that's set by the detecting task. This may seem like an odd idea. After all, Item 38 explains that a future represents the receiving end of a communications channel from a callee to a (typically asynchronous) caller, and here there's no callee-caller relationship between the detecting and reacting tasks. However, Item 38 also notes that a communications channel whose transmitting end is a std::promise and whose receiving end is a future can be used for more than just callee-caller communication. Such a communications channel can be used in any situation where you need to transmit information from one place in your program to another. In this case, we'll use it to transmit information from the detecting task to the reacting task, and the information we'll convey will be that the event of interest has taken place.

The design is simple. The detecting task has a std::promise object (i.e., the writing end of the communications channel), and the reacting task has a corresponding future. When the detecting task sees that the event it's looking for has occurred, it *sets* the `std::promise` (i.e., writes into the communications channel). Meanwhile, the reacting task `waits` on its future. That `wait` blocks the reacting task until the `std::promise` has been set.

Now, both `std::promise` and futures (i.e., `std::future` and `std::shared_future`) are templates that require a type parameter. That parameter indicates the type of data to be transmitted through the communications channel. In our case, however, there's no data to be conveyed. The only thing of interest to the reacting task is that its future has been set. What we need for the `std::promise` and future templates is a type that indicates that no data is to be conveyed across the communications channel. That type is `void`. The detecting task will thus use a `std::promise<void>`, and the reacting task a `std::future<void>` or `std::shared_future<void>`. The detecting task will set its `std::promise<void>` when the event of interest occurs, and the reacting task will `wait` on its future. Even though the reacting task won't receive any data from the detecting task, the communications channel will permit the reacting task to know when the detecting task has "written" its `void` data by calling `set_value` on its `std::promise`.

So given

```
std::promise<void> p;          // promise for
                               // communications channel
```

the detecting task's code is trivial,

```
...                            // detect event

p.set_value();                 // tell reacting task
```

and the reacting task's code is equally simple:

```
...                            // prepare to react

p.get_future().wait();         // wait on future
                               // corresponding to p

...                            // react to event
```

Like the approach using a flag, this design requires no mutex, works regardless of whether the detecting task sets its `std::promise` before the reacting task `waits`, and is immune to spurious wakeups. (Only condition variables are susceptible to that problem.) Like the condvar-based approach, the reacting task is truly blocked after making the `wait` call, so it consumes no system resources while waiting. Perfect, right?

Not exactly. Sure, a future-based approach skirts those shoals, but there are other hazards to worry about. For example, Item 38 explains that between a `std::promise` and a future is a shared state, and shared states are typically dynamically allocated. You should therefore assume that this design incurs the cost of heap-based allocation and deallocation.

Perhaps more importantly, a `std::promise` may be set only once. The communications channel between a `std::promise` and a future is a *one-shot* mechanism: it can't be used repeatedly. This is a notable difference from the condvar- and flag-based designs, both of which can be used to communicate multiple times. (A condvar can be repeatedly notified, and a flag can always be cleared and set again.)

The one-shot restriction isn't as limiting as you might think. Suppose you'd like to create a system thread in a suspended state. That is, you'd like to get all the overhead associated with thread creation out of the way so that when you're ready to execute something on the thread, the normal thread-creation latency will be avoided. Or you might want to create a suspended thread so that you could configure it before letting it run. Such configuration might include things like setting its priority or core affinity. The C++ concurrency API offers no way to do those things, but `std::thread` objects offer the `native_handle` member function, the result of which is intended to give you access to the platform's underlying threading API (usually POSIX threads or Windows threads). The lower-level API often makes it possible to configure thread characteristics such as priority and affinity.

Assuming you want to suspend a thread only once (after creation, but before it's running its thread function), a design using a `void` future is a reasonable choice. Here's the essence of the technique:

```
std::promise<void> p;

void react();                       // func for reacting task

void detect()                       // func for detecting task
{
  std::thread t([]                  // create thread
                {
                   p.get_future().wait();   // suspend t until
                   react();                 // future is set
                });
  ...                               // here, t is suspended
                                    // prior to call to react

  p.set_value();                    // unsuspend t (and thus
                                    // call react)
```

```
         ...                            // do additional work

    t.join();                           // make t unjoinable
  }                                     // (see Item 37)
```

Because it's important that t become unjoinable on all paths out of detect, use of an RAII class like Item 37's ThreadRAII seems like it would be advisable. Code like this comes to mind:

```
void detect()
{
  ThreadRAII tr(                        // use RAII object
    std::thread([]
                {
                  p.get_future().wait();
                  react();
                }),
      ThreadRAII::DtorAction::join      // risky! (see below)
  );

    ...                                 // thread inside tr
                                        // is suspended here

  p.set_value();                        // unsuspend thread
                                        // inside tr

    ...

}
```

This looks safer than it is. The problem is that if in the first "..." region (the one with the "thread inside tr is suspended here" comment), an exception is emitted, set_value will never be called on p. That means that the call to wait inside the lambda will never return. That, in turn, means that the thread running the lambda will never finish, and that's a problem, because the RAII object tr has been configured to perform a join on that thread in tr's destructor. In other words, if an exception is emitted from the first "..." region of code, this function will hang, because tr's destructor will never complete.

There are ways to address this problem, but I'll leave them in the form of the hallowed exercise for the reader.[5] Here, I'd like to show how the original code (i.e., not using ThreadRAII) can be extended to suspend and then unsuspend not just one

---

5 A reasonable place to begin researching the matter is my 8 April 2015 blog post at *The View From Aristeia*, "More on ThreadRAII and Thread Suspension".

reacting task, but many. It's a simple generalization, because the key is to use std::shared_futures instead of a std::future in the react code. Once you know that the std::future's share member function transfers ownership of its shared state to the std::shared_future object produced by share, the code nearly writes itself. The only subtlety is that each reacting thread needs its own copy of the std::shared_future that refers to the shared state, so the std::shared_future obtained from share is captured by value by the lambdas running on the reacting threads:

```cpp
std::promise<void> p;                    // as before

void detect()                            // now for multiple
{                                        // reacting tasks

    auto sf = p.get_future().share();    // sf's type is
                                         // std::shared_future<void>

    std::vector<std::thread> vt;             // container for
                                             // reacting threads

    for (int i = 0; i < threadsToRun; ++i) {
      vt.emplace_back([sf]{ sf.wait();       // wait on local
                            react(); });      // copy of sf; see
    }                                         // Item 42 for info
                                              // on emplace_back

    ...                                     // ThreadRAII not used, so
                                            // program is terminated if
                                            // this "…" code throws!

    p.set_value();                          // unsuspend all threads

    ...

    for (auto& t : vt) {                  // make all threads
      t.join();                           // unjoinable; see Item 2
    }                                     // for info on "auto&"
}
```

The fact that a design using futures can achieve this effect is noteworthy, and that's why you should consider it for one-shot event communication.

Item 40: Use `std::atomic` for concurrency, `volatile` for special memory.

Poor `volatile`. So misunderstood. It shouldn't even be in this chapter, because it has nothing to do with concurrent programming. But in other programming languages (e.g., Java and C#), it is useful for such programming, and even in C++, some compilers have imbued `volatile` with semantics that render it applicable to concurrent software (but only when compiled with those compilers). It's thus worthwhile to discuss `volatile` in a chapter on concurrency if for no other reason than to dispel the confusion surrounding it.

The C++ feature that programmers sometimes confuse `volatile` with—the feature that definitely does belong in this chapter—is the `std::atomic` template. Instantiations of this template (e.g., `std::atomic<int>`, `std::atomic<bool>`, `std::atomic<Widget*>`, etc.) offer operations that are guaranteed to be seen as atomic by other threads. Once a `std::atomic` object has been constructed, operations on it behave more or less as if they were inside a mutex-protected critical section, but the operations are generally implemented using special machine instructions that are more efficient than would be the case if a mutex were employed.

Consider this code using `std::atomic`:

```
std::atomic<int> ai(0);     // initialize ai to 0

ai = 10;                    // atomically set ai to 10

std::cout << ai;            // atomically read ai's value

++ai;                       // atomically increment ai to 11
```

```
--ai;                          // atomically decrement ai to 10
```

During execution of these statements, other threads reading `ai` may see only values of 0, 10, or 11. No other values are possible (assuming, of course, that this is the only thread modifying `ai`).

Two aspects of this example are worth noting. First, in the "`std::cout << ai;`" statement, the fact that `ai` is a `std::atomic` guarantees only that the read of `ai` is atomic. There is no guarantee that the entire statement proceeds atomically. Between the time `ai`'s value is read and `operator<<` is invoked to write it to the standard output, another thread may have modified `ai`'s value. That has no effect on the behavior of the statement, because `operator<<` for `int`s uses a by-value parameter for the `int` to output (the outputted value will therefore be the one that was read from `ai`), but it's important to understand that what's atomic in that statement is nothing more than the read of `ai`.

The second noteworthy aspect of the example is the behavior of the last two statements—the increment and decrement of `ai`. These are each read-modify-write (RMW) operations, yet they execute atomically. This is one of the nicest characteristics of the `std::atomic` types: once a `std::atomic` object has been constructed, all member functions on it, including those comprising RMW operations, are guaranteed to be seen by other threads as atomic.

In contrast, the corresponding code using `volatile` guarantees virtually nothing in a multithreaded context:

```
volatile int vi(0);            // initialize vi to 0

vi = 10;                       // set vi to 10

std::cout << vi;               // read vi's value

++vi;                          // increment vi to 11

--vi;                          // decrement vi to 10
```

During execution of this code, if other threads are reading the value of `vi`, they may see anything, e.g., -12, 68, 4090727—anything! Such code would have undefined behavior, because these statements modify `vi`, so if other threads are reading `vi` at the same time, there are simultaneous readers and writers of memory that's neither `std::atomic` nor protected by a mutex, and that's the definition of a data race.

As a concrete example of how the behavior of std::atomics and volatiles can differ in a multithreaded program, consider a simple counter of each type that's incremented by multiple threads. We'll initialize each to 0:

```
std::atomic<int> ac(0);    // "atomic counter"

volatile int vc(0);        // "volatile counter"
```

We'll then increment each counter one time in two simultaneously running threads:

```
/*----- Thread 1 ----- */    /*------- Thread 2 ------- */

        ++ac;                         ++ac;
        ++vc;                         ++vc;
```

When both threads have finished, ac's value (i.e., the value of the std::atomic) must be 2, because each increment occurs as an indivisible operation. vc's value, on the other hand, need not be 2, because its increments may not occur atomically. Each increment consists of reading vc's value, incrementing the value that was read, and writing the result back into vc. But these three operations are not guaranteed to proceed atomically for volatile objects, so it's possible that the component parts of the two increments of vc are interleaved as follows:

1. Thread 1 reads vc's value, which is 0.

2. Thread 2 reads vc's value, which is still 0.

3. Thread 1 increments the 0 it read to 1, then writes that value into vc.

4. Thread 2 increments the 0 it read to 1, then writes that value into vc.

vc's final value is therefore 1, even though it was incremented twice.

This is not the only possible outcome. vc's final value is, in general, not predictable, because vc is involved in a data race, and the Standard's decree that data races cause undefined behavior means that the code generated by compilers may end up doing literally anything. Compilers don't use this leeway to be malicious, of course. Rather, they perform optimizations that would be valid in programs without data races, and these optimizations yield unexpected and unpredictable behavior in programs where races are present.

The use of RMW operations isn't the only situation where std::atomics comprise a concurrency success story and volatiles suffer failure. Suppose one task computes an important value needed by a second task. When the first task has computed the value, it must communicate this to the second task. Item 39 explains that one way for the first task to communicate the availability of the desired value to the second task is by using a `std::atomic<bool>`. Code in the task computing the value would look something like this:

```
std::atomic<bool> valAvailable(false);

auto imptValue = computeImportantValue();   // compute value

valAvailable = true;                         // tell other task
                                             // it's available
```

As humans reading this code, we know it's crucial that the assignment to `imptValue` take place before the assignment to `valAvailable`, but all compilers see is a pair of assignments to independent variables. As a general rule, compilers are permitted to reorder such unrelated assignments. That is, given this sequence of assignments (where a, b, x, and y correspond to independent variables),

```
a = b;
x = y;
```

compilers may generally reorder them as follows:

```
x = y;
a = b;
```

Even if compilers don't reorder them, the underlying hardware might do it (or might make it seem to other cores as if it had), because that can sometimes make the code run faster.

However, the use of `std::atomics` imposes restrictions on how code can be reordered, and one such restriction is that no code that, in the source code, precedes a write of a `std::atomic` variable may take place (or appear to other cores to take place) afterwards.[6] That means that in our code,

```
auto imptValue = computeImportantValue();   // compute value

valAvailable = true;                         // tell other task
                                             // it's available
```

not only must compilers retain the order of the assignments to `imptValue` and `valAvailable`, they must generate code that ensures that the underlying hardware

---

6 This is true only for `std::atomics` using *sequential consistency*, which is both the default and the only consistency model for `std::atomic` objects that uses the syntax shown in this book. C++11 also supports consistency models with more flexible code-reordering rules. Such *weak* (aka *relaxed*) models make it possible to create software that runs faster on some hardware architectures, but the use of such models yields software that is *much* more difficult to get right, to understand, and to maintain. Subtle errors in code using relaxed atomics is not uncommon, even for experts, so you should stick to sequential consistency if at all possible.

does, too. As a result, declaring `valAvailable` as `std::atomic` ensures that our critical ordering requirement—`imptValue` must be seen by all threads to change no later than `valAvailable` does—is maintained.

Declaring `valAvailable` as `volatile` doesn't impose the same code reordering restrictions:

```
volatile bool valAvailable(false);

auto imptValue = computeImportantValue();

valAvailable = true;   // other threads might see this assignment
                       // before the one to imptValue!
```

Here, compilers might flip the order of the assignments to `imptValue` and `valAvailable`, and even if they don't, they might fail to generate machine code that would prevent the underlying hardware from making it possible for code on other cores to see `valAvailable` change before `imptValue`.

These two issues—no guarantee of operation atomicity and insufficient restrictions on code reordering—explain why `volatile`'s not useful for concurrent programming, but it doesn't explain what it is useful for. In a nutshell, it's for telling compilers that they're dealing with memory that doesn't behave normally.

"Normal" memory has the characteristic that if you write a value to a memory location, the value remains there until something overwrites it. So if I have a normal `int`,

```
int x;
```

and a compiler sees the following sequence of operations on it,

```
auto y = x;            // read x
y = x;                 // read x again
```

the compiler can optimize the generated code by eliminating the assignment to `y`, because it's redundant with `y`'s initialization.

Normal memory also has the characteristic that if you write a value to a memory location, never read it, and then write to that memory location again, the first write can be eliminated, because it was never used. So given these two adjacent statements,

```
x = 10;                // write x
x = 20;                // write x again
```

compilers can eliminate the first one. That means that if we have this in the source code,

```
auto y = x;            // read x
y = x;                 // read x again
```

```
x = 10;              // write x
x = 20;              // write x again
```

compilers can treat it as if it had been written like this:

```
auto y = x;          // read x

x = 20;              // write x
```

Lest you wonder who'd write code that performs these kinds of redundant reads and superfluous writes (technically known as *redundant loads* and *dead stores*), the answer is that humans don't write it directly—at least we hope they don't. However, after compilers take reasonable-looking source code and perform template instantiation, inlining, and various common kinds of reordering optimizations, it's not uncommon for the result to have redundant loads and dead stores that compilers can get rid of.

Such optimizations are valid only if memory behaves normally. "Special" memory doesn't. Probably the most common kind of special memory is memory used for *memory-mapped I/O*. Locations in such memory actually communicate with peripherals, e.g., external sensors or displays, printers, network ports, etc. rather than reading or writing normal memory (i.e., RAM). In such a context, consider again the code with seemingly redundant reads:

```
auto y = x;          // read x
y = x;               // read x again
```

If x corresponds to, say, the value reported by a temperature sensor, the second read of x is not redundant, because the temperature may have changed between the first and second reads.

It's a similar situation for seemingly superfluous writes. In this code, for example,

```
x = 10;              // write x
x = 20;              // write x again
```

if x corresponds to the control port for a radio transmitter, it could be that the code is issuing commands to the radio, and the value 10 corresponds to a different command from the value 20. Optimizing out the first assignment would change the sequence of commands sent to the radio.

volatile is the way we tell compilers that we're dealing with special memory. Its meaning to compilers is "Don't perform any optimizations on operations on this memory." So if x corresponds to special memory, it'd be declared volatile:

```
volatile int x;
```

Consider the effect that has on our original code sequence:

```
auto y = x;          // read x
y = x;               // read x again (can't be optimized away)

x = 10;              // write x (can't be optimized away)
x = 20;              // write x again
```

This is precisely what we want if x is memory-mapped (or has been mapped to a memory location shared across processes, etc.).

Pop quiz! In that last piece of code, what is y's type: int or volatile int?[7]

The fact that seemingly redundant loads and dead stores must be preserved when dealing with special memory explains, by the way, why std::atomics are unsuitable for this kind of work. Compilers are permitted to eliminate such redundant operations on std::atomics. The code isn't written quite the same way it is for volatiles, but if we overlook that for a moment and focus on what compilers are permitted to do, we can say that, conceptually, compilers may take this,

```
std::atomic<int> x;

auto y = x;          // conceptually read x (see below)
y = x;               // conceptually read x again (see below)

x = 10;              // write x
x = 20;              // write x again
```

and optimize it to this:

```
auto y = x;          // conceptually read x (see below)
x = 20;              // write x
```

For special memory, this is clearly unacceptable behavior.

Now, as it happens, neither of these two statements will compile when x is std::atomic:

```
auto y = x;          // error!
y = x;               // error!
```

That's because the copy operations for std::atomic are deleted (see Item 11). And with good reason. Consider what would happen if the initialization of y with x com-

---

7 y's type is auto-deduced, so it uses the rules described in Item 2. Those rules dictate that for the declaration of non-reference non-pointer types (which is the case for y), const and volatile qualifiers are dropped. y's type is therefore simply int. This means that redundant reads of and writes to y can be eliminated. In the example, compilers must perform both the initialization of and the assignment to y, because x is volatile, so the second read of x might yield a different value from the first one.

```
```

piled. Because x is std::atomic, y's type would be deduced to be std::atomic, too (see Item 2). I remarked earlier that one of the best things about std::atomics is that all their operations are atomic, but in order for the copy construction of y from x to be atomic, compilers would have to generate code to read x and write y in a single atomic operation. Hardware generally can't do that, so copy construction isn't supported for std::atomic types. Copy assignment is deleted for the same reason, which is why the assignment from x to y won't compile. (The move operations aren't explicitly declared in std::atomic, so, per the rules for compiler-generated special functions described in Item 17, std::atomic offers neither move construction nor move assignment.)

It's possible to get the value of x into y, but it requires delving a bit deeper into std::atomic's API. The load member function reads a std::atomic's value atomically, while the store member function writes it atomically. To initialize y with x, followed by putting x's value into y, the code can be written like this:

```
std::atomic<int> y(x.load());      // read x

y.store(x.load());                 // read x again
```

This compiles, but the fact that reading x (via x.load()) is a separate function call from initializing or storing to y makes clear that there is no reason to expect either statement as a whole to execute as a single atomic operation.

Given that code, compilers could "optimize" it by storing x's value in a register instead of reading it twice:

```
register = x.load();               // read x into register

std::atomic<int> y(register);      // init y with register value

y.store(register);                 // store register value into y
```

The result, as you can see, reads from x only once, and that's the kind of optimization that must be avoided when dealing with special memory. (The optimization isn't permitted for volatile variables.)

The situation should thus be clear:

- std::atomic is useful for concurrent programming, but not for accessing special memory.

- volatile is useful for accessing special memory, but not for concurrent programming.

Because `std::atomic` and `volatile` serve different purposes, they can even be used together:

```
volatile std::atomic<int> vai;    // operations on vai are
                                  // atomic and can't be
                                  // optimized away
```

This could be useful if `vai` corresponded to a memory-mapped I/O location that was concurrently accessed by multiple threads.

As a final note, some developers prefer to use `std::atomic`'s `load` and `store` member functions even when they're not required, because it makes explicit in the source code that the variables involved aren't "normal." Emphasizing that fact isn't unreasonable. Accessing a `std::atomic` is typically much slower than accessing a non-`std::atomic`, and we've already seen that the use of `std::atomics` prevents compilers from performing certain kinds of code reorderings that would otherwise be permitted. Calling out loads and stores of `std::atomics` can therefore help identify potential scalability chokepoints. From a correctness perspective, *not* seeing a call to `store` on a variable meant to communicate information to other threads (e.g., a flag indicating the availability of data) could mean that the variable wasn't declared `std::atomic` when it should have been.

This is largely a style issue, however, and as such is quite different from the choice between `std::atomic` and `volatile`.

Things to Remember

- `std::atomic` is for data accessed from multiple threads without using mutexes. It's a tool for writing concurrent software.
- `volatile` is for memory where reads and writes should not be optimized away. It's a tool for working with special memory.

CHAPTER 8

Tweaks

For every general technique or feature in C++, there are circumstances where it's reasonable to use it, and there are circumstances where it's not. Describing when it makes sense to use a general technique or feature is usually fairly straightforward, but this chapter covers two exceptions. The general technique is pass by value, and the general feature is emplacement. The decision about when to employ them is affected by so many factors, the best advice I can offer is to *consider* their use. Nevertheless, both are important players in effective modern C++ programming, and the Items that follow provide the information you'll need to determine whether using them is appropriate for your software.

Item 41: Consider pass by value for copyable parameters that are cheap to move and always copied.

Some function parameters are intended to be copied.[1] For example, a member function `addName` might copy its parameter into a private container. For efficiency, such a function should copy lvalue arguments, but move rvalue arguments:

```
class Widget {
public:
  void addName(const std::string& newName)    // take lvalue;
  { names.push_back(newName); }                // copy it

  void addName(std::string&& newName)          // take rvalue;
```

---

1 In this Item, to "copy" a parameter generally means to use it as the source of a copy or move operation. Recall from page 4 that C++ has no terminology to distinguish a copy made by a copy operation from one made by a move operation.

```
  { names.push_back(std::move(newName)); }      // move it; see
    ...                                         // Item 25 for use
                                                // of std::move
private:
  std::vector<std::string> names;
};
```

This works, but it requires writing two functions that do essentially the same thing. That chafes a bit: two functions to declare, two functions to implement, two functions to document, two functions to maintain. Ugh.

Furthermore, there will be two functions in the object code—something you might care about if you're concerned about your program's footprint. In this case, both functions will probably be inlined, and that's likely to eliminate any bloat issues related to the existence of two functions, but if these functions aren't inlined everywhere, you really will get two functions in your object code.

An alternative approach is to make `addName` a function template taking a universal reference (see Item 24):

```
class Widget {
public:
  template<typename T>                              // take lvalues
  void addName(T&& newName)                         // and rvalues;
  {                                                 // copy lvalues,
    names.push_back(std::forward<T>(newName));      // move rvalues;
  }                                                 // see Item 25
                                                    // for use of
    ...                                             // std::forward

};
```

This reduces the source code you have to deal with, but the use of universal references leads to other complications. As a template, `addName`'s implementation must typically be in a header file. It may yield several functions in object code, because it not only instantiates differently for lvalues and rvalues, it also instantiates differently for `std::string` and types that are convertible to `std::string` (see Item 25). At the same time, there are argument types that can't be passed by universal reference (see Item 30), and if clients pass improper argument types, compiler error messages can be intimidating (see Item 27).

Wouldn't it be nice if there were a way to write functions like `addName` such that lvalues were copied, rvalues were moved, there was only one function to deal with (in both source and object code), and the idiosyncrasies of universal references were avoided? As it happens, there is. All you have to do is abandon one of the first rules you probably learned as a C++ programmer. That rule was to avoid passing objects of user-defined types by value. For parameters like newName in functions like addName, pass by value may be an entirely reasonable strategy.

Before we discuss why pass-by-value may be a good fit for newName and addName, let's see how it would be implemented:

```
class Widget {
public:
  void addName(std::string newName)            // take lvalue or
  { names.push_back(std::move(newName)); }     // rvalue; move it

  …

};
```

The only non-obvious part of this code is the application of std::move to the parameter newName. Typically, std::move is used with rvalue references, but in this case, we know that (1) newName is a completely independent object from whatever the caller passed in, so changing newName won't affect callers and (2) this is the final use of newName, so moving from it won't have any impact on the rest of the function.

The fact that there's only one addName function explains how we avoid code duplication, both in the source code and the object code. We're not using a universal reference, so this approach doesn't lead to bloated header files, odd failure cases, or confounding error messages. But what about the efficiency of this design? We're passing *by value*. Isn't that expensive?

In C++98, it was a reasonable bet that it was. No matter what callers passed in, the parameter newName would be created by *copy construction*. In C++11, however, new-Name will be copy constructed only for lvalues. For rvalues, it will be *move constructed*. Here, look:

```
Widget w;

…

std::string name("Bart");

w.addName(name);                  // call addName with lvalue

…

w.addName(name + "Jenne");        // call addName with rvalue
                                  // (see below)
```

In the first call to addName (when name is passed), the parameter newName is initialized with an lvalue. newName is thus copy constructed, just like it would be in C++98. In the second call, newName is initialized with the std::string object resulting from a call to operator+ for std::string (i.e., the append operation). That object is an rvalue, and newName is therefore move constructed.

Lvalues are thus copied, and rvalues are moved, just like we want. Neat, huh?

It is neat, but there are some caveats you need to keep in mind. Doing that will be easier if we recap the three versions of addName we've considered:

```cpp
class Widget {                                    // Approach 1:
public:                                           // overload for
  void addName(const std::string& newName)        // lvalues and
  { names.push_back(newName); }                    // rvalues

  void addName(std::string&& newName)
  { names.push_back(std::move(newName)); }
  …

private:
  std::vector<std::string> names;
};

class Widget {                                    // Approach 2:
public:                                           // use universal
  template<typename T>                             // reference
  void addName(T&& newName)
  { names.push_back(std::forward<T>(newName)); }
  …
};

class Widget {                                    // Approach 3:
public:                                           // pass by value
  void addName(std::string newName)
  { names.push_back(std::move(newName)); }
  …
};
```

I refer to the first two versions as the "by-reference approaches," because they're both based on passing their parameters by reference.

Here are the two calling scenarios we've examined:

```
Widget w;

…

std::string name("Bart");

w.addName(name);                          // pass lvalue

…
w.addName(name + "Jenne");                // pass rvalue
```

Now consider the cost, in terms of copy and move operations, of adding a name to a Widget for the two calling scenarios and each of the three addName implementations we've discussed. The accounting will largely ignore the possibility of compilers optimizing copy and move operations away, because such optimizations are context- and compiler-dependent and, in practice, don't change the essence of the analysis.

- **Overloading:** Regardless of whether an lvalue or an rvalue is passed, the caller's argument is bound to a reference called newName. That costs nothing, in terms of copy and move operations. In the lvalue overload, newName is copied into Widget::names. In the rvalue overload, it's moved. Cost summary: one copy for lvalues, one move for rvalues.

- **Using a universal reference:** As with overloading, the caller's argument is bound to the reference newName. This is a no-cost operation. Due to the use of std::forward, lvalue std::string arguments are copied into Widget::names, while rvalue std::string arguments are moved. The cost summary for std::string arguments is the same as with overloading: one copy for lvalues, one move for rvalues.

  Item 25 explains that if a caller passes an argument of a type other than std::string, it will be forwarded to a std::string constructor, and that could cause as few as zero std::string copy or move operations to be performed. Functions taking universal references can thus be uniquely efficient. However, that doesn't affect the analysis in this Item, so we'll keep things simple by assuming that callers always pass std::string arguments.

- **Passing by value:** Regardless of whether an lvalue or an rvalue is passed, the parameter newName must be constructed. If an lvalue is passed, this costs a copy construction. If an rvalue is passed, it costs a move construction. In the body of the function, newName is unconditionally moved into Widget::names. The cost summary is thus one copy plus one move for lvalues, and two moves for rvalues. Compared to the by-reference approaches, that's one extra move for both lvalues and rvalues.

Look again at this Item's title:

> Consider pass by value for copyable parameters that are cheap to move and always copied.

It's worded the way it is for a reason. Four reasons, in fact:

1. You should only *consider* using pass by value. Yes, it requires writing only one function. Yes, it generates only one function in the object code. Yes, it avoids the issues associated with universal references. But it has a higher cost than the alternatives, and, as we'll see below, in some cases, there are expenses we haven't yet discussed.

2. Consider pass by value only for *copyable parameters*. Parameters failing this test must have move-only types, because if they're not copyable, yet the function always makes a copy, the copy must be created via the move constructor.[2] Recall that the advantage of pass by value over overloading is that with pass by value, only one function has to be written. But for move-only types, there is no need to provide an overload for lvalue arguments, because copying an lvalue entails calling the copy constructor, and the copy constructor for move-only types is disabled. That means that only rvalue arguments need to be supported, and in that case, the "overloading" solution requires only one overload: the one taking an rvalue reference.

   Consider a class with a `std::unique_ptr<std::string>` data member and a setter for it. `std::unique_ptr` is a move-only type, so the "overloading" approach to its setter consists of a single function:

   ```
   class Widget {
   public:
       …
       void setPtr(std::unique_ptr<std::string>&& ptr)
       { p = std::move(ptr); }

   private:
       std::unique_ptr<std::string> p;
   };
   ```

   A caller might use it this way:

---

2 Sentences like this are why it'd be nice to have terminology that distinguishes copies made via copy operations from copies made via move operations.

```
Widget w;

…

w.setPtr(std::make_unique<std::string>("Modern C++"));
```

Here the rvalue std::unique_ptr<std::string> returned from
std::make_unique (see Item 21) is passed by rvalue reference to setPtr, where
it's moved into the data member p. The total cost is one move.

If setPtr were to take its parameter by value,

```
class Widget {
public:

    …

    void setPtr(std::unique_ptr<std::string> ptr)
    { p = std::move(ptr); }


    …

};
```

the same call would move construct the parameter ptr, and ptr would then be
move assigned into the data member p. The total cost would thus be two moves
—twice that of the "overloading" approach.

3. Pass by value is worth considering only for parameters that are *cheap to move.*
   When moves are cheap, the cost of an extra one may be acceptable, but when
   they're not, performing an unnecessary move is analogous to performing an
   unnecessary copy, and the importance of avoiding unnecessary copy operations
   is what led to the C++98 rule about avoiding pass by value in the first place!

4. You should consider pass by value only for parameters that are *always copied.* To
   see why this is important, suppose that before copying its parameter into the
   names container, addName checks to see if the new name is too short or too long.
   If it is, the request to add the name is ignored. A pass-by-value implementation
   could be written like this:

```
class Widget {
public:
  void addName(std::string newName)
  {
    if ((newName.length() >= minLen) &&
        (newName.length() <= maxLen))
    {
      names.push_back(std::move(newName));
    }
```

```
    }

    ...

private:
    std::vector<std::string> names;
};
```

This function incurs the cost of constructing and destroying newName, even if nothing is added to names. That's a price the by-reference approaches wouldn't be asked to pay.

Even when you're dealing with a function performing an unconditional copy on a copyable type that's cheap to move, there are times when pass by value may not be appropriate. That's because a function can copy a parameter in two ways: via *construction* (i.e., copy construction or move construction) and via *assignment* (i.e., copy assignment or move assignment). addName uses construction: its parameter newName is passed to vector::push_back, and inside that function, newName is copy constructed into a new element created at the end of the std::vector. For functions that use construction to copy their parameter, the analysis we saw earlier is complete: using pass by value incurs the cost of an extra move for both lvalue and rvalue arguments.

When a parameter is copied using assignment, the situation is more complicated. Suppose, for example, we have a class representing passwords. Because passwords can be changed, we provide a setter function, changeTo. Using a pass-by-value strategy, we could implement Password like this:

```
class Password {
public:
    explicit Password(std::string pwd)     // pass by value
    : text(std::move(pwd)) {}              // construct text

    void changeTo(std::string newPwd)      // pass by value
    { text = std::move(newPwd); }          // assign text

    ...

private:
    std::string text;                      // text of password
};
```

Storing the password as plain text will whip your software security SWAT team into a frenzy, but ignore that and consider this code:

```
std::string initPwd("Supercalifragilisticexpialidocious");

Password p(initPwd);
```

There are no surprises here: p.text is constructed with the given password, and using pass by value in the constructor incurs the cost of a std::string move construction that would not be necessary if overloading or perfect forwarding were employed. All is well.

A user of this program may not be as sanguine about the password, however, because "Supercalifragilisticexpialidocious" is found in many dictionaries. He or she may therefore take actions that lead to code equivalent to the following being executed:

```
std::string newPassword = "Beware the Jabberwock";

p.changeTo(newPassword);
```

Whether the new password is better than the old one is debatable, but that's the user's problem. Ours is that changeTo's need to use assignment (instead of construction) to copy the parameter newPwd probably causes the function's pass-by-value strategy to explode in cost.

The argument passed to changeTo is an lvalue (newPassword), so when the parameter newPwd is constructed, it's the std::string copy constructor that's called. That constructor allocates memory to hold the new password. newPwd is then move-assigned to text, which causes the memory already held by text to be deallocated. There are thus two dynamic memory management actions within changeTo: one to allocate memory for the new password, and one to deallocate the memory for the old password.

But in this case, the old password ("Supercalifragilisticexpialidocious") is longer than the new one ("Beware the Jabberwock"), so there's no need to allocate or deallocate anything. If the overloading approach were used, it's likely that none would take place:

```
class Password {
public:
  …

  void changeTo(const std::string& newPwd)        // the overload
  {                                                // for lvalues

    text = newPwd;              // can reuse text's memory if
                                // text.capacity() >= newPwd.size()
  }

  …
```

```
private:
  std::string text;                                        // as above
};
```

In this scenario, the cost of pass by value includes an extra memory allocation and deallocation—costs that are likely to exceed that of a `std::string` move operation by orders of magnitude.

Interestingly, if the old password were shorter than the new one, it would typically be impossible to avoid an allocation-deallocation pair during the assignment, and in that case, pass by value would run at about the same speed as pass by reference. The cost of assignment-based parameter copying can thus depend on the values of the objects participating in the assignment! This kind of analysis applies to any parameter type that holds values in dynamically allocated memory. Not all types qualify, but many—including `std::string` and `std::vector`—do.

This potential cost increase generally applies only when lvalue arguments are passed, because the need to perform memory allocation and deallocation typically occurs only when true copy operations (i.e., not moves) are performed. For rvalue arguments, moves almost always suffice.

The upshot is that the extra cost of pass by value (compared to pass by reference) for functions that copy a parameter using assignment depends on the type being passed, the ratio of lvalue to rvalue arguments, whether the type uses dynamically allocated memory, and, if so, the implementation of that type's assignment operators and the likelihood that the memory associated with the assignment target is at least as large as the memory associated with the assignment source. For `std::string`, it also depends on whether the implementation uses the small string optimization (SSO—see Item 29) and, if so, whether the values being assigned fit in the SSO buffer.

So, as I said, when parameters are copied via assignment, analyzing the cost of pass by value is complicated. Usually, the most practical approach is to adopt a "guilty until proven innocent" policy, whereby you use overloading or universal references instead of pass by value unless it's been demonstrated that pass by value yields acceptably efficient code for the parameter type you need.

Now, for software that must be as fast as possible, pass by value may not be a viable strategy, because avoiding even cheap moves can be important. Moreover, it's not always clear how many moves will take place. In the `Widget::addName` example, pass by value incurs only a single extra move operation, but suppose that `Widget::add-Name` called `Widget::validateName`, and this function also passed by value. (Presumably it has a reason for always copying its parameter, e.g., to store it in a data structure of all values it validates.) And suppose that `validateName` called a third function that also passed by value…

You can see where this is headed. When there are chains of function calls, each of which employs pass by value because "it costs only one inexpensive move," the cost for the entire chain of calls may not be something you can tolerate. Using by-reference parameter passing, chains of calls don't incur this kind of accumulated overhead.

An issue unrelated to performance, but still worth keeping in mind, is that pass by value, unlike pass by reference, is susceptible to *the slicing problem*. This is well-trod C++98 ground, so I won't dwell on it, but if you have a function that is designed to accept a parameter of a base class type *or any type derived from it*, you don't want to declare a pass-by-value parameter of that type, because you'll "slice off" the derived-class characteristics of any derived type object that may be passed in:

```
class Widget { … };                          // base class

class SpecialWidget: public Widget { … };    // derived class

void processWidget(Widget w);    // func for any kind of Widget,
                                 // including derived types;
    …                            // suffers from slicing problem


SpecialWidget sw;


    …


processWidget(sw);               // processWidget sees a
                                 // Widget, not a SpecialWidget!
```

If you're not familiar with the slicing problem, search engines and the Internet are your friends; there's lots of information available. You'll find that the existence of the slicing problem is another reason (on top of the efficiency hit) why pass by value has a shady reputation in C++98. There are good reasons why one of the first things you probably learned about C++ programming was to avoid passing objects of user-defined types by value.

C++11 doesn't fundamentally change the C++98 wisdom regarding pass by value. In general, pass by value still entails a performance hit you'd prefer to avoid, and pass by value can still lead to the slicing problem. What's new in C++11 is the distinction between lvalue and rvalue arguments. Implementing functions that take advantage of move semantics for rvalues of copyable types requires either overloading or using universal references, both of which have drawbacks. For the special case of copyable, cheap-to-move types passed to functions that always copy them and where slicing is not a concern, pass by value can offer an easy-to-implement alternative that's nearly as efficient as its pass-by-reference competitors, but avoids their disadvantages.

Item 42: Consider emplacement instead of insertion.

If you have a container holding, say, `std::strings`, it seems logical that when you add a new element via an insertion function (i.e., `insert`, `push_front`, `push_back`, or, for `std::forward_list`, `insert_after`), the type of element you'll pass to the function will be `std::string`. After all, that's what the container has in it.

Logical though this may be, it's not always true. Consider this code:

```
std::vector<std::string> vs;           // container of std::string

vs.push_back("xyzzy");                 // add string literal
```

Here, the container holds `std::strings`, but what you have in hand—what you're actually trying to `push_back`—is a string literal, i.e., a sequence of characters inside quotes. A string literal is not a `std::string`, and that means that the argument you're passing to `push_back` is not of the type held by the container.

`push_back` for `std::vector` is overloaded for lvalues and rvalues as follows:

```
template <class T,                            // from the C++11
          class Allocator = allocator<T>>     // Standard
class vector {
public:
    ...
    void push_back(const T& x);               // insert lvalue
    void push_back(T&& x);                     // insert rvalue
    ...
};
```

In the call

```
vs.push_back("xyzzy");
```

compilers see a mismatch between the type of the argument (`const char[6]`) and the type of the parameter taken by `push_back` (a reference to a `std::string`). They address the mismatch by generating code to create a temporary `std::string` object from the string literal, and they pass that temporary object to `push_back`. In other words, they treat the call as if it had been written like this:

```
vs.push_back(std::string("xyzzy"));    // create temp. std::string
                                       // and pass it to push_back
```

The code compiles and runs, and everybody goes home happy. Everybody except the performance freaks, that is, because the performance freaks recognize that this code isn't as efficient as it should be.

To create a new element in a container of `std::strings`, they understand, a `std::string` constructor is going to have to be called, but the code above doesn't make just one constructor call. It makes two. And it calls the `std::string` destructor, too. Here's what happens at runtime in the call to `push_back`:

1. A temporary `std::string` object is created from the string literal "xyzzy". This object has no name; we'll call it *temp*. Construction of *temp* is the first `std::string` construction. Because it's a temporary object, *temp* is an rvalue.

2. *temp* is passed to the rvalue overload for `push_back`, where it's bound to the rvalue reference parameter x. A copy of x is then constructed in the memory for the `std::vector`. This construction—the *second* one—is what actually creates a new object inside the `std::vector`. (The constructor that's used to copy x into the `std::vector` is the move constructor, because x, being an rvalue reference, gets cast to an rvalue before it's copied. For information about the casting of rvalue reference parameters to rvalues, see Item 25.)

3. Immediately after `push_back` returns, *temp* is destroyed, thus calling the `std::string` destructor.

The performance freaks can't help but notice that if there were a way to take the string literal and pass it directly to the code in step 2 that constructs the `std::string` object inside the `std::vector`, we could avoid constructing and destroying *temp*. That would be maximally efficient, and even the performance freaks could contentedly decamp.

Because you're a C++ programmer, there's an above-average chance you're a performance freak. If you're not, you're still probably sympathetic to their point of view. (If you're not at all interested in performance, shouldn't you be in the Python room down the hall?) So I'm pleased to tell you that there is a way to do exactly what is needed for maximal efficiency in the call to push_back. It's to not call push_back. push_back is the wrong function. The function you want is emplace_back.

emplace_back does exactly what we desire: it uses whatever arguments are passed to it to construct a std::string directly inside the std::vector. No temporaries are involved:

```
vs.emplace_back("xyzzy");    // construct std::string inside
                             // vs directly from "xyzzy"
```

emplace_back uses perfect forwarding, so, as long as you don't bump into one of perfect forwarding's limitations (see Item 30), you can pass any number of arguments of any combination of types through emplace_back. For example, if you'd like to create a std::string in vs via the std::string constructor taking a character and a repeat count, this would do it:

```
vs.emplace_back(50, 'x');    // insert std::string consisting
                             // of 50 'x' characters
```

emplace_back is available for every standard container that supports push_back. Similarly, every standard container that supports push_front supports emplace_front. And every standard container that supports insert (which is all but std::forward_list and std::array) supports emplace. The associative containers offer emplace_hint to complement their insert functions that take a "hint" iterator, and std::forward_list has emplace_after to match its insert_after.

What makes it possible for emplacement functions to outperform insertion functions is their more flexible interface. Insertion functions take *objects to be inserted*, while emplacement functions take *constructor arguments for objects to be inserted*. This difference permits emplacement functions to avoid the creation and destruction of temporary objects that insertion functions can necessitate.

Because an argument of the type held by the container can be passed to an emplacement function (the argument thus causes the function to perform copy or move construction), emplacement can be used even when an insertion function would require no temporary. In that case, insertion and emplacement do essentially the same thing. For example, given

```
std::string queenOfDisco("Donna Summer");
```

both of the following calls are valid, and both have the same net effect on the container:

```
vs.push_back(queenOfDisco);     // copy-construct queenOfDisco
                                // at end of vs

vs.emplace_back(queenOfDisco);  // ditto
```

Emplacement functions can thus do everything insertion functions can. They some-times do it more efficiently, and, at least in theory, they should never do it less effi-ciently. So why not use them all the time?

Because, as the saying goes, in theory, there's no difference between theory and prac-tice, but in practice, there is. With current implementations of the Standard Library, there are situations where, as expected, emplacement outperforms insertion, but, sadly, there are also situations where the insertion functions run faster. Such situa-tions are not easy to characterize, because they depend on the types of arguments being passed, the containers being used, the locations in the containers where inser-tion or emplacement is requested, the exception safety of the contained types' con-structors, and, for containers where duplicate values are prohibited (i.e., `std::set`, `std::map`, `std::unordered_set`, `std::unordered_map`), whether the value to be added is already in the container. The usual performance-tuning advice thus applies: to determine whether emplacement or insertion runs faster, benchmark them both.

That's not very satisfying, of course, so you'll be pleased to learn that there's a heuris-tic that can help you identify situations where emplacement functions are most likely to be worthwhile. If all the following are true, emplacement will almost certainly out-perform insertion:

- **The value being added is constructed into the container, not assigned.** The example that opened this Item (adding a `std::string` with the value `"xyzzy"` to a `std::vector vs`) showed the value being added to the end of `vs`—to a place where no object yet existed. The new value therefore had to be constructed into the `std::vector`. If we revise the example such that the new `std::string` goes into a location already occupied by an object, it's a different story. Consider:

```
std::vector<std::string> vs;          // as before

...                                    // add elements to vs

vs.emplace(vs.begin(), "xyzzy");      // add "xyzzy" to
                                       // beginning of vs
```

For this code, few implementations will construct the added `std::string` into the memory occupied by `vs[0]`. Instead, they'll move-assign the value into place. But move assignment requires an object to move from, and that means that a temporary object will need to be created to be the source of the move. Because the primary advantage of emplacement over insertion is that temporary objects are neither created nor destroyed, when the value being added is put into the container via assignment, emplacement's edge tends to disappear.

Alas, whether adding a value to a container is accomplished by construction or assignment is generally up to the implementer. But, again, heuristics can help.

Node-based containers virtually always use construction to add new values, and most standard containers are node-based. The only ones that aren't are `std::vector`, `std::deque`, and `std::string`. (`std::array` isn't, either, but it doesn't support insertion or emplacement, so it's not relevant here.) Within the non-node-based containers, you can rely on `emplace_back` to use construction instead of assignment to get a new value into place, and for `std::deque`, the same is true of `emplace_front`.

- **The argument type(s) being passed differ from the type held by the container.** Again, emplacement's advantage over insertion generally stems from the fact that its interface doesn't require creation and destruction of a temporary object when the argument(s) passed are of a type other than that held by the container. When an object of type T is to be added to a *container*<T>, there's no reason to expect emplacement to run faster than insertion, because no temporary needs to be created to satisfy the insertion interface.

- **The container is unlikely to reject the new value as a duplicate.** This means that the container either permits duplicates or that most of the values you add will be unique. The reason this matters is that in order to detect whether a value is already in the container, emplacement implementations typically create a node with the new value so that they can compare the value of this node with existing container nodes. If the value to be added isn't in the container, the node is linked in. However, if the value is already present, the emplacement is aborted and the node is destroyed, meaning that the cost of its construction and destruction was wasted. Such nodes are created for emplacement functions more often than for insertion functions.

The following calls from earlier in this Item satisfy all the criteria above. They also run faster than the corresponding calls to `push_back`.

```
vs.emplace_back("xyzzy");     // construct new value at end of
                              // container; don't pass the type in
                              // container; don't use container
                              // rejecting duplicates

vs.emplace_back(50, 'x');     // ditto
```

When deciding whether to use emplacement functions, two other issues are worth keeping in mind. The first regards resource management. Suppose you have a container of `std::shared_ptr<Widget>`s,

```
std::list<std::shared_ptr<Widget>> ptrs;
```

and you want to add a `std::shared_ptr` that should be released via a custom deleter (see Item 19). Item 21 explains that you should use `std::make_shared` to create std::shared_ptrs whenever you can, but it also concedes that there are situations where you can't. One such situation is when you want to specify a custom deleter. In that case, you must use new directly to get the raw pointer to be managed by the std::shared_ptr.

If the custom deleter is this function,

```
void killWidget(Widget* pWidget);
```

the code using an insertion function could look like this:

```
ptrs.push_back(std::shared_ptr<Widget>(new Widget, killWidget));
```

It could also look like this, though the meaning would be the same:

```
ptrs.push_back({ new Widget, killWidget });
```

Either way, a temporary std::shared_ptr would be constructed before calling push_back. push_back's parameter is a reference to a std::shared_ptr, so there has to be a std::shared_ptr for this parameter to refer to.

The creation of the temporary std::shared_ptr is what emplace_back would avoid, but in this case, that temporary is worth far more than it costs. Consider the following potential sequence of events:

1. In either call above, a temporary std::shared_ptr<Widget> object is constructed to hold the raw pointer resulting from "new Widget". Call this object *temp*.

2. push_back takes *temp* by reference. During allocation of a list node to hold a copy of *temp*, an out-of-memory exception gets thrown.

3. As the exception propagates out of push_back, *temp* is destroyed. Being the sole std::shared_ptr referring to the Widget it's managing, it automatically releases that Widget, in this case by calling killWidget.

Even though an exception occurred, nothing leaks: the Widget created via "new Widget" in the call to push_back is released in the destructor of the std::shared_ptr that was created to manage it (*temp*). Life is good.

Now consider what happens if emplace_back is called instead of push_back:

```
ptrs.emplace_back(new Widget, killWidget);
```

1. The raw pointer resulting from "new Widget" is perfect-forwarded to the point inside emplace_back where a list node is to be allocated. That allocation fails, and an out-of-memory exception is thrown.

2. As the exception propagates out of `emplace_back`, the raw pointer that was the only way to get at the `Widget` on the heap is lost. That `Widget` (and any resources it owns) is leaked.

In this scenario, life is *not* good, and the fault doesn't lie with `std::shared_ptr`. The same kind of problem can arise through the use of `std::unique_ptr` with a custom deleter. Fundamentally, the effectiveness of resource-managing classes like `std::shared_ptr` and `std::unique_ptr` is predicated on resources (such as raw pointers from `new`) being *immediately* passed to constructors for resource-managing objects. The fact that functions like `std::make_shared` and `std::make_unique` automate this is one of the reasons they're so important.

In calls to the insertion functions of containers holding resource-managing objects (e.g., `std::list<std::shared_ptr<Widget>>`), the functions' parameter types generally ensure that nothing gets between acquisition of a resource (e.g., use of `new`) and construction of the object managing the resource. In the emplacement functions, perfect-forwarding defers the creation of the resource-managing objects until they can be constructed in the container's memory, and that opens a window during which exceptions can lead to resource leaks. All standard containers are susceptible to this problem. When working with containers of resource-managing objects, you must take care to ensure that if you choose an emplacement function over its insertion counterpart, you're not paying for improved code efficiency with diminished exception safety.

Frankly, you shouldn't be passing expressions like "`new Widget`" to `emplace_back` or `push_back` or most any other function, anyway, because, as Item 21 explains, this leads to the possibility of exception safety problems of the kind we just examined. Closing the door requires taking the pointer from "`new Widget`" and turning it over to a resource-managing object in a standalone statement, then passing that object as an rvalue to the function you originally wanted to pass "`new Widget`" to. (Item 21 covers this technique in more detail.) The code using `push_back` should therefore be written more like this:

```
std::shared_ptr<Widget> spw(new Widget,     // create Widget and
                            killWidget);     // have spw manage it

ptrs.push_back(std::move(spw));              // add spw as rvalue
```

The `emplace_back` version is similar:

```
std::shared_ptr<Widget> spw(new Widget, killWidget);
ptrs.emplace_back(std::move(spw));
```

Either way, the approach incurs the cost of creating and destroying `spw`. Given that the motivation for choosing emplacement over insertion is to avoid the cost of a temporary object of the type held by the container, yet that's conceptually what `spw` is, emplacement functions are unlikely to outperform insertion functions when you're adding resource-managing objects to a container and you follow the proper practice of ensuring that nothing can intervene between acquiring a resource and turning it over to a resource-managing object.

A second noteworthy aspect of emplacement functions is their interaction with `explicit` constructors. In honor of C++11's support for regular expressions, suppose you create a container of regular expression objects:

```
std::vector<std::regex> regexes;
```

Distracted by your colleagues' quarreling over the ideal number of times per day to check one's Facebook account, you accidentally write the following seemingly meaningless code:

```
regexes.emplace_back(nullptr);    // add nullptr to container
                                  // of regexes?
```

You don't notice the error as you type it, and your compilers accept the code without complaint, so you end up wasting a bunch of time debugging. At some point, you discover that you have inserted a null pointer into your container of regular expressions. But how is that possible? Pointers aren't regular expressions, and if you tried to do something like this,

```
std::regex r = nullptr;           // error! won't compile
```

compilers would reject your code. Interestingly, they would also reject it if you called `push_back` instead of `emplace_back`:

```
regexes.push_back(nullptr);       // error! won't compile
```

The curious behavior you're experiencing stems from the fact that `std::regex` objects can be constructed from character strings. That's what makes useful code like this legal:

```
std::regex upperCaseWord("[A-Z]+");
```

Creation of a `std::regex` from a character string can exact a comparatively large runtime cost, so, to minimize the likelihood that such an expense will be incurred unintentionally, the `std::regex` constructor taking a `const char*` pointer is `explicit`. That's why these lines don't compile:

```
std::regex r = nullptr;           // error! won't compile

regexes.push_back(nullptr);       // error! won't compile
```

In both cases, we're requesting an implicit conversion from a pointer to a `std::regex`, and the `explicitness` of that constructor prevents such conversions.

In the call to `emplace_back`, however, we're not claiming to pass a `std::regex` object. Instead, we're passing a *constructor argument* for a `std::regex` object. That's not considered an implicit conversion request. Rather, it's viewed as if you'd written this code:

```
std::regex r(nullptr);            // compiles
```

If the laconic comment "compiles" suggests a lack of enthusiasm, that's good, because this code, though it will compile, has undefined behavior. The `std::regex` constructor taking a `const char*` pointer requires that the pointer be non-null, and `nullptr` emphatically fails that requirement. If you write and compile such code, the best you can hope for is that it crashes at runtime. If you're not so lucky, you and your debugger could be in for a special bonding experience.

Setting aside `push_back`, `emplace_back`, and bonding for a moment, notice how these very similar initialization syntaxes yield different results:

```
std::regex r1 = nullptr;          // error! won't compile

std::regex r2(nullptr);           // compiles
```

In the official terminology of the Standard, the syntax used to initialize `r1` (employing the equals sign) corresponds to what is known as *copy initialization*. In contrast, the syntax used to initialize `r2` (with the parentheses, although braces may be used instead) yields what is called *direct initialization*. Copy initialization is not permitted to use `explicit` constructors. Direct initialization is. That's why the line initializing `r1` doesn't compile, but the line initializing `r2` does.

But back to `push_back` and `emplace_back` and, more generally, the insertion functions versus the emplacement functions. Emplacement functions use direct initialization, which means they may use `explicit` constructors. Insertion functions employ copy initialization, so they can't. Hence:

```
regexes.emplace_back(nullptr);    // compiles. Direct init permits
                                  // use of explicit std::regex
                                  // ctor taking a pointer

regexes.push_back(nullptr);       // error! copy init forbids
                                  // use of that ctor
```

The lesson to take away is that when you use an emplacement function, be especially careful to make sure you're passing the correct arguments, because even `explicit` constructors will be considered by compilers as they try to find a way to interpret your code as valid.

Things to Remember

- In principle, emplacement functions should sometimes be more efficient than their insertion counterparts, and they should never be less efficient.
- In practice, they're most likely to be faster when (1) the value being added is constructed into the container, not assigned; (2) the argument type(s) passed differ from the type held by the container; and (3) the container won't reject the value being added due to it being a duplicate.
- Emplacement functions may perform type conversions that would be rejected by insertion functions.

Index

underlying type for, 69-71
equals sign (=), assignment vs. initialization, 50
errata list for this book, 7
error messages, universal reference and, 195
event communication
    boolean flags, 264
    condition variables and, 262
    cost and efficiency of polling, 265
    future as mechanism for, 266-270
example classes/templates
    (see also std::)
    Base, 79-82, 112
    Bond, 119
    Derived, 79, 81-82
    Investment, 119, 122
    IPv4Header, 213
    IsValAndArch, 226
    MyAllocList, 64
    MyAllocList<Wine>, 65
    Password, 288-290
    Person, 180-182, 184, 189, 191, 193, 196
    Point, 24, 100, 101, 106
    Polynomial, 103-105
    PolyWidget, 239
    RealEstate, 119
    ReallyBigType, 145
    SomeCompilerGeneratedClassName, 229
    SpecialPerson, 183, 192
    SpecialWidget, 291
    std::add_lvalue_reference, 66
    std::basic_ios, 75
    std::get, 257
    std::pair, 93
    std::remove_const, 66
    std::remove_reference, 66
    std::string, 160
    std::vector, 24, 166, 292
    std::vector<bool>, 46
    Stock, 119
    StringTable, 113
    struct Point, 24
    TD, 31
    ThreadRAII, 254, 257
    Warning, 83
    Widget, 3, 5, 50, 52, 64, 78, 80, 83, 106-108,
        109, 112, 115, 130-132, 148-155, 162,
        168-170, 202, 210, 219, 224, 260,
        281-288, 291
    Widget::Impl, 150-153

Widget::processPointer, 78
Wine, 65
example functions/templates
    (see also std::)
    addDivisorFilter, 217, 223
    arraySize, 16
    authAndAccess, 25-28, 26-27
    Base::Base, 113
    Base::doWork, 79
    Base::mf1, 81-82
    Base::mf2, 81-82
    Base::mf3, 81-82
    Base::mf4, 81-82
    Base::operator=, 113
    Base::~Base, 112
    calcEpsilon, 47
    calcValue, 261
    cbegin, 88
    cleanup, 96
    compress, 237
    computerPriority, 140
    continueProcessing, 70
    createInitList, 23
    createVec, 32, 35
    cusDel, 146
    delInvmt2, 123
    Derived::doWork, 79
    Derived::mf1, 81-82
    Derived::mf2, 81-82
    Derived::mf3, 81-82
    Derived::mf4, 81-82
    detect, 268, 270
    doAsyncWork, 241-242
    doSomething, 83
    doSomeWork, 57, 221
    doWork, 96, 251, 255
    dwim, 37-38
    f, 10-16, 18, 22-23, 32, 34, 59, 90, 95,
        164-166, 199, 208, 247
    f1, 17, 29, 60
    f2, 17, 29, 60
    f3, 60
    fastLoadWidget, 136
    features, 43
    findAndInsert, 88
    func, 5, 39, 197-198, 201
    func_for_cx, 19
    func_for_rx, 19
    func_for_x, 19

J

"Jabberwocky", allusion to, 289
John 8:32, allusion to, 164
joinability, testing std::threads for, 255
joinable std::threads
    definition of, 250
    destruction of, 251-253
    testing for joinability, 255

K

Kaminski, Tomasz, xiv
Karpov, Andrey, xiv
keywords, contextual, 83
Kirby-Green,Tom, xiv
Kohl, Nate, xiv
Kreuzer, Gerhard, xiv, xv
Krügler, Daniel, xiii

L

lambdas
    auto&& parameters and decltype in, 229-232
    bound and unbound arguments and, 238
    by-reference captures and, 217-219
    by-value capture, drawbacks of, 219-223
    by-value capture, pointers and, 219
    creating closures with, 216
    dangling references and, 217-219
    default capture modes and, 216-223
    definition of, 5, 215
    expressive power of, 215
    generic, 229
    implicit capture of the this pointer, 220-222
    init capture, 224-229
    inlining and, 236
    lambda capture and objects of static storage duration, 222
    move capture and, 238
    overloading and, 235
    polymorphic function objects and, 239
    variadic, 231
    vs. std::bind, 232-240
        bound arguments, treatment of, 238
        inlining and, 236
        move capture and, 239
        polymorphic functions objects and, 239
        readability and, 232-236
        unbound arguments, treatment of, 238

Lavavej, Stephan T., xiii, 139
legacy types, move operations and, 203
lhs, definition of, 3
Liber, Nevin ":-)", xiv
literal types, definition of, 100
load balancing, 244
local variables
    by-value return and, 173-176
    when not destroyed, 120
Long, Ashley Morgan, xv
lvalues, definition of, 2

M

Maher, Michael, xv
make functions
    avoiding code duplication and, 140
    custom deleters and, 142
    definition of, 139
    exception safety and, 140-142, 298
    parentheses vs. braces, 143
"Mary Poppins", allusion to, 289
Matthews, Hubert, xiv
memory
    consistency models, 274
    memory-mapped I/O, definition of, 276
Merkle, Bernhard, xiii
Mesopotamia, 109
"Modern C++ Design" (book), xiii
most vexing parse, definition of, 51
move capture, 224
    emulation with std::bind, 226-229, 239
    lambdas and, 239
move operations
    defaulting, 113-114
    definition of, 3
    generic code and, 206
    implicitly generated, 109-112
    legacy types and, 203
    Pimpl Idiom and, 152-153
    std::array and, 204
    std::shared_ptr and, 126
    std::string and, 205
    strong guarantee and, 205
    templates and, 206
move semantics, definition of, 157
move-enabled types, 110
move-only type, definition of, 119

efficiency of, 125, 133
  move operations and, 126
  multiple control blocks and, 129
  size of, 126
  vs. std::weak_ptr, 134
std::string, move operations and, 205
std::swap, 93
std::system_error, 242
std::threads
  as data members, member initialization
    order and, 254
  destroying joinable, 251-253
  implicit join or detach, 252
  joinable vs. unjoinable, 250
  RAII class for, 253-257, 269
std::true_type, 187
std::unique_ptr, 118-124
  conversion to std::shared_ptr, 124
  deleters and, 120-123, 126
    vs. std::shared_ptr deleters, 155
  efficiency of, 118
  factory functions and, 119-123
  for arrays, 124
  size of, 123
std::vector, 24, 166, 292
  std::vector constructors, 56
  std::vector::emplace_back, 167
  std::vector::push_back, 166, 292
std::vector<bool>, 43-46
  std::vector<bool>::operator[], 46
  std::vector<bool>::reference, 43-45
std::weak_ptr, 134-139
  caching and, 136
  construction of std::shared_ptr with, 135
  cycles and, 137
  efficiency of, 138
  expired, 135
  observer design pattern and, 137
  vs. std::shared_ptr, 134
Steagall, Bob, xiv
Stewart, Rob, xiv
strong guarantee
  definition of, 4
  move operations and, 205
  noexcept and, 91
Summer, Donna, 294
Supercalifragilisticexpialidocious, 289
Sutter, Herb, xiv
system threads, 242

T

T&&, meanings of, 164
tag dispatch, 185-188
task-based programming, definition of, 241
tasks
  load balancing and, 244
  querying for deferred status, 248
  vs. threads, 241-245
template
  alias templates, 63-65
  aliases, 63
  classes, definition of, 5
  disabled vs. enabled, 189
  functions, definition of, 5
  instantiations, deleting, 77
  move operations and, 206
  names, perfect forwarding and, 211
  parentheses vs. braces in, 57
  standard operators and type arguments for,
    235
  type deduction, 9-18
    array arguments and, 15-17
    for pass by value, 14-15
    for pointer and reference types, 11-14
    for universal references, 13-14
    function arguments and, 17
    vs. auto type deduction, 18-19
terminology and conventions, 2-6
testing std::threads for joinability, 255
"The Hitchhiker's Guide to the Galaxy", allusion to, 30
"The View from Aristeia" (blog), xv, 55, 269
thread handle destructor behavior, 258-262
thread local storage (TLS), definition of, 247
thread-based programming, definition of, 241
threads
  destruction, 252
  exhaustion, 243
  function return values and, 242
  hardware, 242
  implicit join or detach, 252
  joinable vs. unjoinable, 250
  OS threads, 242
  setting priority/affinity, 245, 252, 268
  software, 242
  suspending, 268-270
  system threads, 242
  testing for joinability, 255
  vs. tasks, 241-245

About the Author

Scott Meyers is one of the world's foremost experts on C++. A sought-after trainer, consultant, and conference presenter, his *Effective C++* books (*Effective C++*, *More Effective C++*, and *Effective STL*) have set the bar for C++ programming guidance for more than 20 years. He has a Ph.D. in computer science from Brown University. His website is *aristeia.com*.

Colophon

The animal on the cover of *Effective Modern C++* is a *Rose-crowned fruit dove* (*Ptilinopus regina*). This species of dove also goes by the names pink-capped fruit dove or Swainson's fruit dove. It is distinguished by its striking plumage: grey head and breast, orange belly, whitish throat, yellow-orange iris, and grey green bill and feet.

Distributed in lowland rainforests in eastern Australia, monsoon forests in northern Australia, and the Lesser Sunda Islands and Maluku Islands of Indonesia, the Rose-crowned fruit dove's diet consists of various fruits like figs (which it swallows whole), palms, and vines. Camphor Laurel, a large evergreen tree, is another food source for the fruit dove. They feed—in pairs, small parties, or singly—in rainforest canopies, usually in the morning or late afternoon. To hydrate, they get water from leaves or dew, not from the ground.

The fruit dove is considered vulnerable in New South Wales due to rainforest clearing and fragmentation, logging, weeds, fire regime–altered habitats, and the removal of Laurel Camphor without adequate alternatives.

Many of the animals on O'Reilly covers are endangered; all of them are important to the world. To learn more about how you can help, go to animals.oreilly.com.

The cover image is from Wood's *Illustrated Natural History*, bird volume. The cover fonts are URW Typewriter and Guardian Sans. The text font is Adobe Minion Pro; the heading font is Adobe Myriad Condensed; and the code font is Dalton Maag's Ubuntu Mono.

Learn from experts.
Find the answers you need.

Sign up for a **10-day free trial** to get **unlimited access** to all of the content on Safari, including Learning Paths, interactive tutorials, and curated playlists that draw from thousands of ebooks and training videos on a wide range of topics, including data, design, DevOps, management, business—and much more.

Start your free trial at:
oreilly.com/safari

(No credit card required.)

Milton Keynes UK
Ingram Content Group UK Ltd.
UKHW050909051024
449280UK00002B/3